W. W. COTTERMAN

BUSINESS SYSTEMS
AND
DATA PROCESSING PROCEDURES

BUSINESS SYSTEMS

AND

DATA PROCESSING PROCEDURES

FRANK J. CLARK
Director of Data Processing
Genesee Community College

RONALD GALE
Manager of Laboratory Education
IBM

ROBERT GRAY
Executive Director of New York State Society of CPA's
Associate Professor, Accounting, SUNY

PRENTICE-HALL, INC., Englewood Cliffs, New Jersey

© 1972
Prentice-Hall, Inc.
Englewood Cliffs, N.J.

10   9   8   7   6   5   4   3   2   1

ISBN: 0-13-107680-9

Library of Congress Catalog Card Number: 79-157725

Printed in the United States of America

PRENTICE-HALL INTERNATIONAL, INC. *London*
PRENTICE-HALL OF AUSTRALIA, PTY. LTD. *Sydney*
PRENTICE-HALL OF CANADA, LTD. *Toronto*
PRENTICE-HALL OF INDIA PRIVATE LIMITED *New Delhi*
PRENTICE-HALL OF JAPAN, INC. *Tokyo*

CONTENTS

PREFACE

Current applications of computers as well as new business, industrial, and national needs have made it necessary for data processing students to understand the total environment in which they will be working. Concepts of business systems provide a broad background for success in entry occupations.

This text has been prepared to provide an understanding of today's business systems. It has been developed from lectures in a two-year college, intensive industrial education programs, and the practical experiences of a consulting firm.

The objectives of this text are to:

... prepare a broad foundation in systems concepts for the data processing student to enable him to learn whatever new systems concepts or new generation of computer hardware that he will meet in his vocational career.

... provide short exercises in problem solving that are directed at various elements in a system rather than assignments to design total systems (projects that would consume more than a semester).

... give students skills to make them competitive in the employment market and productive on their first job.

If possible, the systems courses using this text should be structured to allow sufficient laboratory time during which the instructor may assist students individually with the exercises and problem assignments.

It is not within the scope of an introductory book on systems to require the beginning student to design a total system but rather to provide him with an overview of several types of systems:

Commercial—a bank

Industrial—a manufacturing company

Transportation—a bus line

Research—with manufacturing tasks subcontracted out

Education—a junior college

The content is presented in a logical and psychological order with exercises given at the end of each chapter that are concerned with the particular part of a system or procedure under consideration. This is similar to an assignment in the accounting cycle such as the adjusted trial balance, income statement, balance sheet, etc.

The fourteen chapters contain enough material for one semester's study. One chapter should be assigned per week and time set aside for midterm exams, final review or evaluation of projects, and the final exam.

The first half of the text is concerned with elements of a system, the procedures, equipment, and personnel (Chapters 1-7).

The second half of the text is concerned with the activities of the systems analyst with the view to improving systems as a continuous process (Chapters 8-14).

We would like to acknowledge the assistance of International Business Machines Corporation, Mahar Business Forms Inc., Association for Systems Management, Liberty National Bank, and Goodyear Publishing Company who have provided us with many useful illustrations and photographs. We also are grateful for Figure 8.5 from Professor Charles Grech of Dutchess Community College, Poughkeepsie, New York.

Frank J. Clark
Ronald Gale
Robert Gray

CHAPTER **1**

HISTORY AND DEVELOPMENT OF BUSINESS SYSTEMS

1.1

Businessmen in the Ancient World

Our ancient ancestors were curious and restless. The more goods they could accumulate, the more they traded and the farther they traveled in search of new markets. For example, when improvements in agriculture finally created surpluses, storage areas and warehouses were developed. The possibility of bringing surpluses to distant populations helped lead to advances in the technologies of transportation of crops by water or overland caravans. Ancient Mediterranean peoples, among others, established far-flung depots and colonies. The Romans developed impressive long-distance overland routes, transportation networks, continuous markets, and extensive production systems, and enacted laws governing business transactions. Even before them, the Phoenicians had developed overseas routes to remote England and Ireland, and among the Babylonians promissory notes and installment payments were common.

Because these ancient business systems relied on calculation and documentation, businessmen helped to spread the skills of arithmetic and writing, as the markings on ancient jars and clay

1

tablets indicate. Businessmen, however, were not the heroes that we read about in Roman and Greek epics. In fact, businessmen were frequently despised by peoples such as the Spartans and Romans, who idolized warriors and emphasized hero worship. We never read about a typically tired soldier, but often about tired, anemic, and worried tradesmen. At one time the ruling families of Rome were prohibited from engaging in trade by law.

Ancient warriors were quick to purchase arms, and frequently merchants were overwhelmed and robbed even by the men with whom they had just been trading. Trading activity in this age of ceaseless warfare involved other hazards. For example, a merchant approaching a city might find it blockaded or even in ruins. Some merchants resorted to studying the flights of birds and other omens to predict the outcome of a business venture. Others allied themselves with warriors, hijacking ships and caravans for materials they could not or did not wish to manufacture or buy elsewhere.

The centuries following the decline of Rome were characterized by severe cultural, political, and economic stagnation; the few continuous markets that survived were for a narrow range of commodities: weapons, foods, and some luxuries.

The Age of Exploration, starting in the thirteenth century, witnessed travels and voyages of discovery intended specifically to develop new markets. The travels of Marco Polo to the Far East is only one example.

After the establishment of colonies in the New World, these new sources of raw materials and new markets for finished goods intensified the need for the development of large-scale production and distribution of goods. Since this kind of business activity required massive capital investment, the Age of Exploration was followed by a period in which commercial wealth, represented by bankers and investment houses, quickly surpassed aristocratic wealth.

1.2

**The First
Business Studies**

At the dawn of the Scientific Age (around 1700), some intelligent minds extended rational analysis to business procedures. The resultant innovations eventually led to the concepts of business systems as we know them today. Some noteworthy milestones are:

2

1699—De la Hire in France analyzed the simple activity of a workman carrying a workload up a flight of stairs. De la Hire determined that if the workman instead loaded the bricks in a container, walked (unburdened) up the stairs, then descended by means of a rope and pulley that lifted the load at the same time, the workman could use his weight to increase his output four times.

1801—The German Polytechnic School was founded for the education of directors and persons employed in the management of public works. One objective of the school was to improve the nation's manufacturing activities and other branches of industry.

1824—Charles Dupin in Paris initiated industrial education classes for workmen, foremen, and supervisors.

1832—Charles Babbage, in England, began systematic studies of the importance of machines, tools, and tool design; mass production of goods; the division of labor, both physical and mental; plant locations and size; unions; profit-sharing; calculating machines; and a new concept called "a fair day's wage for a fair day's work."

Other eighteenth-century and nineteenth-century studies were crude forerunners of today's work measurement studies. Observation of miners, builders, and other manual laborers at work led to the general conclusion that a man cannot sustain continuous use of his muscles, but output could be increased with frequent short intervals of rest during a working day.

1.3

The Rise of the Social Ethic

The rapid growth of American productivity during the eighteenth and nineteenth centuries eventually created a conflict between two distinct commercial types: the *frontiersmen*, who typified what is often referred to as the *individual ethic*, and the *specialist*, who typifies the *social ethic*. On one hand was the opportunity for individuals to exploit natural resources on the American frontier. On the other hand, the growing need for men to bring their special skills together to achieve a common goal became more pressing. (After all, the weaver needs the farmer's

3

food, the bricklayer needs the weaver's clothing and the farmer's food, and so on.) As it became clearer that America's frontiers and resources were finite, and as the population grew and technology advanced, greater work specialization made it increasingly necessary for men to collaborate.

Both the individualistic and social ethics exert pressures on today's business systems, for the creativity of individuals and the solidarity of a business system are both invaluable assets. Today's businesses are continually trying to enhance the individual's role within the business system. For the moment we shall focus on the social or interpersonal aspects of a business enterprise.

1.4

Frederick W. Taylor

Frederick W. Taylor, just before the turn of the century, observed, "In the past man has been first; in the future the system must be first."

As a factory foreman, Taylor had been overloaded with work and forced to make decisions in areas where he had little or no expertise. After these early experiences Taylor worked to eliminate one-man control by assigning responsibility to supervisory personnel on the basis of their specializations. Instead of eight foremen supervising eight groups of workmen, for example, eight specialists were employed to supervise all the workmen. (See Figs. 1.1 and 1.2.)

Figure 1.1 shows a clear line of authority from shop superintendent to foreman to worker. In Fig. 1.2, the workers are responsible to eight different specialists. In Chapter 2 we will note some problems that this type of structure may present. However, with this structure or *functional organization*, Taylor hoped to promote cooperation *not* individualism among the supervising personnel. Individuals were subordinate to the system.

Science in business management, not the rule of thumb, was Taylor's objective. The expected results of this approach were harmony, not discord, maximum output, not restricted output, and the development of each man to his greatest efficiency and prosperity. For these reasons Taylor has been called the "Father of Scientific Management."

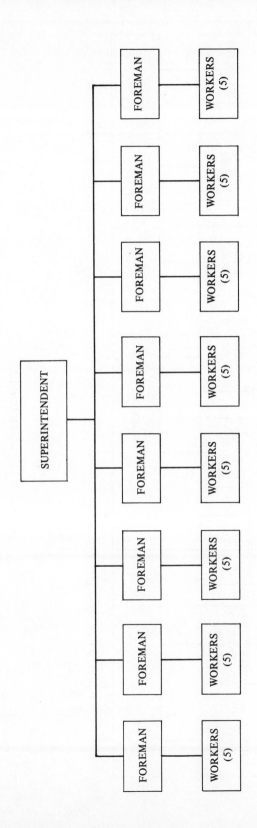

FIGURE 1.1.

5

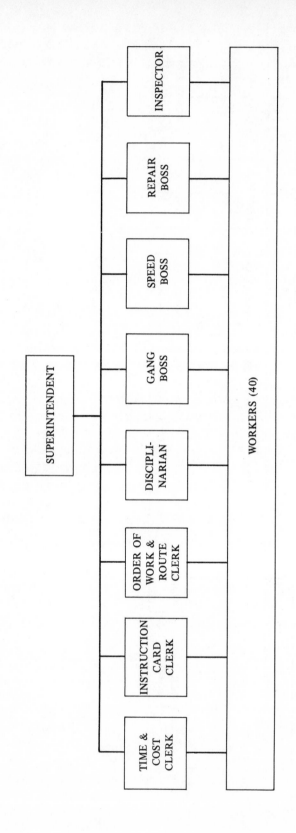

FIGURE 1.2.

1.5

The Increase in Business Systems Complexity

Taylor lived during a period of great economic expansion in the United States. Rapid, inexpensive, overland transportation facilities were growing. Population and industry rapidly spread across the country. Seaboard cities were tied to inland cities by telegraph. Huge warehouses were erected as buffers against sudden demands. Businessmen no longer bothered to study omens, or worry so much about the safe arrival of their cargos. Manufacturers, farmers, and markets were in constant touch with each other and "middlemen" accelerated trading between buyers and sellers, who only needed to see each other infrequently or not at all.

The Industrial Revolution was bringing complicated equipment into the factories. With Taylor and others like him, it was necessary that each time a job was performed it was performed in exactly the same manner. Exceptions were permitted only when a supervisor felt that the change would increase the worker's output.

Standardized instructions specifying and categorizing the similar elements found in different operations were developed as ways of increasing the benefits of specialization.

The Industrial Revolution brought a division of labor within factories and offices that required persons to be rapidly trained to perform specialized tasks for the efficient operation of a business enterprise. The skilled worker had replaced the worker with a strong back.

Business systems became dependent upon human capabilities and machine functions. As business volumes grew, more equipment and more people were added, and work became further subdivided.

Business systems were increasingly subdivided into many subsystems: a payroll system, a sales-order billing system, an inventory system, and so on. Every new file, form, report, or record required new special procedures.

A radical breakthrough in handling this overwhelming fragmentation and multiplication of operations was achieved with the introduction of electronic computers, which made possible the rapid processing of massive amounts of paperwork at greatly reduced costs.

At first, the basic structures of business subsystems and the

7

relationships within them were little affected by computers. But after such improvements as high-speed input/output devices, increased processing speeds, and massive storage devices, an effective integration of data processing activities took place, so that a single transaction, such as the receipt of an item with its accompanying packing slip, could cause a whole chain of reactions throughout several automated subsystems. The packing slip updated the inventory bin, the accounts payable file, production scheduling, shipping, accounting, and so on.

1.6

**Operations
Research**

    In the mid 1930's Congress was trying to learn the value of rivers, harbors, and irrigation projects. For example, if navigational benefits may be derived from a system of canals, are there additional recreational benefits from any lakes that were created by the canal system? Congressional Committees were *researching operations* on public projects.

    During World War II, studies were made to determine the best use of Britain's airpower, and later, the mathematical techniques employed were used to improve the operations of the North Atlantic convoys. Techniques like these were the beginnings of Operations Research and were soon adopted by business systems in the United States. As the Industrial Revolution replaced the strong back with the skilled worker, computers and techniques like Operations Research, PERT, and CPM (see Chapter 14) replaced skilled muscle-power with skilled and disciplined brain-power. A trend toward professionalism in business management had begun.

    After World War II there was a trend away from the "Hero" manager and policy-making by the wealthy who controlled business systems. Today, officers in a business system are frequently men who have several college degrees and have advanced through the ranks.

    Good presidents, officers, managers, and foremen do not 'happen'; they must be trained for leadership. Machinists or salesmen, for example, do not always make the best foremen or managers (nor do they all want to be).

    Today's leaders do not need to know how every part of a business system works, nor do they need to own it outright. They must know how best to use it.

CHAPTER 2

NATURE AND SCOPE
OF A MODERN
BUSINESS ENTERPRISE

2.1

Types of Business Enterprises

Broadly defined, a business enterprise consists of persons, materials, and/or equipment properly organized to *produce* and/or *distribute* goods or *services*.

Business enterprises fall into the three general categories italicized in the last paragraph.

Production

Some examples of business enterprises that are engaged in production are:

Home appliance industries that manufacture refrigerators, washing machines, light bulbs, etc;

Agriculture, or the production of grains, dairy products, etc;

Mining, or the production of such raw materials as iron, copper, tin, petroleum, etc; and

Construction-trades engaged in building schools, homes, factories, and highways.

Distribution

This type of business enterprise assists other types of businesses in the marketing of their goods and services.

Transportation systems carry raw materials to manufacturing locations and the finished products to markets; some transportation systems such as bus, railroad, or subway lines serve the general public.

Communication systems distribute messages and records of business transactions, market conditions, and so on, over such media as telegraph, telephone, radio, and television.

Service

Service enterprises also provide assistance to other types of business. A few examples are:

Maintenance and repair of equipment;

Insurance of business properties against loss by fire, flood, or theft;

Communication systems which may also be properly called service enterprises; and

Medical services to insure the well-being of people employed by a business enterprise.

2.2

Economic Environment of a Business Enterprise

All modern societies have economic activities involved with the production and distribution of goods and services. In the United States these activities have two important characteristics, *a risk of loss*, and *an opportunity for profit*.

A *risk of loss*. We noted earlier that the ancient trader faced risks of piracy or of finding his market blockaded or even destroyed by enemies. Today, risks are still present. Technological changes, foreign competition, or even a public fancy can cause losses in the markets.

Profit motives are a driving force behind business enterprises in capitalist countries. Profits provide:

Incentive to work efficiently;

Standards to compare with other business enterprises; and

Revenue for future investment, growth, and change.

When the planning of production and distribution of goods and services are left to private individuals, who do so for profit, the economy is usually referred to as a capitalist or free-enterprise economy.

A basic concept of American capitalism is the freedom of the individual's choice in determining the kind of business enterprise he wishes to engage in. However, no economy can be described as entirely capitalist. There are nonprofit enterprises such as educational institutions, Blue Cross/Blue Shield, the foundations, and so on. Further, government agencies operate some nonprofit services such as water-supply systems, county planning services, and police and fire departments.

Other modern economic systems, such as socialism and communism, are also engaged in the production and distribution of goods and services, but their business environment restricts individuals' freedom of choice, and fundamentally differs from capitalism in the following respects:

Socialism is commonly ascribed to systems in which there is state ownership, control, and operation of basic industries such as coal, steel, and transportation, and in which the state, as a result, exerts considerable influence over other sections of the state's economy which are marked by private enterprise.

Communism is characterized by complete state ownership, control, and operation of all production and distribution of goods and services.

2.3

Environmental
Factors
Regardless of *isms*, business activity in all economic systems is affected by environmental factors, i.e.,

Company policies and procedures

Government laws and regulations

Production factors

Marketing of goods and services

Technological advances

Social climate

Company Policy and Procedures

A *policy* is a statement which guides administrative actions and establishes general lines of authority, responsibility, and standards. One policy might, for example, dictate the maintenance of a central filing system, another policy might establish the payroll on a biweekly basis, and another might call for employee education programs. Policies are generally set forth in company manuals, are supplemented by memos and correspondence from the company's executives, and are administered and enforced by company's officers and managers.

A *procedure* is a prescribed sequence of logical steps taken to perform routine and repetitive actions—for example, the method for gathering together all employee time cards before processing a payroll program on the computer. Procedures are also usually presented in company manuals and are often used to supplement, or may even comprise, an employee's "on-the-job" training.

Government Laws and Regulations

In addition to its policies and procedures, governmental laws and the rules of regulatory agencies also influence the activities of a business enterprise. The laws most significantly affecting the activities of a business usually concern fair trade practices, wages, hours of work, labor relations, and (in capitalist nations) stock and financial operations, the prevention of the formation of trusts and monopolies, and the control of conglomerates. Recent laws designed to prevent environmental pollution also have far-reaching implications for businesses, especially for manufacturers who must dispose of large amounts of waste products.

The legal departments of business enterprises are responsible for the awareness and interpretation of these laws which are administered by agencies of the government and enforced by the courts.

Factors of Production

The productive level of a business depends heavily on the availability of *materials*, of an *expert labor force*, and of working *capital*. Each of these factors influences the costs of products and services, and thus the selling price must cover at least the costs of production and distribution—and at the same time be reasonable and competitive—if the business is to survive.

An expensive machine or a highly skilled labor force may increase costs, but in return provide large volumes of output or a superior product. Production factors must be carefully examined and decisions must be made on how to produce goods or provide a service efficiently and cheaply. It is clear that the efficiency and output of a power plant on the Niagara Falls, the Victorian Falls, or the Dnieper River depends upon the equipment that the owner is willing to supply, the talent, brainpower, and educational preparation of its management and the skills and energies of its work force.

Marketing Factors

A market is a formal and organized gathering of buyers and sellers of goods, and marketing is the process of buying or selling in a market. The requirements of marketing are materials for sale, distribution networks, and a system of recorded transactions.

There must be a demand for goods and services if a business activity is to survive. Markets develop as a response to a need. The need may be real such as food and shelter, or psychological, created by a strong advertising effort or combination of the real and the psychological. Markets also develop as a result of a technological advance. For example, a newly discovered vaccine providing immunity against a disease creates a new market in pharmaceuticals.

Markets are influenced by such things as customer demand and in capitalist nations the quality and prices of competing products.

Technological Advances

Technological advances can affect not only markets and the survival of a business enterprise, but also lead to new equipment, new labor skills, management skills, and business procedures. Technological advances not only open up new opportunities for the business enterprises, but also improve benefits to society in general. The availability of more and improved goods and services has provided a higher standard of living. In addition, long hours and dangerous conditions for labor are often reduced.

Social Climate

In the ancient warrior societies, the businessman lived an uncertain existence. His materials could be plundered enroute to his markets. His work force could be conscripted or forced into military service or slaughtered by an invader. This precarious position in society can be contrasted with the power of businessmen of the latter nineteenth century in America.

Public concern over the social evils of the "sweat shops" and child labor and the Great Depression of the 1930's did a great deal to curb the power of these individuals. Since World War II, the need for people trained in scientific management brought ambitious men from varying socio-economic backgrounds into positions of leadership in large corporations. They are gradually replacing the unfettered "rugged individualist" of the nineteenth century as planners and decision makers.

2.4

Recent Trends   Today's businessmen are also concerned with the rights of minority groups and the preservation of our natural resources. In response to the environmental factors we have been discussing, dramatic changes have taken place in the present century; i.e., specialization in business enterprise, mass production of goods and services, and automation.

Specialization in Business Enterprises

We have noted in Chapter 1 that scientific management in F. W. Taylor's time was concerned with maximizing the productivity of workers through specialization or division of labor. A direct result of this specialization of labor is the dependence of one work station upon another.

A tour through any factory can easily demonstrate this *intradependency*. For example, the manufacture of magnetic-core memory of computers requires such work stations as shown in Fig. 2.1. At each of these work stations, specialists must perform their operations properly if production is to be done efficiently. Each job is important and depends upon the work done at another station.

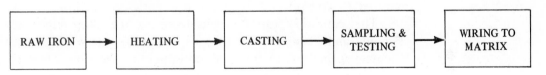

FIGURE 2.1.

The production of magnetic-core memory is itself a specialized business enterprise. It depends upon other business enterprises to survive. Another business enterprise must provide the wires for the matrix upon which these core memory bits will reside, another must supply the raw materials, e.g., iron, another must provide transportation to and from this factory, and several other business enterprises engaged in the manufacture of computers will need these finished core matrices for their own products.

This dependence of one business enterprise upon another is called *interdependency*. It arises from the specialization of business enterprises within the total economy.

Specialization in production as well as the specialization of labor has made possible the *mass production* of standard products.

Mass Production

Mass production is characterized by the manufacturing of large volumes of identical items. Automobile production is an example.

A part, such as the brake band, can be produced on a specialized machine that can rapidly produce identical copies of the same band. These identical copies not only find their way to the wheels of new automobiles, but they can also be shipped to service stations and repair shops to be used as replacement parts for worn brake bands.

Considering the many standardized parts in any given automobile model it is easy to visualize how specializations in machines and labor support and promote mass production.

Automation

Automation is the automatic control of a process or a machine. With the introduction of computers into factories, great output of materials can be produced with only a few workers required to control and maintain automatic production systems.

The computer can be considered as the shop supervisor assigning and keeping track of jobs, measuring the work of each machine against standards, and coordinating the flow of work. Production reports provide the computer with information on the final product. Any desirable changes or modifications can then be prepared by the computer programmer (see Fig. 2.2).

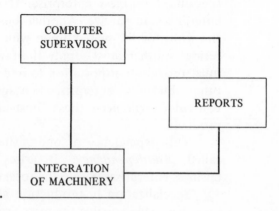

FIGURE 2.2.

Integration of machinery means uniting the separate work stations into one single automatic unit. One extremely complicated electronic work unit is called a *transfer machine* because it transfers materials from one work station to another. This transfer machine is as long as a football field, includes 500 work stations, and is part of an automated factory that produces automobiles.

Artificial intelligence is a term used to describe a machine's ability to "learn" a production operation. In some operations, closed circuit television cameras performing as the machine's "eyes" may help to correct initial errors. Once these errors have been corrected the machine performs its assignments perfectly.

2.5

The Structure of a Business Enterprise— Organization Charts

Organization charts are a conventional method of graphically illustrating the relationships of people in a business enterprise.

Organization charts are useful tools to anyone responsible for improving or monitoring the activities of a business enterprise. These charts typically indicate a division of labor within the enterprise, lines of delegated authority as well as relationships that are non-authoritarian, lines of communication, and the degree of specialization. In addition, the nature of the business enterprise itself is often implied in the organization chart.

Line Organization

The earliest and simplest type of personnel organization is represented in the line organization chart (Fig. 2.3) in which the lines of authority flow directly down from the general manager to the workers. There are no research groups, or advisory committees attached. Workers are directly accountable to their respective foremen who are in turn accountable to the factory superintendent who reports to the general manager. Department chiefs on each level are independent of others on the same level.

Functional Organization

We noted in Chapter 1 (Fig. 1.2), that under F. W. Taylor's functional organization, the supervisory activity of the foreman was broken down into categories and assigned to specialists.

17

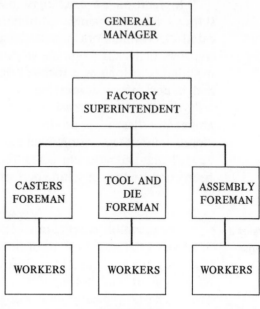

FIGURE 2.3.

Authority still flows from the top down in the functional organization, but specialists have a limited authority over personnel at lower levels. Critics of this functional organization argue that because its lines of authority are not clear, the results are conflict or confusion over who is "*boss*" and there is no unity of command.

Line and Staff Organization

Many small business enterprises fall into the simple line organization category, and some manufacturing activities use the functional organization model. Most large business organizations, however, have a greater complexity. Their greater diversity requires auxiliary advisory staff personnel. This leads to *line-and-staff* organizations which typically combine features of both the line and functional structures. Delegation of authority insures necessary control, and staff specialization provides accountability through special responsibilities.

A staff position is advisory in nature; the advice of staff personnel is used in the development of plans and programs that aid in decision-making. An example of staff personnel is a research scientist.

A line position carries out decisions handed down from above and makes decisions appropriate to that level of authority. An example of a line person is a manager involved in the production of goods and services.

Additional staff functions are usually required simply because the officers and managers of large business enterprises do not possess *all* the expertise needed to direct complex organizations. Thus in Fig. 2.4, the product research and development team might be staffed with scientists. Men with intensive education and long experience in finance would make up the financial research and budget forecasting team. Professional educators are frequently found directing employee education programs; and the labor relations group is usually staffed with lawyers.

The complexity of a modern business enterprise can be further emphasized by considering an organization chart such as that of the Ferrous-Cube Company, a manufacturer of magnetic-core memory units for computers (Fig. 2.5).

In all of our preceding organization charts, the flow of authority has been from top to bottom. This is not precisely the case in all situations. In the Ferrous-Cube Company, the basis for decision-making on budgets and on research comes from staff committees. In a sense, these committees delegate authority *upwards*.

Authority—the power to make decisions that guide the actions of others—is often expressed in a superior-subordinate arrangement. However, the members of the Finance and Research Committees of the Ferrous-Cube Company, by applying highly specialized skills to problem analyses, can produce solutions more reliable than those obtainable from any other person or group of persons in the organization. In this manner authority can be ascribed to professional expertise, and decision-making power may be delegated upward to top management.

Departing from business enterprises for a brief look at professional associations helps to make the concept of authority

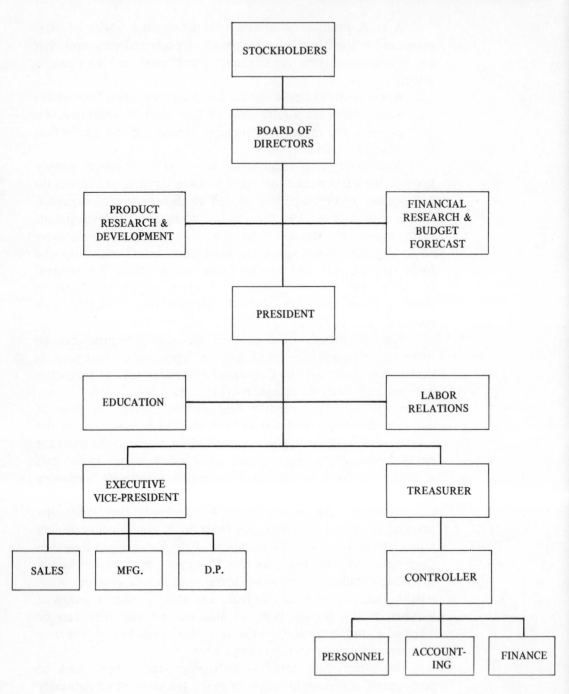

FIGURE 2.4.

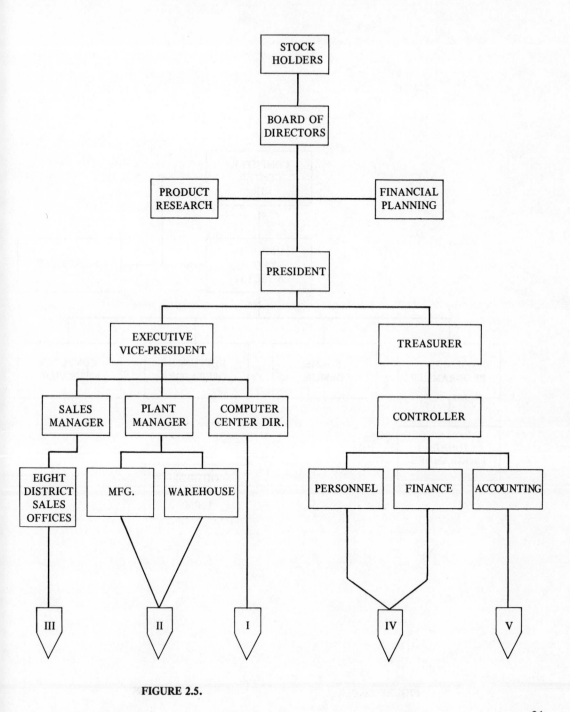

FIGURE 2.5.

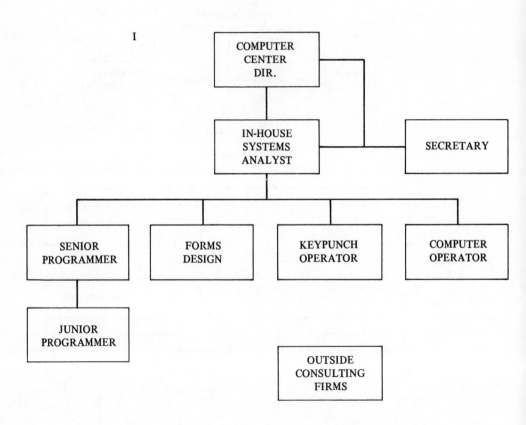

FIGURE 2.6.

II

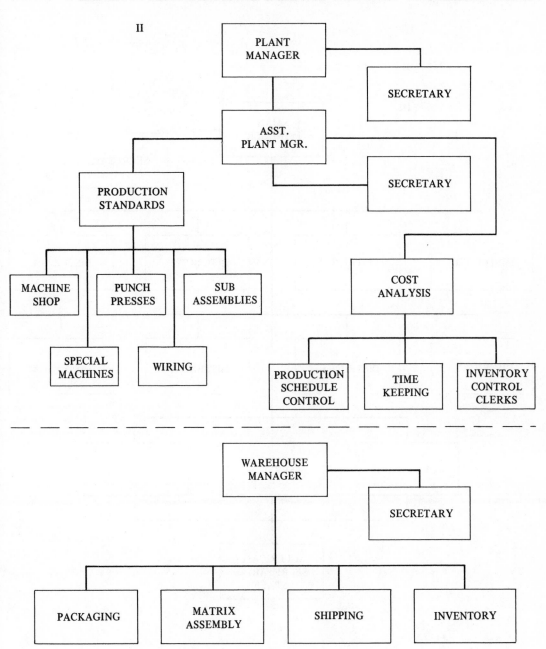

FIGURE 2.7.

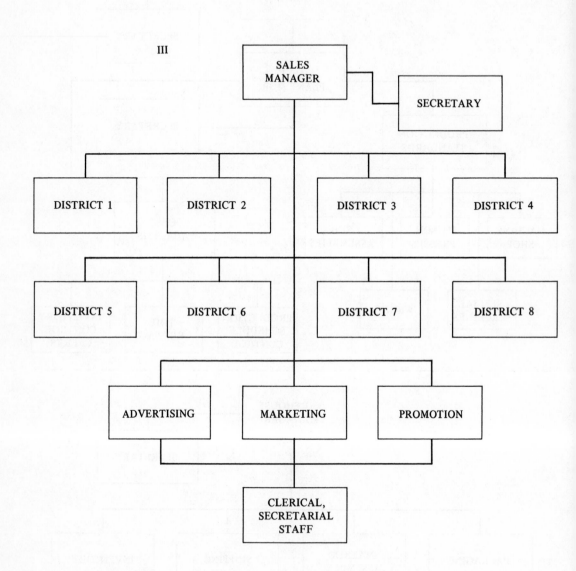

FIGURE 2.8.

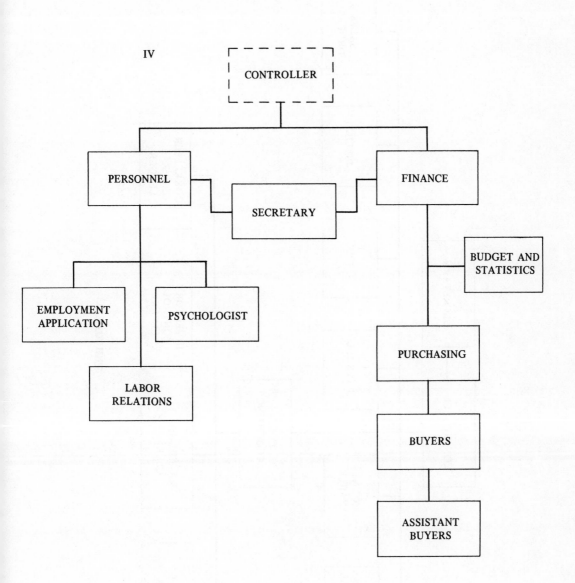

FIGURE 2.9.

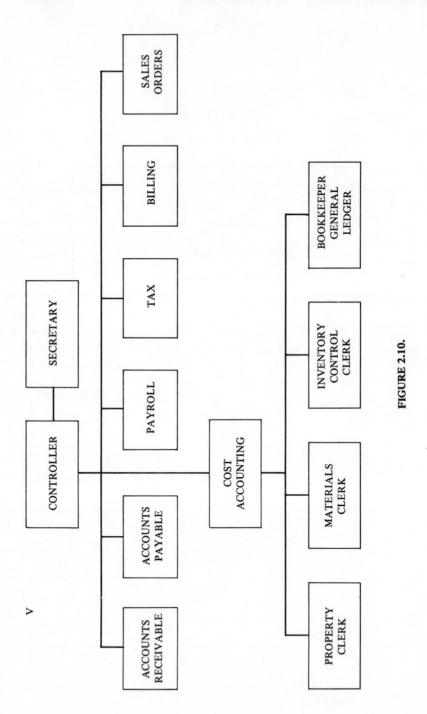

FIGURE 2.10.

upwards clearer. Scientists, doctors, lawyers, and teachers do not consider themselves employees of the professional groups or societies to which they belong. Decision-making in such areas as educational standards for membership, and autonomy over subject matter, is conducted at the group and committee level within the organization. These groups and committees set policy and authority for the administration of these policies is delegated upwards to the officers who have been elected by the membership.

Business systems begin with a source of power–human creative power. The channels of this power should be expressed in properly maintained organization charts. Furthermore, in rapidly expanding companies it is crucial to keep these organization charts up to date. Poor or invalid charts create difficulties and conflicts among staff personnel as well as contributing to poor communications. Functions and areas of specializations must be properly grouped and the lines of delegated authority must be clearly drawn or the system will eventually fail to handle information flow adequately.

The Nature of the Business Activity

The nature of the business activity can usually be learned from company manuals. There are two basic types of company manuals: one on procedures and instructions and another on job specifications.

Procedures or instructions are the rules or guidelines under which work is performed; they set standards for work measurement and are designed to elicit the best possible results from personnel and equipment.

Job specifications describe the function of each employee in the business enterprise and can be used as a guide in training new employees.

A job specification is often a statement of the human qualifications necessary to do the job and includes:

Education

Experience

Training

Judgement

Initiative

Physical effort

Physical skills

Responsibilities

Communication skills

Emotional characteristics

Unusual sensory demands, such as sight, hearing, etc.

2.6

The Structure of a Business System— Systems Model

In addition to organization charts and manuals, it is also useful to graphically illustrate the nature and scope of a business enterprise in a drawing or model of the system. A simple form of this type of illustration is found in Fig. 2.11.

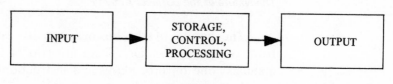

FIGURE 2.11.

Consider a department store. *Inputs* are sales slips, cash, a document indicating a charge, a document indicating a returned item, and so on. *Storage* consists of inventory bins for merchandise and the journals or ledgers which keep the records of monies collected or disbursed. *Processing* refers to counting the cash receipts, the sales slips, selling merchandise, recording transactions in the appropriate ledgers, and so on. *Control* involves such activities as deciding what items to sell, making certain that inventories are properly stocked, and setting reasonable prices for items. *Outputs* include merchandise sold, sales analysis reports, and taxes paid to state and federal agencies.

Figure 2.12 expands the concept of the systems model.

28

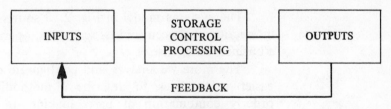

FIGURE 2.12.

Expanding our general diagram further to apply it to a specific business enterprise, consider a shoe manufacturing business. Several kinds of skills are needed to operate this enterprise, and special equipment is also needed. These persons and equipment can be thought of as *resources* (see Fig. 2.13).

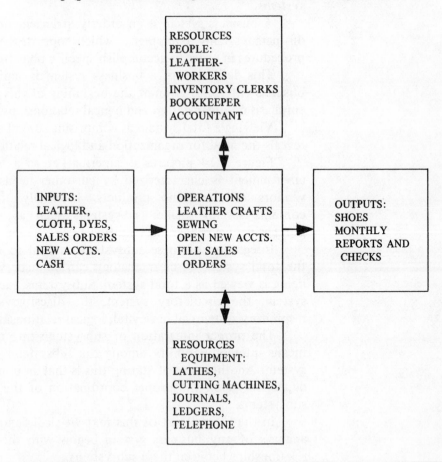

FIGURE 2.13.

29

The systems model in Fig. 2.13 shows the relationships and interactions between inputs, resources, operations, and outputs of a business enterprise.

The more we analyze and configurate business activities, the easier it becomes to describe a methodical arrangement and orderly combination of parts making up the whole. We have implied that this orderly arrangement was not typical in the past nor is it always true today. However, it is a modern trend to configurate and otherwise graphically describe the flow of information through a business enterprise. Because we are concerned with orderly arrangements of all business activities, we shall from this point on, refer to business enterprises as *business systems*.

A business system is an orderly arrangement or organization of persons and equipment which operates under a set of procedures in order to accomplish specific objectives.

This definition of a business system is similar to that of a business enterprise given at the beginning of this chapter with the emphasis on organization and logical relationships.

Viewing a total system as comprising several small subsystems reveals the need for organization and logical relationships.

Figure 2.14 pictures a supermarket as a total system. Its environment is characterized by customer needs and competing vendors of the same products. Internally, the supermarket contains several smaller subsystems such as inventory, sales, purchasing, payroll, and accounting.

Integration of these subsystems is vital to the functions of the total system. A clear analogy can be made when the human being is viewed as a total system. Subsystems, such as the nervous system, the circulatory system, the digestive system, and the respiratory system, all have vital, logical relationships to each other.

The proper integration of subsystems into any total system means intercompatibility among the subsystems within the total system. Another way of stating this is that an integrated system is dependent upon the proper coordination of the functions of its subsystems.

In the second part of this text we shall demonstrate that the analysis of any business system begins with the analysis of the relationships between these subsystems.

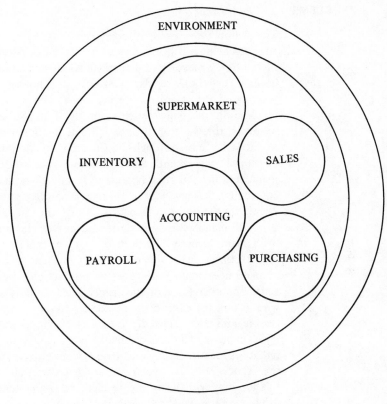

FIGURE 2.14.

EXERCISES 1. In what way might a committee on computer utilization headed by the director of the computer center delegate authority upwards?

2. (a) List the staff positions illustrated in the organization charts of the Ferrous-Cube Company (Fig. 2.5).
   (b) Distinguish between a line position and a staff position in the Ferrous-Cube Company.

3. Chart a total system and its environment, as in Fig. 2.14, for a local newspaper publisher.

4. Describe and explain the influence of basic environmental factors on the business activities of a local automobile dealer.

5. Contrast the basic environmental factors which affect the automobile dealer in Exercise 4 with those which affect the operation of the school you are enrolled in.

PROBLEMS   1. *The Wilson Company*

The Wilson Company is a rapidly growing and progressive corporation. At the present time it has in excess of 500 stockholders. The Board of Directors of the firm is made up of nine members elected entirely from the stockholder group. They hold regular quarterly stockholders' meetings, as well as a meeting of the Board once every week. The Board of Directors is heavily involved in the daily activities of the firm. Since it has many potential products, the Director of Research and Development reports directly to the Board of Directors through the Chairman of the Board. As new products are developed the Board itself decides when the product is ready for manufacturing and sales. Because of its many new and potential products, the corporation has an unusually large Legal Department, which also reports directly to the Board of Directors through the Chairman.

All manufacturing is carried on in two separate plants, each headed up by a Plant Manager. Each Plant Manager reports to the Vice-President of Manufacturing, who supervises the two Plant Managers directly as well as prepares new products for the first production runs directly through his own staff. The sales force of the firm is headed up by a Vice-President of Sales who in turn has divided the marketing area into two separate regions. These two regions are headed up by Sales Managers who have a small staff of representatives who work directly with independent manufacturing representatives located throughout the respective marketing areas. The function of the offices of the Sales Managers is to train and maintain working relationships with many independent sales representatives who handle their products. Both the Vice-President of Manufacturing and the Vice-President of Sales report directly to the company's President. Also reporting to the President is the Treasurer of the company who handles all financial transactions involving long- and short-term borrowing. He exercises final authorization for payment of all invoices. The Controller of the company reports directly to the Treasurer, and all office functions relating to record-keeping, cost-accounting, and related areas are directly under his control. The Secretary of the company performs the typical functions of a corporate secretary and reports directly to the President.

Required: From the preceding description of the relationships between the stockholders, the Board of Directors, and the various functions described, draw an organization chart which accurately portrays these relationships.

2. *Contact Airlines Inc.*

Contact Airlines, Inc. is a 20-year-old feeder-type airline which has been characterized by rapid growth. The Directors and Officers have been concentrating on building safe and reliable service from medium-size metropolitan areas to the industrial and large population centers of an eight-state area. Management believes that if it can cover the area adequately, it can persuade the Federal Department of Transportation to award a contract to the more profitable trunk lines.

With such goals in mind, the company has concentrated on upgrading its pilot training and maintenance programs. By borrowing large sums they were able to purchase the most modern short-range passenger jets, which were comfortable and appealing to the public. The Department of Transportation did not look favorably on the purchase but the company was able to overcome their objections. It was estimated that those aircraft would be serviceable for about eight years before better craft would be available.

The company had filed with the Department of Transportation for a trunk line but as yet the decision had not been made. Representatives of the Department suggested that the major airlines were already serving the route adequately. They also pointed out that several medium-sized cities in the airline's area appeared to need more service. The airline countered by pointing out that these cities lacked adequate municipal airports and that in two areas the voters had turned down a proposed bond issue to improve the existing airports.

At a recent board meeting, Contact's President expressed his concern about the proposed trunk line. He pointed out that a newly completed superhighway between two cities they serve has cut the automobile travel time considerably, and that airline-ticket sales on this route have dropped noticeably as a result. He also reviewed with the board the plans for a proposed superhighway that would link several cities that the airline now serves. This, as well as frequent discussion about monorail systems means, according to the President, that short-haul airline travel will decline and that long-haul routes are essential.

Required: Discuss the environmental factors that affect the activities of Contact Airlines, Inc.

3. The Publishing Company

The printing of a book such as this one is one example of a business activity. The publisher's cash resources are utilized for the book's production and for the selling activities related to its availability. Paper and inks must be purchased, photographic plates set, and artists and editors must expend effort in preparation for its printing. Journeymen and apprentice printers operate the equipment in the production process.

Assume a publishing company to have divided their activities into two categories as follows:

Publishing	*Printing*
Editors	Journeymen printers
Artists	Offset plates prepared
Inventory (ink, paper, etc.)	Composition
Sales	Proofreading
Advertising	Printing
	Binding

This is a brief overview of the process of publishing a book which can be described as the combination of resources and inputs resulting in outputs such as this text.

Required: Draw a systems model displaying the above process (refer to Fig. 2.13).

CHAPTER 3

COMMUNICATIONS

3.1

Information, Messages, and Meaning

Communication is the transfer of information from source to destination. *Information* may be a fact, such as today's date, an instruction from a foreman to a machine operator, an opinion on politics, and so on. In any event, real communication only takes place when the sender's message is understood by the recipient. A person, whom we shall refer to as the recipient, is typically the *destination* of a message in a business system. Some messages can be expressed entirely with numbers—for example, a dollar amount, the humidity index, the percentage, interest of a loan, quotas, and so on. Although some of this *statistical information* can be misleading, *quantitative messages* usually mean exactly the same thing to the sender and to the recipient of the message. For example, if wage negotiations produce a $600 increase, both employees and employer understand precisely what $600 is.

A *message*—a specific communication which is spoken, written, or given by signal—is made up of symbols whose meanings both the sender and recipient must agree upon. Messages are ordinarily characterized as either nonverbal or verbal. *Non Verbal* communications include shaking hands, a tap on the shoulder, a pat on the back, pointing a finger, winking an eye, nodding the head, and smiling.

Verbal symbols may be either spoken or written words. The spoken word, "pencil," is another kind of symbol representing the same concept in the mind of the recipient. In this paragraph, the symbol "pencil" was first typewritten by the authors, then transferred through the medium of a printed page, and finally perceived by the reader (the "recipient") as one of the words in this paragraph.

About one-fourth of the words we use in daily speech have more than one meaning. With over a half-million words available to English-speaking people, one would expect the dictionary to function as a manual of meanings, yet even the word "meaning" has more than one meaning in the "manual of meanings." We all see things differently—probably because we all cannot occupy the same place at the same time and because our educations and personal experiences are so varied. Meanings of words vary even by geographic area; sometimes meanings change over a period of time; and some words simply drop out of daily use.

In order to improve communications, professionals in all fields aim for precision in their vocabulary. When carefully chosen, some technical terms are virtually self-defining. *"Processing unit,"* for example, identifies a specific piece of computer hardware, and the words, "2020 Central Processing Unit," offer no semantic problems because they form the label of a specific and unique item.

Emotions affect the meaning of communications. Abrupt or discourteous messages may impair communications, confuse or alter meanings, or provoke a negative reaction in the recipient. The sender must always keep in mind that the recipient is really another system, different from his own.

3.2

The Dynamics of Communication

Figure 3.1 shows three major components of communication:

The *source*, which creates the message

The *medium*, which transfers the message

The *destination*, which receives the message

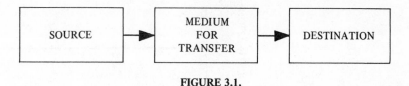

FIGURE 3.1.

Channels (represented by arrows in Fig. 3.1) are routes over which information travels. The chain of command implicit in the downward arrow in Fig. 3.4 contains many channels. The "grapevine" which usually transmits rumors is also a channel, but an informal and relatively unreliable one.

A *Network* is an arrangement of channels. *Media* are specific types of channels—the human voice, paper forms, telephone, radio, television, etc. *Sources* and *destinations* of messages within a business system are people working in the system.

If communications were a perfected art encountering no problems in its performance, there would be no need to analyze its component parts. However, this is not always the case. Communications break down, and messages are too often distorted, misunderstood, or not received at all. When messages are poorly constructed, or when the destination is inattentive or hostile, communications break down, for hostility and fear are self-reinforcing emotions which reduce productivity. Distorted views can spread throughout a group and even result in open conflict between levels in a business system. Because this sometimes happens and because no business system can function without adequate communication, we shall take a closer look at the component parts in a communication process.

Feedback

In 1938, Claude Shannon of Bell Laboratories graphically expressed the relationships between the basic elements of communication in terms of a network. In the "Shannon Circuit" (Fig. 3.2), feedback clearly makes communication a two-way activity between source and destination.

To understand this we must define feedback as that function of a system which automatically brings back information about a situation under consideration to the source of that information. Thermostat control of a home heating system provides a fair analogy. The furnace burns fuel generating heat measured by a

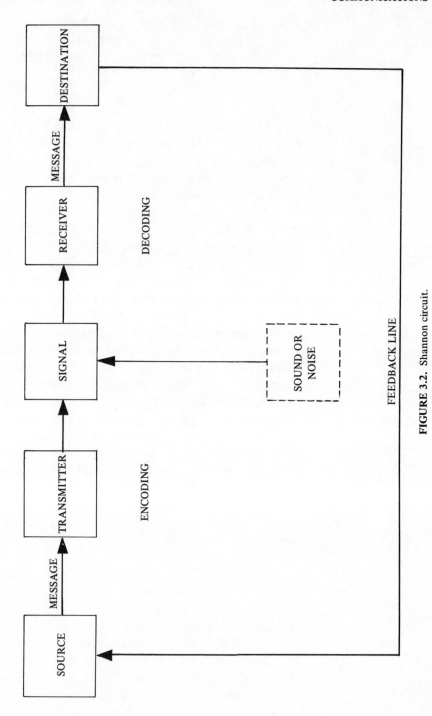

FIGURE 3.2. Shannon circuit.

thermometer. If the temperature rises above a predetermined level, the thermostat signals directly to the furnace that the amount of burning fuel is to be reduced. If the temperature falls below that level, the thermostat signals the furnace to burn more fuel.

Low feedback occurs at times in large university classes if professors rarely see their students individually. "Student aids" sometimes serve as buffers between a professor and his students in such cases, and communication is often a one-way activity until an examination is given. This approaches the military situation, in which in the interest of optimum efficiency and discipline, a command can be questioned only under pain of court martial. Thus, where feedback is not tolerated, absolute authority is often the rule. Under these *zero-feedback* conditions, the sender may never know if this message is understood, and if the destination is remote, must usually make an expensive, supplementary effort to determine how accurate the response is at the point of action. Therefore, provision must be made for feedback after vital business messages have been transmitted and received. This facilitates checking reports for accuracy and for measuring results against expectations.

3.3

Business Communications– General Criteria

In modern communication networks, messages may travel from man to man, from man to machine, from machine to man, or from machine to machine. In business systems, we are primarily interested in man-to-man communications.

We noted earlier that the goal of communication is the transfer of meaning. Both the articulate manager and the trainee who listens attentively make valuable contributions toward that goal.

The goals of business communications are:

1. to create an exact correspondence between the message that originates in the mind of the sender and the message that is received in the mind of the recipient;
2. to promote a unity of purpose between all members of the business system;
3. to motivate people for the accomplishment of management's objectives.

The Source

The person creating the message should:

1. organize his thoughts, considering the best possible arrangement of his main ideas, and stress effectively the purpose of the message;
2. know his destination, the ability of the recipient to comprehend the message as well as the recipient's status, attitudes, and beliefs—the message should not be sender-oriented, but adapted to the recipient's ability to understand (see "Empathy," page 41); and
3. use facts and evidence to justify the objectives of the message and avoid offering unsupported opinions.

The Destination

The person receiving the message should:

1. be alert and attentive, increasing his attention span as required by the message;
2. analyze the message and note its main points; and
3. be open-minded and unprejudiced regarding the message in order to comprehend the sender's objectives.

3.4

Aids and Obstacles to Effective Communication

To their recipients, messages may sometimes seem like interruptions of normal work activities. Managers usually have several reports a day to digest as well as receiving many verbal directions. Workers likewise are chiefly involved in clerical activities or in the production of materials and services. To be effective, therefore, business communications should be brief and to the point.

Because the communications network is vital to any business system, standards for all messages must be exact and uniform. The meanings of terms must be agreed upon, they must be precise, and semantic problems must be avoided. Senders and destinations must be "in tune" with each other to insure understanding.

Empathy

The source or person initiating a communication should place himself in the position of the person receiving the communication. This *empathy,* an attempt to duplicate in oneself the ideas and feelings of others, helps to determine whether one is communicating in a way in which his message will be understood. If his message is not understood, communication, by definition, has not taken place.

Redundancy

Redundant messages contain words that can be eliminated without loss of essential information. Adjectives, especially those of the eloquent variety, offer a good example of redundancy. In the statement, "I would feel *greatly* humiliated to be *put in the attitude of* a candidate and *then* fail to secure a nomination," redundant words are in italics.

Entropy

In an electronic system, entropy refers to electrical disturbances that degrade a signal. "Noise" in communications systems in general can also be described as entropy—the measure of disorder in a message.

To avoid "noise" or unwanted data, encoding information for a transmitter and decoding it from a receiver must be performed by competent personnel using properly maintained hardware. If the medium is a simple typewritten memo, the typist must be proficient and the typewriter in good working order. If the medium is a computer program, the programmer must possess the appropriate programming skills and the computer must be functioning properly.

The effectiveness of business communications can be expressed by a formula:

Effective Communication = Message – (Entropy + Redundancy)

This formula also expresses the concept that effective communication in a business system is a function of the orderliness of the system and that the degree of *order*, not volume of *information*, should increase as the direct result of a good communication network.

3.5

Types of Networks   *Networks,* which we have defined as arrangements of channels or routes over which messages travel, reflect not only the relative orderliness in business communications (or lack thereof), but may also be used to study the morale and performance of people in a business system (see Fig. 3.3).

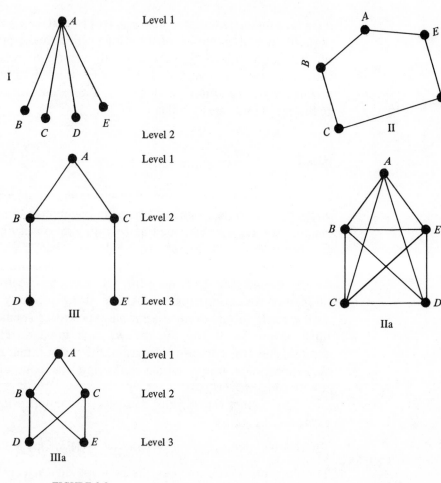

FIGURE 3.3.

Network I contains four workers and one supervisor.

Networks II and IIa describe leaderless equalitarian groups.

Networks III and IIIa both contain two supervisory levels.

In network I, performance is quick and accurate but morale is very poor. Leadership in network I is clear but the group is not a participative nor equalitarian one.

In network II communication is possible between two adjacent people. In network IIa all members are free to talk and listen to each other. In network II morale is very high but work performance is slow and accuracy is low. In IIa, typical of some project groups involving a team of engineers or scientists, morale is high and work performance is improved over network II because there are no limitations on a free exchange of ideas. Network IIa provides for membership control and a greater probability that errors will be corrected.

These advantages can offset the possibility that work speeds in IIa might be slower than in II.

Network III is typical of many business systems and can be easily related to Fig. 2.4 in Chapter 2. Network III provides a focus for all communications within the system and an intermediary level at B and C for coordination of different activities.

Network IIIa has some similarities to the functional plan of F. W. Taylor. Communication lines at the second and third levels can cross to provide accountability to several supervisors depending upon their specialization (see Fig. 1.2). The chief criticism of this network is the possible confusion created by reporting to several supervisors. When lines of authority cross it is often uncertain exactly who is the superior.

No set pattern of communication networks can be applied to all situations. The selection of the network depends upon the nature of the task to be performed and the attitudes and job skills of the people who are to perform that task.

3.6

Internal Communications

There are three types of internal communications within a business system:

Downward   Upward   Horizontal

Downward Communication

Downward communication (see Fig. 3.4, and compare network III in Fig. 3.3) may consist of spoken words, written bulletins, memos, company manuals, or performance evaluations. Personal contacts bypassing the chain of command when top management tours its shops and talks with workers is also a form of downward communication.

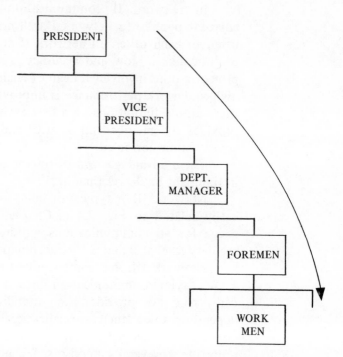

FIGURE 3.4.

Messages conveying information downward may contain new instructions or new knowledge. Sometimes these messages are directions or orders and sometimes they are more consultive in nature. Among their objectives may be:

Explanation of new procedures,

Employee motivation, or

Education or reclassification of employees.

If there are many management levels in the organization for messages to pass through, management may try to overemphasize rather than underemphasize their messages. In these situations care must be taken to avoid redundancy.

Upward Communications

Upward communications (see Fig. 3.5) often consist of messages of accountability and provide management with another tool for control of business operations. Emphasis here is on feedback and an exchange of opinions between different levels in a business structure.

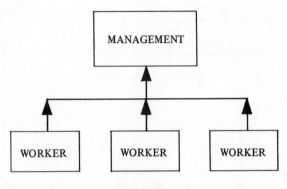

FIGURE 3.5.

Upward communications are usually work-oriented. They may be messages concerned with:

Production reports

Cost reports

Performance reports

Project reports

Conferences with supervisors in the chain of command

Suggestions

Grievance procedures

To control a business system, messages must be sent both downward to the point of action and upward to the source of authority and power. In Fig. 3.6, an organization chart of a small manufacturing company, first notice that none of the lines of communications cross. (Crossed channels of communications may indicate conflict within the structure.) The downward arrows represent the paths of messages from authority centers to operations personnel. The upward arrows represent the paths of messages which feed back information to centers of authority.

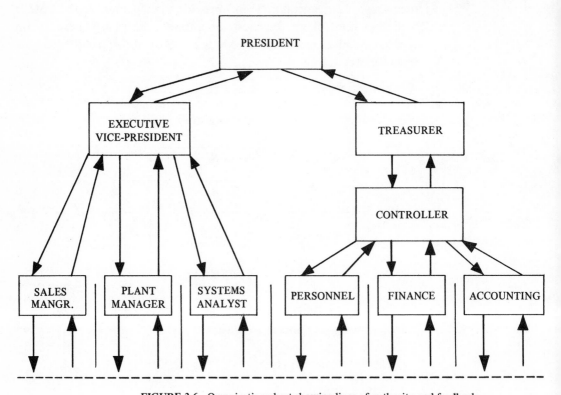

FIGURE 3.6. Organization chart showing lines of authority and feedback.

Horizontal Communication

Horizontal communication takes place between departments or between staff groups, or between line and staff functions. (See Fig. 3.7 and refer to networks II and IIa in Fig. 3.3.) In Fig. 3.7,

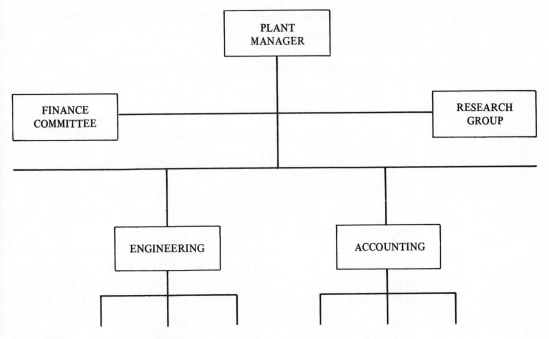

FIGURE 3.7.

assume that the accounting, engineering, finance, and research departments are in "horizontal communications" with each other. We could then rearrange these blocks on the organization chart to show the channels of communication as in Fig. 3.8.

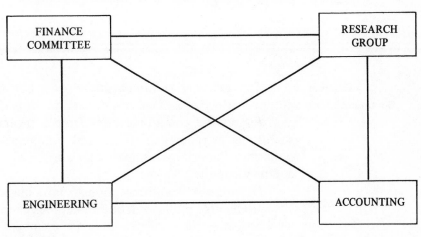

FIGURE 3.8.

Some pertinent questions that can be quickly resolved by this type of communication network are:

What kinds of projects are to be instigated?

What part of the budget will be used for the development of new products?

What are the costs of modifying existing products?

How does new technology affect existing products?

Horizontal communications may vary from formal reports on work progress to informal talks in which departments share their experiences with one another.

Horizontal communications improve cooperation and coordination between departments and can be helpful in reducing superfluous downward communications. For example, in Fig. 3.8, highly skilled specialists in each of the four groups working together provide a basis for deciding on new products, production methods, schedules, marketing, costs, and profits. Since few persons possess equally developed skills in accounting, finance, engineering, and science, horizontal communications provide the coordination of talents essential for this sort of leadership in large, complex organizations.

3.7

External Communications

The *external communications* of a business system can be grouped into two general categories: *functional* and *promotional.*

Functional communications from a business system include such items as reports to federal and state regulatory agencies and published financial statements that are made available in journals and newspapers.

Promotional communications from a business system include advertisements, public relations materials, newspaper and magazine articles, and even speeches by members of the system—as guest lecturers at local events.

EXERCISES   1. Give some examples of nonverbal communication you may encounter while driving your car.

2. List *one* example of verbal communication which has a precise definition in the vocabulary of a professional in data processing and which may not communicate anything to a landscape artist.

3. How may emotions affect the communication from your professor to you?

4. Using the Shannon Circuit (Fig. 3.2) as a guide, describe the process of taking an examination.

5. Criticize the following memo:

> To: Director of Data Processing
> From: Controller
> Subject: Machine Purchase Proposal 2/10/71
>   File No. 2103
>   Your proposal of 2/10/71 for the purchase and acquisition of additional equipment shows a complete lack of knowledge of the scarcity of company resources in this period of tight money as well as ignorance and lack of knowledge of sound investment policy. Although I can see the need for one of the machines, the other appears to be completely unjustified for reasons stated above.

Consider factors the sender of a message should be aware of as well as empathy, redundance, and entropy.

PROBLEMS   1. *The Holland Company*

The Holland Company manufactures a single product, sheet-metal industrial shelves. You are asked to analyze the information flow concerning the basic raw material used in production. The amount of sheet metal ordered is decided on the basis of information received from several sources. The typical sequence is as follows:

   i. The Vice-President of Sales obtains monthly forecasts from his field representatives.

   ii. The Vice-President of Sales relates these forecasts to industrial economic conditions and compiles a 3-month sales forecast.

   iii. The Plant Manager, who receives a copy of the 3-month sales forecast each month, determines production requirements after checking inventory levels of finished goods on hand and work-in-process.

49

iv. The Purchasing Department receives a copy of the production schedule and from this determines the amount of raw material required for production. After determining the amount of raw sheet metal on hand from the Stores Control Manager, the availability of sheet metal from suppliers, various shipping schedules, and the prices for various quantities, purchase orders are issued to the appropriate suppliers.

v. When the raw material is shipped, the supplier sends an invoice directly to the Holland Company, and it is forwarded to the company's Controller, who matches it up with a copy of the purchase order received from Purchasing and with a copy of the receiving report from Stores Control. One of the Controller's clerks checks the quantity and price of the goods ordered against the invoice and the amount and specifications shown on the receiving report against the purchase order. Next the Controller forwards all documents to the company's Treasurer. The Treasurer reviews the documents and authorizes the payment of the invoice amount.

Required: Draw a diagram to show the flow of information.

2. Federal Corporation

In the assembly room of Federal Corporation the Assembly Foreman feels that one of his assembly groups is not performing at an optimum level. There seems to be frequent dissension among the workers and production is erratic. He describes the assembly operation to you as follows:

i. The job to be accomplished is the assembly of parts A-1, A-2, C-10, and K-4. This is a subassembly of a brake system.

ii. There are 7 people in this assembly area, 6 of them divided into two equal work groups. Three people in group 1 assemble parts A-1 and A-2, directed by one of the three as a working group leader. This subassembly, called A-3, is passed directly to group 2, who work adjacent to group 1. Group 2 is composed of 3 people with one acting as a working group leader. This group adds parts C-10 and K-4 for a completed unit, which goes directly to the Inspector, who has a work bench about 20 feet away. The Inspector reports to the Quality Control Foreman. Any faulty assembly work is returned to the appropriate group leader for correction. The seventh person under the foreman's authority also assembles parts A-1 and A-2 on a separate work bench next to the others, but his parts are transferred to an assembly area in another part of the plant to be used in a larger brake system.

Required:
(a) Draw an information network for the assembly area described above (refer to Fig. 3.3).
(b) Write a narrative of the kinds of problems in productivity and morale you would expect to find in this situation.

(c) What changes do you think should be made? Why?

(d) Draw an information network to reflect the changes recommended in (c) above.

3. *The Urban Bus Company*

The Urban Bus Company, a local city bus system, called in a management consultant to aid them in determining changes that customers might desire in the bus system. After considerable discussion, the consultant decided to conduct a survey of bus passengers by sending interviewers on the buses to ask riders a selected set of questions. As a result of the survey, tabulated in Fig. 3.9, the company purchased several new buses, increased the number of daily trips, and altered some of the routes.

REVEALED BUS CHANGE PREFERENCES

	Percent
Cleaner-newer	27.
Run more often	25.
Run later	15.
Special service	14.
Better Service (convenient)-better routing	10.
Fares reduction	6.
Reduced fare tokens for multiple users	1.5
New routes	1.5
	100.0

FIGURE 3.9.

Required:

(a) Display the above communication system by the use of a Shannon Circuit (Fig. 3.2). Write a brief paragraph on each block in the Shannon Circuit explaining its relationship to the communications between the Urban Bus Company and its passengers.

(b) Explain how the method used by the consultant may or may not be structured to meet the requirements or avoid the problems presented on p. 39 and Sec. 3.4.

CHAPTER **4**

FORMS DESIGN AND CONTROL

4.1

Forms—Definition and Purpose

Information usually travels through a business system on paper forms, frequently on punched cards. Such forms are media that can aid in the collection of data, provide the necessary information for the accomplishments of objectives, support decision-making, announce new policies and procedures and generally control and improve operations.

A form is a piece of paper that contains some preprinted information and blank spaces for the insertion of data. Forms should be designed to meet the communications needs of a system.

The function or purpose of a form should be clear to anyone who has to fill in data on it. For example, an application for employment must contain spaces for statistics vital for the employer's evaluation of the applicant. An invoice (see Fig. 4.1) should indicate such things as quantity, description, customer name, and so on.

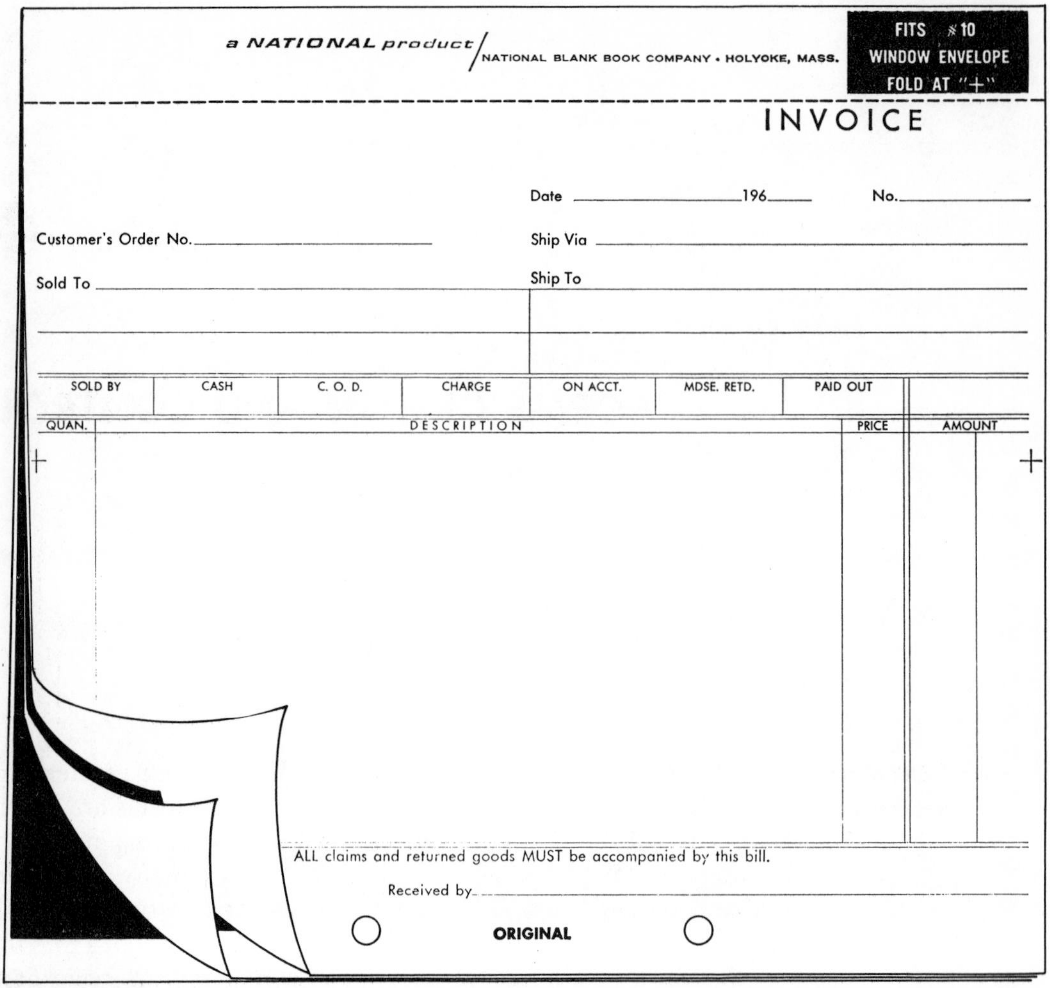
a NATIONAL product / NATIONAL BLANK BOOK COMPANY • HOLYOKE, MASS.

FITS #10 WINDOW ENVELOPE FOLD AT "+"

INVOICE

Date ______ 196__ No.______

Customer's Order No.______ Ship Via ______

Sold To ______ Ship To ______

SOLD BY	CASH	C. O. D.	CHARGE	ON ACCT.	MDSE. RETD.	PAID OUT

QUAN.	DESCRIPTION	PRICE	AMOUNT

ALL claims and returned goods MUST be accompanied by this bill.

Received by______

ORIGINAL

FIGURE 4.1.

4.2 Types of Forms

Forms may be prepared on single separate sheets of paper, and they may contain margins punched for insertion in binders. Forms may be continuous such as the type used on computers and containing holes punched at the sides to facilitate travel through the computer's high-speed printers (see Figs. 4.2 and 4.7).

DURA PROG 01
RS - 4

CUSTOMER, MASTER SHEET   PAGE   OF

| TRANS CODE | ACCT. NO. | BR. | | BILL TO BRANCH | DATE | COMPANY CODE | DISCOUNT CODE | PRIOR CODE |

SEE DISCOUNT SHEET

ACCOUNT NAME

ATTN. A/P DEPT.

ADDRESS LINE 1

ADDRESS LINE 2

CUST. DEPT. NO.

ADDRESS LINE 3

CUST. STORE NO.

CITY

STATE   ZIP

SHIPPER NO. 1

W G T   FROM   TO

SHIPPER NO. 2

W G T   FROM   TO

| P. P. CD. | TRAF. CD. | INV. CD. | ST. TAX | LOC. TAX |

SPECIAL INSTRUCTION ORDER

SPECIAL INSTRUCTIONS INVOICE

| ST. CD. | CITY CD. | TER. | SLSM | | CREDIT CODE | CREDIT LIMIT |

* COMPANY NO'S.	PARCEL POST CODES	INVOICE CODE	TRAFFIC CODE	PRIORITY CODE	TRANSACTION CODE
01 = ESTEE LAUDER	1 = P. P. 1-40 LBS.	1 = ORIGINAL WITH CTN.	1 = CLASS 100	1 = PRIORITY	07 = NEW
02 = ARAMIS	2 = P. P. 1-20 LBS.	2 = DUPL. WITH CTN.	7 = CLASS 70	2 = REGULAR	08 = CHANGE
03 = CLINIQUE	3 = P. P. 1-30 LBS.	3 = ORIGINAL & DUPL. WITH CTN.			09 = CANCEL
04 = AZURL	8 = P. P. ONLY -	4 = TWO PACKING SLIPS			
	SPLIT SHIP IF NECESSARY	5 = PACKING SLIP IN ENV.			
	9 = NO. P. P.				

| CREDIT AUTH. | NEW ACCT. AUTH. | CHANGE AUTH. | |

FIGURE 4.2.

Forms may be bound and attached to a pad (see Fig. 4.3). As indicated in the forms distribution chart of Fig. 4.18, colors may be used to expedite forms distribution.

11527

Date _____ 19 _____

Sold to _____

Address _____

MASTER METER DUPLICATOR

AUTOMATICALLY
PRINTED

FULLY SEALED IN

TO INSURE YOU
OF ACCURACY

T. T. SALESMAN   Time _____   A.M.
                                                                      P.M.
    SLIP NO.

YOUR SALE NO.	GALLON READING-FINISH	10ths
PREVIOUS SALE NO.	GALLON READING-START	
	GALLONS DELIVERED	

PRODUCT	GALS.	PRICE	TOTAL AMT.

Received
Payment $_____   _____
                                    Tank Truck Salesman

CUSTOMER SIGN HERE AFTER DELIVERY ONLY—ABOVE GALLONS RECEIVED

ECON-O-FORM NO. 80-T

INSERT FACE DOWN   ▼   BOTTOM END FIRST

FIGURE 4.3.

The original and several copies of an individual form may be grouped into a set. These multiple copies may be interleaved with carbon paper, or the forms may be of the carbonless variety produced by the NCR Company.

An accordion-like or fanfold arrangement has copies of the form connected at the sides (see Fig. 4.4).

UARCO
Fanfold continuous
forms

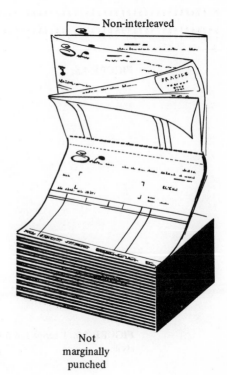

FIGURE 4.4. UARCO fan-fold continuous forms.

A punched card (Fig. 4.5) fits our description of a form in that it contains spaces for the insertion of information.

Post cards, envelopes, tags, and mailing labels are examples of forms that are usually kept in large supply in the office supplies department. (See Fig. 4.6.)

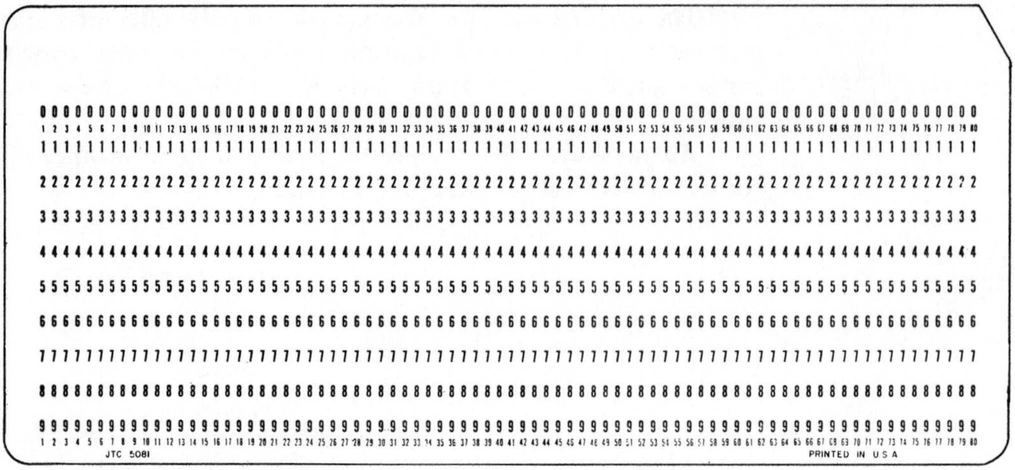

FIGURE 4.5.

FIGURE 4.6. 1 across fan fold style.

4.3

Forms Design *General Considerations*

The wages or salaries paid to persons who use forms are more important than costs of the forms themselves. People who prepare or receive forms in a business system must work with documents that communicate clearly. Therefore, the first and most important question to be asked before a form is designed is: Is this form needed, and if so, why? Other questions that are to also be answered are:

> *What* are the functions of the form? Are these functions duplicated?
>
> *When* will the form be used?
>
> *How many* copies are needed and where do these copies go? Are the copies stored, or destroyed after use?
>
> *Who* will use the form? Who fills it out? Who reads and processes the information once the form has been completed?

If the answers to questions like these indicate that a new form is necessary, then other determinations must also be made:

> What kind of paper is to be used? If the form is internal—that is, if it does not travel outside of the work stations in a business system—then its production should be as inexpensive as possible.
>
> Are the forms to be run off on a computer? If so, continuous forms provided with punched marginal holes appropriately spaced for the computer's printer are needed. (See Fig. 4.7.)
>
> Are single sheets required, or are sets of two or more required?
>
> If multiple copies are required, will the sheets be interleaved with carbon paper, or are carbonless paper forms to be used? If sets are to be used, how will the copies in one set be fastened together for the computer run? by crimping? by stapling? (See Fig. 4.8.)
>
> How are consecutive copies or sets to be numbered? If the forms are to be found on a pad, will the individual sheets or sets of sheets be numbered in sequence? If the forms are to be run off on the computer, will the computer print out the sequence numbers?

FIGURE 4.7.

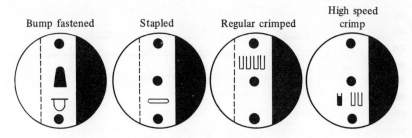

FIGURE 4.8. Fastening methods.

The purpose of any form is to communicate, and the effectiveness of this communication lies in the design of the form. Sufficient space must be allowed for data, which should be collected and presented in an orderly manner. Captions and headings must be easy to read, and instructions (if any) should be brief and easy to follow.

In Fig. 4.9, instructions are found in each box. Notice how the instructions that apply to the completion of the form may also be used by a keypunch operator, who can put the appropriate data into a punched card.

CIRCLE ONE NUMBER FOR EACH QUESTION.

WHAT MACHINE ARE YOU MOST FAMILIAR WITH?	Col. 25
Keypunch	1
Sorter	2
Reproducer	3
Collator	4
Interpreter	5
Accounting machine	6
Computer	7

WHAT IS YOUR AREA OF DATA PROCESSING SPECIALIZATION?	Col. 26
Business	1
Industrial	2
Scientific	3
Educational	4

HIGHEST DEGREE EARNED IN A COLLEGE OR UNIVERSITY	Col. 27
Associate	1
Bachelor's	2
Masters	3
Doctorate	4

FIGURE 4.9.

61

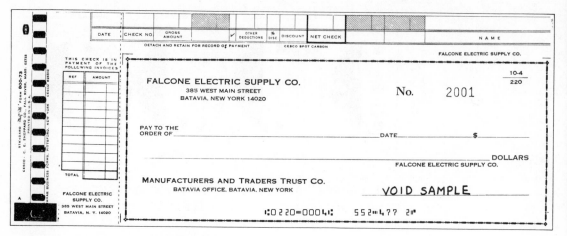

FIGURE 4.10.

Special Considerations

The size of a form is often crucial to electronic data processing. For example, checks usually should be a minimum of $2\frac{3}{4}$ by $6''$ so that they may be processed by the bank's check sorter (Fig. 4.10).

Postal regulations may be a consideration in the designing of window envelopes and mailing labels.

Type

Type should be legible, not ornate, so that any preprinted data on the form may be easily read and understood. The best kind of type to use is one that can be reproduced in a photocopy process—i.e., duplicated, enlarged, or compressed without loss of readability.

Heading Format

The *heading format* (Fig. 4.11), the *ballot-box format,* (Fig. 4.12) and the caption-on-line format (Fig. 4.12a) are all easily understood. If a form is "busy" or must contain a great deal of inserted data, the *angled-heading-type* (see Fig. 4.13) is one very satisfactory method of representing long headings.

	NAVIGATION				ELECTRICAL					FUEL				
MONTH	COMPASS	SEXTANT	CHARTS	TABLES	WIRING	TRANSISTORS	CAPACITORS	DIODES	SWITCHES	R-F-231	R-F-232	R-F-301	R-F-650	R-F-651
JULY														
AUGUST														
SEPTEMBER														

FIGURE 4.11.

Application completed?	☐ Yes	☐ No
Physical exam completed?	☐ Yes	☐ No
References in to personnel?	☐ Yes	☐ No
School transcripts to personnel?	☐ Yes	☐ No
Payroll number assigned?	☐ Yes	☐ No

FIGURE 4.12.

Employee number _____   Department _____

Building number _____   Shop number _____

Seniority _____   Shop union name _____

FIGURE 4.12a.

OFFICE EQUIPMENT	POLICE DEPT.	FIRE DEPT.	WATER WORKS	CITY ENGINEERING	CLERICAL	URBAN RENEWAL	PARKS DEPARTMENT	HEALTH & WELFARE	COMMENTS
DESKS									
CHAIRS									
FILE CABINETS									
STAPLERS									
STATIONERY									

FIGURE 4.13.

Layout

Forms should be designed on layout sheets that clearly indicate the type of printing desired and the exact location of each printed character. Some type of graph paper is helpful if the form is not a punched card.

Margins and headings should be penciled in lightly. All spaces for the insertion of information or signatures should be made large enough to avoid cluttering.

It is usually wise to draw an extra copy of the layout sheet for the vendor's use. Otherwise, care must be taken in the preparation and duplication of layout forms. For example, a blue preprinted form will not reproduce well in some photocopy processes.

The IBM Printer Spacing Chart (Fig. 4.14) is very useful in designing forms to be used by computers. Each box corresponds to one character as printed by the computer; the spacing of lines on this layout form also matches that of computer printers. Figure 4.14 shows the exact print positions and lines for a student's list of courses prepared on a Printer Spacing Chart. Notice the headings and spaces for the insertion information (to be printed by the computer).

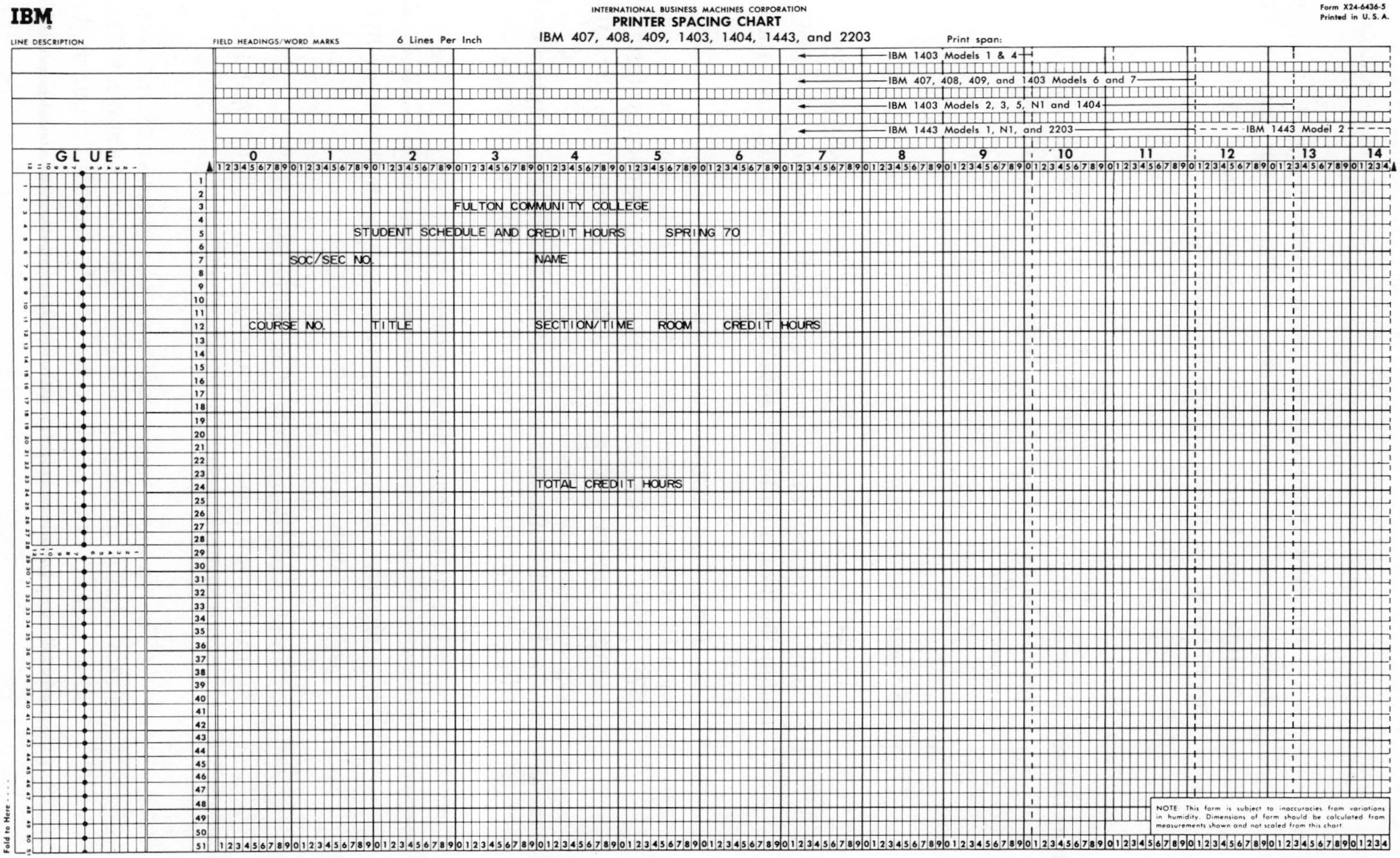
IBM
LINE DESCRIPTION
FIELD HEADINGS/WORD MARKS
6 Lines Per Inch
INTERNATIONAL BUSINESS MACHINES CORPORATION
PRINTER SPACING CHART
IBM 407, 408, 409, 1403, 1404, 1443, and 2203
Print span:
IBM 1403 Models 1 & 4
IBM 407, 408, 409, and 1403 Models 6 and 7
IBM 1403 Models 2, 3, 5, N1 and 1404
IBM 1443 Models 1, N1, and 2203
IBM 1443 Model 2
Form X24-6436-5
Printed in U. S. A.
GLUE
FULTON COMMUNITY COLLEGE
STUDENT SCHEDULE AND CREDIT HOURS SPRING 70
SOC/SEC NO.
NAME
COURSE NO.
TITLE
SECTION/TIME
ROOM
CREDIT HOURS
TOTAL CREDIT HOURS
NOTE: This form is subject to inaccuracies from variations in humidity. Dimensions of form should be calculated from measurements shown and not scaled from this chart.
Fold to Here

FIGURE 4.14.

The IBM Multiple-Card Layout Form in Fig. 4.15 is used to design fields used on punched cards. Printer Spacing Charts, Multiple-Card Layout Forms, and similar aids may be obtained from forms vendors or computer manufacturers.

4.4

Forms Control

Storing forms and requesting new forms should be the responsibility of a *forms administration* or *office supplies department*.

Numbering and Coding

To facilitate the functions of forms control, forms may contain *identification numbers* and *sequence numbers*. The identification number is sometimes grouped with the title of the form.

Fig. 4.16 shows two numbers: 021523 is the form identification number and is grouped with the title of the form; 679 refers to the 679th copy of this particular form. These numbers can be associated with the dollar amount, the date, and the customer for a specific transaction.

For identification in an inventory of forms, and to expedite forms distribution, the forms identification number can be coded according to a subject, function, and type.

The *subject code* may indicate:

1. a physical object in the system, such as an item in an inventory bin, a vehicle, a piece of machinery, etc.
2. a person in the system, such as a new employee, a retired employee, a dependent of an employee, etc.
3. a condition about something or someone in the system, such as maintenance, theft, illness, travel, etc.

The *function code* indicates the purpose of the form and states what is to happen to, or on behalf of, the subject. The *type code* indicates the media to be used, for example, punched cards, envelopes, padded paper, stock paper, etc. The coding sequence in

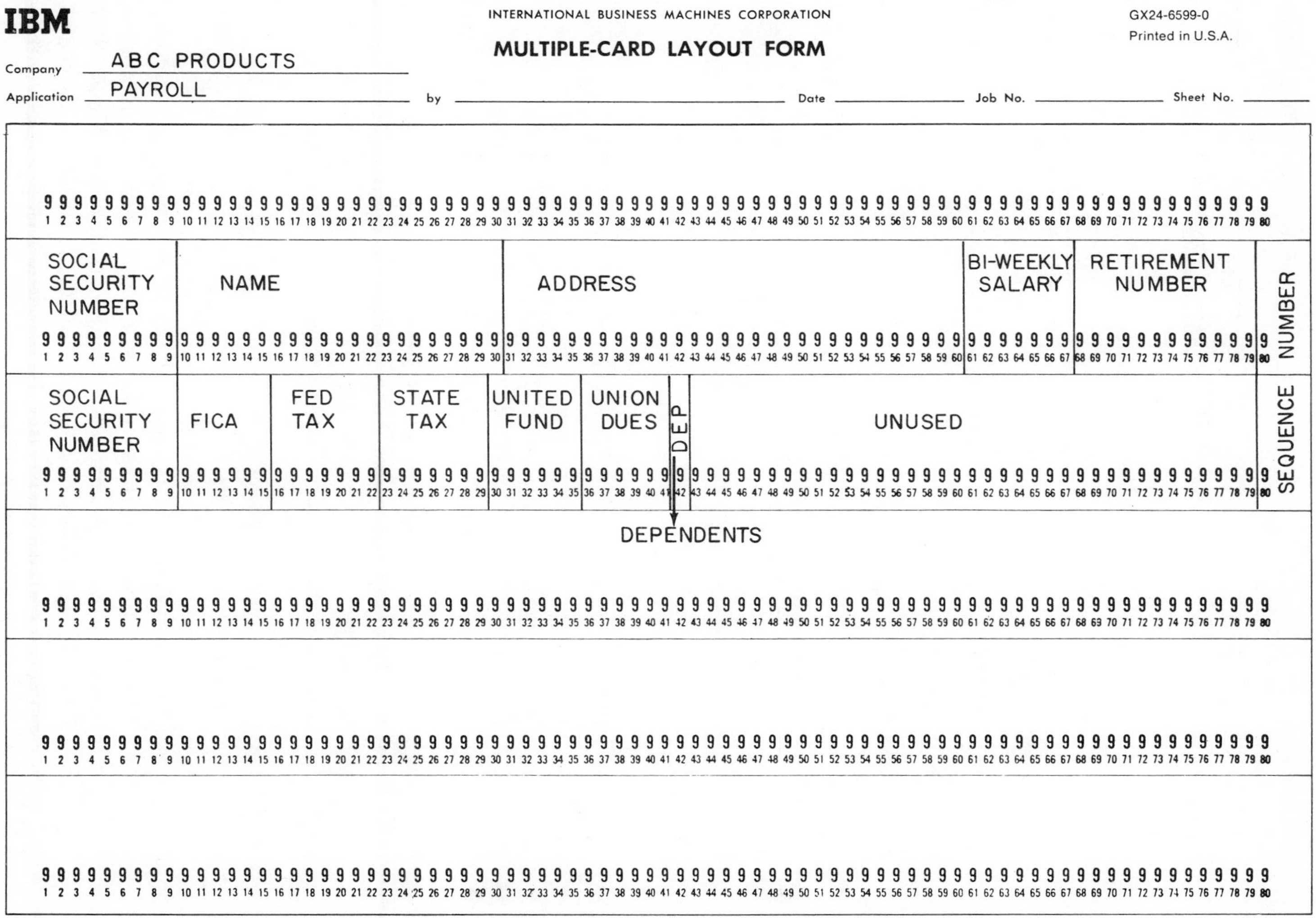
IBM
INTERNATIONAL BUSINESS MACHINES CORPORATION
MULTIPLE-CARD LAYOUT FORM
GX24-6599-0
Printed in U.S.A.
Company ABC PRODUCTS
Application PAYROLL
by
Date
Job No.
Sheet No.
SOCIAL SECURITY NUMBER
NAME
ADDRESS
BI-WEEKLY SALARY
RETIREMENT NUMBER
NUMBER
SOCIAL SECURITY NUMBER
FICA
FED TAX
STATE TAX
UNITED FUND
UNION DUES
DEP
UNUSED
SEQUENCE
DEPENDENTS

FIGURE 4.15.

INVOICE   NO. 679

021523

DATE _____

CUSTOMER NAME   _____

ADDRESS   _____

TERMS   _____

REMITTANCE   _____

QTY	ITEM #	DESCRIPTION	PRICE EXT.	TOTAL
				TAX ____
			PAY THIS AMOUNT	____

FIGURE 4.16.

Fig. 4.17 is an example that uses six digits to identify a form. Thus the subject of the form under consideration is "cash," the function "receipt," and the type is $8\frac{1}{2}$ x 11" bond paper.

Forms Distribution

When forms are properly filled out, they must be distributed to the proper departments for processing. For this purpose, a forms distribution chart is a useful graphic aid. Figure 4.18 illustrates the destinations of some of the forms under our coding scheme. Various colors may be associated with departments to further expedite distribution.

68

00-09 *SUBJECT CODE*	10-19 *FUNCTION CODE*
00 Parts	10 Application
01 Cash	11 Authorization
02 Invoice	12 Schedule
03 Packing slip	13 Report
04 Payroll checks	14 Inspection
05 Employment	15 Request
06 Time sheets	16 Acknowledge
07 Purchase order	17 Payment
08 Re-order	18 Deduction
09 Transportation	19 Receipt

20-29
TYPE CODE

20 Padded form
21 Continuous (for computer)
22 Punched cards
23 8½″ × 11″ Bond paper
24 Envelope
25 Tag
26 Label
27 Ballot
28 Unused
29 Unused

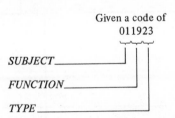

Given a code of
011923

SUBJECT_____
FUNCTION_____
TYPE_____

FIGURE 4.17.

Forms Storage and Ordering

Forms should be stored in properly marked bins or on shelves. When the quantity of a particular form is depleted to a predetermined level, a refill purchase order should be sent to the forms vendor. The lack of a particular form can cause bottlenecks in such situations as a sales-order or billing cycle and even more chaotic problems with payroll checks. After a new form has been

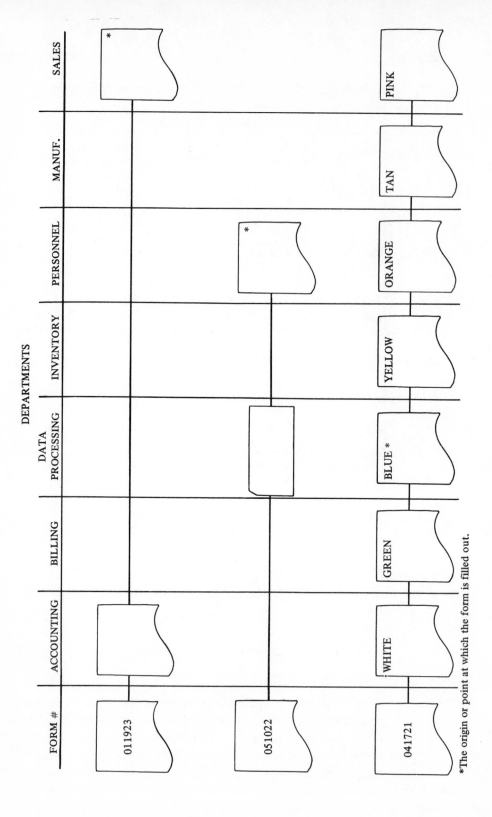

FIGURE 4.18. Forms distribution chart.

*The origin or point at which the form is filled out.

70

approved and designed to meet a communication need in the system, it must be ordered.

If a business system has the capability to print its own forms, proofreading and internal delivery schedules are usually worked out without too much difficulty. When the form to be ordered is a standard type which an outside vendor is prepared to supply, delivery usually requires less time than an entirely new custom-made form requires.

When ordering forms from an outside forms vendor, several problems must be considered. In ordering such forms as payroll checks, for example, the buyer and the forms vendor share the responsibility of insuring that new forms are printed on time. This means that orders for new forms must be submitted with a sufficient amount of *lead time*—the time required for producing a proof, proofreading, reading the corrected proof, and final delivery.

Figure 4.19 shows one example of the time relationships involved in the delivery of standard and custom-made forms.

DAYS

FORMS	1	3	17	20	25	40
STANDARD		REORDER		DELIVERY		
CUSTOM	DESIGNED	ORDER	PROOF	APPROVAL	CORRECTED PROOF	DELIVERY

FIGURE 4.19.

Reorders should be anticipated and vendors given sufficient advance notice so that delivery dates will meet the requirements of the system.

EXERCISES 1. State the objective of a well-designed form.

2. (a) What is the purpose of a form identification number?
   (b) Give an example of the breakdown or meaning of an identification number.

3. (a) What is a forms distribution chart?
   (b) What are its major characteristics?
   (c) What are the advantages in using a forms distribution chart?

71

4. What questions should be asked before a form is designed?

5. List the conditions under which the following form formats can be used:
   (a) The heading-format
   (b) Ballot-box format
   (c) Caption-on-line format
   (d) Angled-heading format

6. In designing a form which aids can be used when the forms are to be used:
   (a) on a computer? Why?
   (b) with mechanical or hand-filled-in methods?

PROBLEMS   1. *The Parkway Corporation*

The Parkway Corporation has several types of forms in use. Because considerable confusion often exists in the routing of forms, you have been asked to prepare a forms distribution chart and to design a recommended form coding system. In the Accounting Department you find the following forms and reports in use:

Form	*Destination*
Monthly balance sheet	President
Monthly profit and loss	Treasurer
Monthly profit and loss	Controller
Selling expense analysis	Vice-President–Sales
" " "	President
Factory cost budget analysis	Vice-President–Manufacturing
" " " "	Plant Superintendent
Factory departmental budget analysis (3 depts.)	Plant Superintendent
" " "	Department heads
Monthly profit-and-loss forecast	President
" " " " "	Treasurer

Required: Design and fill in a forms distribution chart appropriate to the above situation.

2. *Burr Truck and Trailer Sales Inc.*

The form in Fig. 4.20 is used as a truck-repair order. It serves many purposes within the organization, and its major uses are:

72

BURR TRUCK & TRAILER SALES, INC.								

Table content of the form:

BURR TRUCK & TRAILER SALES, INC.
3125 VESTAL ROAD   VESTAL, N. Y. 13850
DIAL 729 - 2211

CUMMINS   STRICK TRAILERS   OSHKOSH   DETROIT   TERMS:
DIESEL   SALES-SERVICE-PARTS TRUCKS   DIESEL   CASH

SALE AMOUNT	QUAN	PARTS

NAME	ORDER WRITTEN BY	DATE
ADDRESS	TIME RECEIVED A.M. P.M.	TERMS
CITY	PHONE WHEN READY	TIME PROMISED A.M. P.M.	CUSTOMER'S ORDER NO.
YEAR	TYPE OR MODEL	UNIT NO.	SERIAL NO.	LICENSE NO.	SPEEDOMETER

REPAIR ORDER - LABOR INSTRUCTIONS

INTERNAL SUMMARY				
ACCT.	CHARGE	COST	TOTAL LABOR	
			TOTAL PARTS	
			SERVICE CALL	
			TOTAL GAS, OIL, GREASE	

WE ARE NOT RESPONSIBLE FOR LOSS OR DAMAGE TO CARS OR ARTICLES LEFT IN CARS IN CASE OF FIRE, THEFT OR ANY OTHER CAUSE BEYOND OUR CONTROL.

GAS, OIL, GREASE	AMT.
GALS. @ GAS	
QTS. @ OIL	
LBS. @ GREASE	
TOTAL GAS, OIL, GREASE →	

MACHINE SHOP	
MISC	
TAX	

← TOTAL PARTS

(Courtesy of The Standard Register Company)

FIGURE 4.20.

(a) as a list of work instructions for the mechanics;

(b) as a list of parts used by the mechanics in repairing the truck—also used to reduce the inventory control (amount and quantity);

(c) as a list of the amounts of gas, oil, and grease used in servicing the vehicle—also used to reduce gas, oil, and grease inventory;

(d) as labor-item record on each repair for all repair orders for a time period "tied" into total labor for the period;

(e) as a record of miscellaneous services, such as service calls and labor or service performed at a specialized shop;

(f) as a customer invoice (when the form is completed);

(g) as a permanent record of work performed—for warranty requirements; and

(h) as a work instruction (when signed by the customer).

Required: Critically review the form in Fig. 4.20 and suggest appropriate changes or additions.

3. *Inventory Control*

You have been requested by your supervisor to aid in the construction of a system to organize the flow of information in the Inventory Control Section of your firm. Specifically, he has assigned you a problem of designing three forms to be used in recording materials received and issued from stores inventory. Because of the rapid growth of the firm, many present methods and procedures are no longer adequate for the current level of business. Your supervisor suggests that you design a new standard purchase requisition, purchase order, and receiving report. You have never performed this type of task before, nor are you completely familiar with these types of forms. You therefore investigate the nature of the three proposed forms and the purposes that they can reasonably expect to fulfill. You find the following information:

A. *Purchase requisition*—a written request to the Purchasing Department to order materials or services specified thereon. For goods regularly kept in the material stores area, the purchase requisition may be issued by the materials clerk. This clerk would issue such a requisition for a particular material when the balance-on-hand (shown by the Materials Ledger account) falls below the prescribed minimum. On occasion for special materials and services, the purchase requisition may be issued by supervisory personnel, such as the Foreman or Office Manager. One copy goes to the Purchasing Department; another copy is retained by the person issuing the request.

Your analysis of the requirements of your company indicate the purchase requisition should show the following information:

1. title of form;
2. department requesting the items described thereon;
3. requisition number;
4. date;
5. where the goods should be delivered;
6. who should be notified when they are delivered;
7. what the materials are to be used for (production, replacement parts, etc.);
8. amount of this type of material on hand;
9. approximate amount of usage for 1 month;
10. date of required delivery;
11. description of material ordered;
12. the quantity ordered;
13. the price.

In addition to the above information the purchase requisition should have provision for the authorization of the order by a responsible person.

B. *Purchase order*—used by the Purchasing Department to order materials or services from outside vendors. The original of this form goes to the supplier, while one copy is retained by the Purchasing Department for follow-up purposes and is subsequently used to verify the supplier's invoice by the Accounting Department. A third copy could be sent to the Receiving Department to serve as notice that shipment will be received as specified thereon.

Your investigation reveals that the purchase order should have the following information contained thereon:

1. name of form;
2. provision should be made for numbering the form;
3. company name;
4. date;
5. name and address of the supplier or vendor;
6. means by which goods are to be shipped;
7. quantity;
8. complete description of materials;
9. unit price and total amount of order; and
10. an authorized person's signature.

C. *Receiving form*—normally issued by an authorized person in the Receiving Department to provide a record of the materials received in that area. One copy should go to the Purchasing Department, a second copy should go to the person who requested the goods, and one copy should be retained by the Receiving Department as a permanent record of goods received.

Required: Design appropriate forms for A and B. For C, the student is free to include what he thinks are pertinent entries. This should include at least:

1. *the quantity;*
2. *the description of materials received;*
3. *the name and address of the vendor or supplier.*

CHAPTER 5

RECORDS AND FILES

5.1

Records   A *record* is a group of related facts treated as a unit. Records should not be confused with forms, which, we noted in Chapter 4, are preprinted pieces of paper containing spaces for the insertions of information.

A bank deposit slip will serve to make clear the distinction between a record and a form.

Before it is filled out (see Fig. 5.1), the bank deposit slip is a form—a piece of paper containing blank spaces for the insertion of information. After the depositor fills out this slip of paper (see Fig. 5.2) and turns it over to the bank teller with his deposit, it becomes a *record* of that specific transaction. In the bank deposit *record* in Fig. 5.2, the depositor's name and account number, the date, the amount of money in bills, coin, Canadian currency, and checks, and the total amount deposited are a group of related facts to be treated as a unit.

ThriftiCheck DEPOSIT TICKET

FRANK J. CLARK

CHECKS AND OTHER ITEMS ARE RECEIVED FOR DEPOSIT
SUBJECT TO THE RULES AND REGULATIONS OF THIS BANK.
PLEASE BE SURE ALL ITEMS ARE PROPERLY ENDORSED.

DATE _____ 19 ____

**LIBERTY NATIONAL BANK
AND TRUST COMPANY**
BATAVIA, NEW YORK

⑈0 2 20⑈⑈00 ⑈ 2⑈:   0 78 3⑈⑈ 58 7⑈⑈

	DOLLARS	CENTS
BILLS		
COIN		
CANADIAN		
CHECKS 1		
2		
3		
TOTAL CHECKS		
TOTAL		

FIGURE 5.1.

ThriftiCheck DEPOSIT TICKET

FRANK J. CLARK

CHECKS AND OTHER ITEMS ARE RECEIVED FOR DEPOSIT
SUBJECT TO THE RULES AND REGULATIONS OF THIS BANK.
PLEASE BE SURE ALL ITEMS ARE PROPERLY ENDORSED.

DATE ___*Oct 1*___ 19 *70*

**LIBERTY NATIONAL BANK
AND TRUST COMPANY**
BATAVIA, NEW YORK

⑈0 2 20⑈⑈00 ⑈ 2⑈:   0 78 3⑈⑈ 58 7⑈⑈

	DOLLARS	CENTS
BILLS	18	00
COIN		
CANADIAN		
CHECKS 1	20	00
2	45	00
3		
TOTAL CHECKS	65	00
TOTAL	83	00

FIGURE 5.2.

5.2

**Records
Management**

Records of a business system accumulate. As an organization becomes larger and top management becomes further away from the daily transactions, control over the flow of information about the systems activities becomes a specialized function of one person or a small group of persons.

78

This specialized function of the management of records should provide:

1. *Accessibility*—quick access to active records and those inactive records which it is company policy to retain.
2. *Retention*—efficient and effective flow of the information from its creation through use to its destruction.
3. *Storage*—appropriate storage devices and accessible depository areas for both permanent and temporary records.

Accessibility

Accessing records can be facilitated by a logical arrangement or sequence, such as ascending numerical order by social security number, or date, or item number, or department number.

Request frequency is an important factor affecting accessibility. Thus anyone responsible for records management must know how soon an invoice needs to be examined after it has been received. Will it be requested after it has been in storage for a month? After a year?

In general:

Sales orders are processed as soon as they are received.

Accounts receivable records are usually interrogated monthly in order to bill customers.

Inventory records are usually verified annually.

Company charters are usually reviewed only when legal action is involved.

Active records such as sales orders and accounts receivable must be made easily available to all those responsible for processing them. Inactive records such as company charters can be stored in safes or bank vaults.

Retention

The question of *what* records are to be retained and *how long* they are to be retained can be answered in part by the internal requirements or policies of a system and external requirements such as government regulations.

Government regulations require tax, social security, stock transactions, workmen's compensation, payroll, and interstate commerce records to be retained by a business system and laws require that these records be available to various federal and state agencies for inspection.

Records of estimates, engineering records, plans, and business charters are to be regarded as permanent in nature and should never be destroyed.

Records of the individual transactions of a business system— payment vouchers, invoices, freight bills, etc.—should be retained for as long as internal policy dictates.

To avoid the accumulation of unnecessary records, all records should be destroyed when their retention period has ended. Even then, the destruction of any record requires proper authorization.

Storage

The manner in which records are stored is often crucial to the operation of a system. A logical arrangement which meets standard protection requirements is mandatory. Records should be kept either in steel containers, in filing cabinets, on metal shelves, or in safes; the depository should be fire- and floodproof.

Where volume is large and request frequency is great, an efficient method is microfilm storage, which reduces storage space by about 90 per cent and lasts as long as (or longer than) paper; moreover, microfilmed records are acceptable as legal documents. The potential growth of a company's records must be anticipated over a period of time and sufficient storage space allotted for the expected extra volume.

To help control accessibility, retention and storage, a *record inventory and retention schedule* should be developed. Figure 5.3 illustrates such a schedule in which record categories are arranged alphabetically.

5.3

Files   A *file* is a collection of records which have a common characteristic or function. For example, a personnel file

80

RECORD INVENTORY AND RETENTION SCHEDULE

NAME	FORM NUMBER	SEQUENCE NUMBER	RETENTION DATE	PROBABLE FREQUENCY	LOCATION	COMMENTS
Accounts Payable						
Packing slips	031325	–	01/01/71	Weekly	File-A/R-1	None
Vouchers	011720	5001-9999	04/21/72	Monthly	File-A/P-1	None
Accounts Receivable						
Invoices	021523	0420-7999	01/01/71	Monthly	File-A/R-2	None
Payroll						
Time sheets	061321	0001-4999	–	Quarterly	File-E-3	Back-up for 941a report

FIGURE 5.3. Record inventory and retention schedule.

contains employees' histories and training records; a payroll file contains records of hours worked and rates paid; a work-order file contains the job records of machines and their operators; and so on.

Files are important business tools because they contain the histories of activities or of communications in a business system.

Filing is the operation of inserting a record in its proper sequence in a file. In manual systems and in some types of EDP (electronic data processing) applications, where many records are to be inserted into a file, arranging the insertions into proper sequence before filing saves time by eliminating thumbing back and forth across a file.

File Permanence

Files are frequently categorized as *permanent* or *temporary*. A master file containing year-to-date earnings, state and federal taxes, etc., is one kind of *permanent file*, while a transaction file containing weekly hours worked and rates paid, usually retained only for as long as company policy dictates, may be described as a *temporary file*.

The permanent master file in Fig. 5.4 is periodically updated. The time/rate cards are one-time-only transaction cards and kept in a storage area only perhaps until the 941a FICA quarterly report is run on the computer.

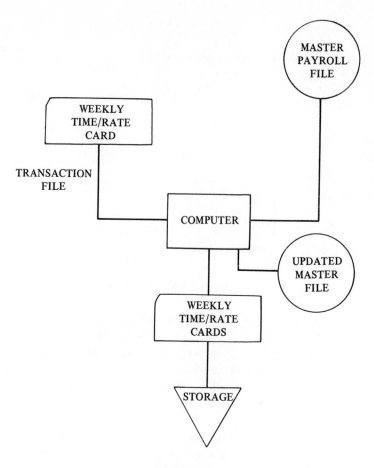

FIGURE 5.4.

5.4

File Design   Files and their records should be designed and organized so
that they might be read or processed easily. As the record
processing needs of a business system increase, so does the
dependence of any one subsystem upon another. The outputs
from a sales-order subsystem become the inputs for the inventory
subsystem. The outputs from inventory (and thus from sales-
orders also) become the inputs for the billing subsystem, and so
on. Because several computer programs may require the same files
for processing, certain files usually become more active than
others.

Designing a file and its associated records requires careful consideration of four basic factors:

File activity

File size

Input

Output

File Activity

In designing the organization of any file, the percentage of active records is one of the important facts to be considered. If a small percentage of records will be processed at one time, the file should be organized to permit random access to any one record without having to interrogate all of the other records in the file.

Also, peak and slack periods must be projected. For example, in a seasonal business such as garment manufacturing, some accounts receivable files will be processed more frequently during winter months than during summer months.

If the file has a high activity rate, or most of its records are to be processed at any one time, then a sequential arrangement of records might be the most efficient organization for that file.

File Size

File size plays an important role in determining the design and organization of a file as well as the type and amount of storage required. Predicted growth of the file should be considered as well as current size.

A massive file containing policy records for a large insurance company would require a different design and organization than the payroll file for a high school faculty and administrators.

Input

The types of source documents that supply the input to a file are an important consideration. The file should be organized so that the input can be processed efficiently.

Output

When files are processed, reports or documents of some type are often generated. The file should be designed in such a way that the information required for the desired outputs is readily obtainable.

5.5

File Identification

The beginning and end of every file should be clearly identified in both manual and EDP systems.

This may be done by adding two additional records to the file: a header, or first record, and a trailer, or last record (see Fig. 5.5).

HEADER
DETAIL
DETAIL
TRAILER

FIGURE 5.5.

Header Records

The header record is labeled with such information as:

The file *name*

The file *creation date*

The file *retention date*—the date when the file must be destroyed

The file *device number*—for example, the file cabinet number; or, in EDP files, the tape reel number, disk pack number, or punched card drawer number

The *record length* or, in EDP files, the *number of positions* in each record

Detail Records

Detail records, which make up the bulk of the file, contain data required for processing—an amount of money to be deposited, a balance in an accounts receivable record, and so on. Detail records also contain such identification as employee number, name, address, etc., and are usually placed in some logical sequence, for example, in alphabetical order by name, or in numerical order by Social Security number.

Trailer Records

The trailer record identifying the end of a file, may also separate it from the next adjacent file. Trailer records may also contain such summary information as the number of records in the file (a good means of verifying that all records in the file have been processed, or that none have been lost).

5.6

File Storage Devices

The function of the file usually dictates the storage device to be used. For example, while employees' records are confidential, they are often needed for quick reference. Thus, to insure both confidentiality and accessibility, manila folders, each containing one employee's application, birth certificate, promotion history, education and training data, etc., can be kept in *file cabinets* (Fig. 5.6) in the personnel office.

A *rotary card system* is a small wheel or drum mounted on a frame (Fig. 5.7). A card in this file may contain a brief record of work orders, customer names, inventory numbers, addresses, credit ratings, salesmen's names and routes, etc. The rotary file enables quick access to each record by simple rotation of the wheel or drum.

The *punched card file cabinet* (Fig. 5.8) contains drawers especially designed for containing punched card records. Magnetic disk packs and magnetic tapes containing records and files should also be kept in safe storage areas (Fig. 5.9 a, b).

EDP Records and Files

Because computer costs for processing files can be high, we will take a closer look at the organization of EDP files with a view to the efficient accessing and processing of their records.

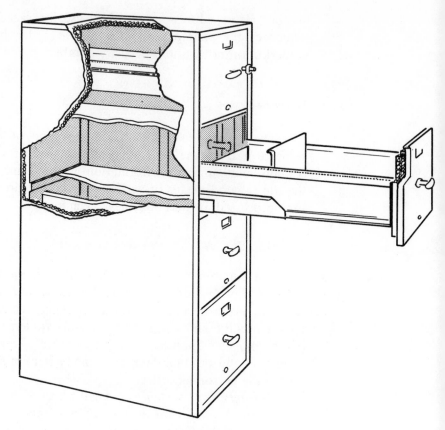

FIGURE 5.6.

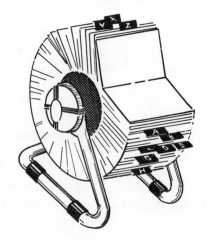

FIGURE 5.7.

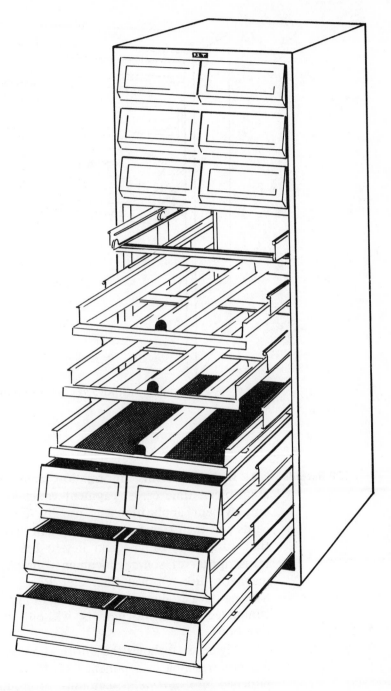

FIGURE 5.8.

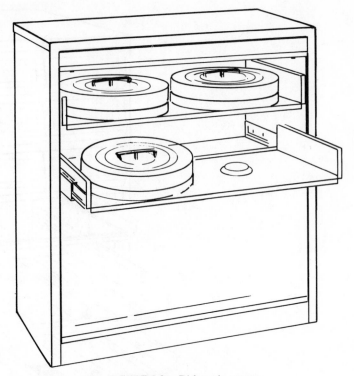

FIGURE 5.9a. Disk pack storage.

5.7

EDP Records

In EDP systems, information from source documents—such as invoices, time cards, payment vouchers, shipping notices, and employment applications—is usually transcribed onto punched cards and then transferred to magnetic tape or disk and stored in that form. Key-to-tape and key-to-disk equipment permits the transcription of source documents directly to magnetic tape or magnetic disk. Optical Character Recognition (OCR) and Mark Sensing devices allow the processing of appropriately designed and completed source documents without the necessity of transcription.

Figure 5.10 shows the information on the deposit slip in Fig. 5.2 now residing in a punched card. Groups of related facts are punched into *card fields*, columns, or groups of columns reserved

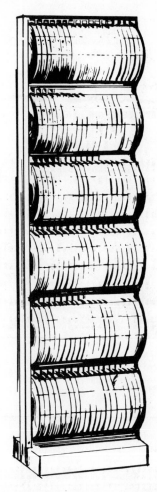

FIGURE 5.9.b. Tape reel storage.

for specific information. Fields names may be preprinted onto cards to facilitate key punching, verifying, and card handling (see Fig. 5.11).

Card design involves planning the kinds of fields, their lengths, and their arrangement in the punched card. The multiple Card Layout Form (Fig. 4.15, in Chapter 4) is frequently used as an aid in designing punched card records. Each card column contains one character, or *position* (i.e., letter, number, space, or punctuation mark), in the layout form; punches in the card columns are made in the *Hollerith Code* (see Appendix A).

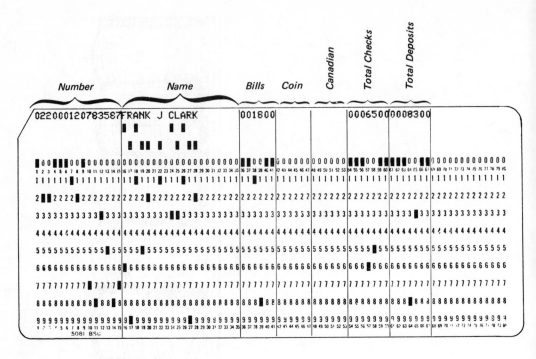

FIGURE 5.10.

FIGURE 5.11.

5.8

Blocking EDP   Records stored on magnetic tape or disk are separated from
Records   one another by a blank space called an *inter-record gap* (IRG). As
inter-record gaps occupy valuable space and lengthen processing
time, the number of gaps is usually minimized by grouping records
together and writing them on tape or disk as a *block* (sometimes
called a *physical record*). Such grouping of records is called
blocking and the number of records in a block is called the
blocking factor. The individual records in a block are called *logical
records*. The block in the top part of Fig. 5.12 contains one logical
record; the block in the lower part of Fig. 5.12 contains three
logical records.

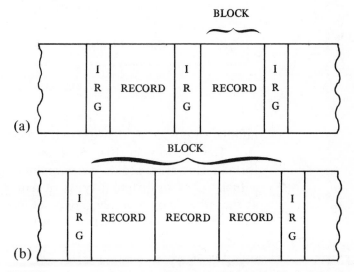

FIGURE 5.12. (a) Unblocked logical records; (b) 3 blocked logical records.

5.9

Data Sets   We have already defined a *file* as a collection of records
which have a common characteristic or function. An EDP file is
usually referred to as a *data set*, which may be defined as a
collection of logical records or data records, residing on punched
cards, magnetic tape, magnetic disk, or similar storage media.

Records in a data set may be similar to each other or they may vary in size, form, or content.

For example, records in a data set containing bank depositors are usually uniform in format and size. Information found in these records typically consists of account number, name, address and balance (see Fig. 5.13).

ACCT #	NAME	ADDRESS	BALANCE	RECORD 1
ACCT #	NAME	ADDRESS	BALANCE	RECORD 2
ACCT #	NAME	ADDRESS	BALANCE	RECORD 3

FIGURE 5.13.

When records in a data set all consist of exactly the same number of positions, they are said to be *fixed-length records*.

The records in Fig. 5.14 are an example of this record format. However, a data set containing fixed-length records may actually contain different types of data records, each type as long as the other. For example, a data set made up of input records for a billing system might contain these two different types:

Invoices

Work Orders

INVOICE	CUST #	ITEM #	QTY	PRICE	SLSMAN #	DATE
WORK-ORDER	CUST #	PARTS	LABOR	SERVICEMAN	COST	DATE

FIGURE 5.14.

Records in other data sets may vary in size, form and content. Student records in a university are an example:

Record for Student A	*Record for Student B*
Student number	Student number
Name	Name
Address	Address
English	English
Mathematics	Social studies
Social studies	Accounting
Biology	Data processing
	Business systems
	Physical education
	6 points transfer credit in Accounting from ABC Junior College

Student records A and B differ in size and content: student B has taken more courses than student A, and has been credited with 6 hours in Accounting from another educational institution. When data records in a data set differ in size, as in this case, they are called *variable-length records*.

As noted earlier, blocking records saves space and computer processing time. Since both fixed-length and variable-length records can be blocked, a data set composed of records follows one of four possible formats:

Unblocked
  fixed-length
  variable-length

Blocked
  fixed-length
  variable-length

Unblocked Fixed-length

When a data set is composed of fixed-length records and the records are unblocked, the logical record is the same size as the block, and each block is the same size (see upper part of Fig. 5.12).

Unblocked Variable-length

When a data set is composed of unblocked variable-length records, each record must include a field indicating its size. This *length field* is necessary so that the program processing the data set can determine the length of the record. Usually the length field is the first field in the record (see Fig. 5.15). For unblocked variable-length records, a blocksize is the same size as its logical record.

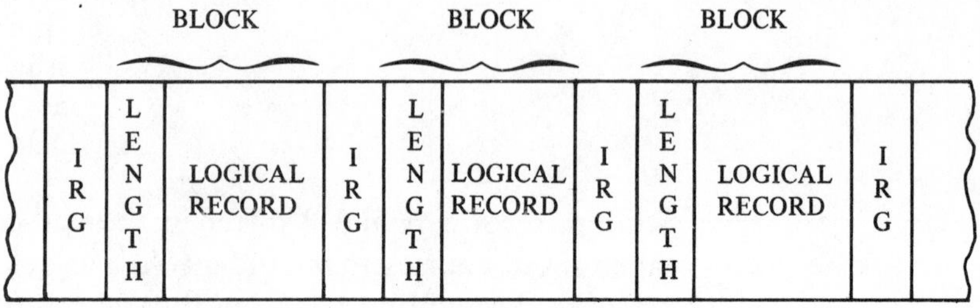

BLOCK				BLOCK				BLOCK		
I R G	L E N G T H	LOGICAL RECORD	I R G	L E N G T H	LOGICAL RECORD	I R G	L E N G T H	LOGICAL RECORD	I R G

FIGURE 5.15.

Blocked Fixed-length

When fixed-length records are blocked (see Fig. 5.16), the *size of the block* is defined as the blocking factor multiplied by one record length. Given a 40-character record, a blocking factor of 5, then 40 × 5 equals a blocksize of 200 characters. All blocks will be the same size with the possible exception of the last block. For example, a data set of 91 records in blocks of three will contain only one record in its last block. In such a case some computer systems pad out the last block with two *dummy* or blank records, while other systems permit a short block at the end of a data set.

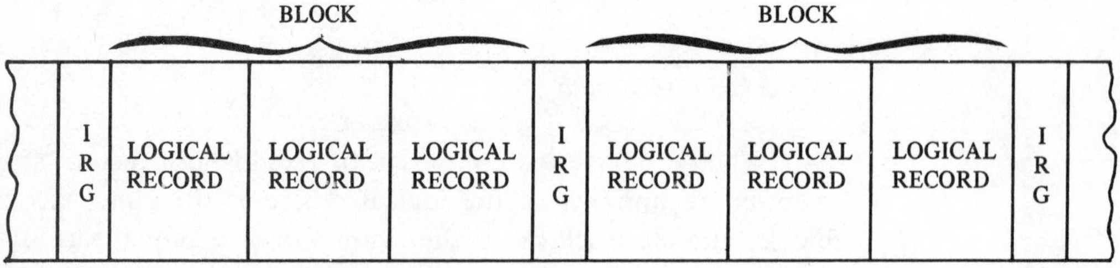

BLOCK				BLOCK			
I R G	LOGICAL RECORD	LOGICAL RECORD	LOGICAL RECORD	I R G	LOGICAL RECORD	LOGICAL RECORD	LOGICAL RECORD	I R G

FIGURE 5.16.

94

Blocked Variable-length

When variable-length records are blocked, it is necessary to include a length field to the *block* (usually at the beginning of the block) in addition to the length fields in the individual logical records (see Fig. 5.17).

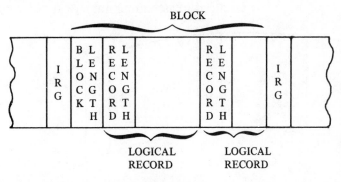

FIGURE 5.17.

5.10

Data Set Organization

As data sets are basically *files*, the remarks made earlier about file design (Sec. 5.4) apply to them also. In addition, three basic forms of data set organizations are common to many computing systems:

Sequential

Direct-access

Indexed sequential

Sequential Organization

A *sequential data set* is processed starting with the first record, and each succeeding record is processed in turn. Records are read from the device on which they are stored in the same sequence in which they were written on the device. Sequential data sets may be stored on any external storage device such as punched cards, magnetic tape, or magnetic disk.

Frequently data records are sorted so that they are stored in ascending (or descending) value of some *key field*, a field containing the identification of the record such as a Social Security number identifies the person to whom it belongs.

A good example of a sequential file is the reel of magnetic tape in Fig. 5.18, in which data records (or blocks of records) are arranged in ascending numerical order by ID number.

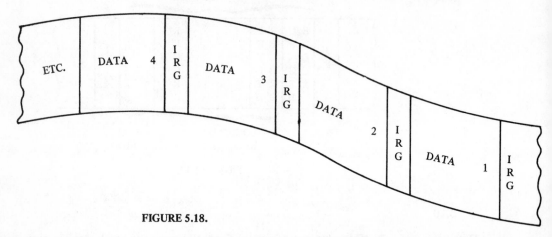

FIGURE 5.18.

The bank depositor's file mentioned earlier (see Fig. 5.13) can be very conveniently processed for updating interest in this type of data set organization. Updating the sequential data set is simply a matter of entering all deposit and withdrawal transactions. However, the input, or *transaction data set*, must first be sorted into the same order and on the same key field as the sequential data set. (See Fig. 5.19.)

In sequential processing the entire master file must be read into the computer. Thus, inserting new records or deleting inactive records requires rewriting the entire data set. Records may not be skipped; rather, each record must be processed in strict sequence. It is usually advisable, therefore, to let transactions accumulate until a reasonably sized batch is available for processing.

Direct-access Organization

A *direct-access data set* contains records that are accessible without reading or writing all the other records in the data set.

96

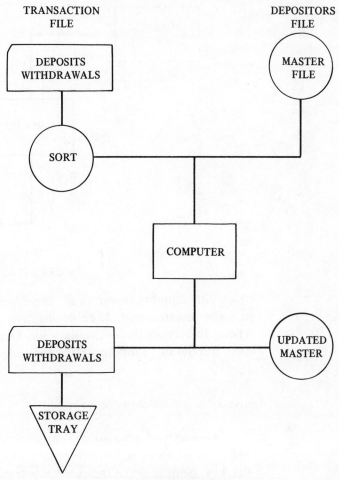

FIGURE 5.19.

Direct-access organization requires a magnetic disk, magnetic drum, or a storage device such as the data cell. Consider the student file referred to earlier (Sec. 5.9). If the Bursar's office is interested in one student who has not paid his course fees, it is far less costly in terms of computer time to go directly to the record of the student under consideration than to search the entire file until that record can be found. By assigning each student an identification number corresponding with the location of his record on the disk pack, or by utilizing some kind of randomizing routine to calculate that location, the read/write head on the disk drive can be sent directly to the desired record (see Fig. 5.20).

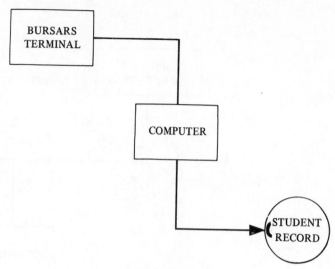

FIGURE 5.20.

With direct-access data set organization, new student records may be inserted and those of inactive students deleted without having to recopy the entire data set. Data records may be written onto the file in a random, rather than sequential, manner.

Indexed Sequential Organization

An *indexed sequential data set* is composed of data records and a set of indexes. Data records are sorted in ascending order on the key field, and the indexes keep track of the location of each record on the device.

An indexed sequential data set must reside on a direct-access device, and may be processed sequentially or directly. New records may be inserted and inactive records deleted without recopying the entire data set.

EXERCISES

1. Distinguish between a *form* and a *record*.

2. What does "IRG" mean?

3. What should records management provide for in a business system?

4. What influences the length of time records should be retained?

5. Define a *card field*.

6. Give examples of a *source document*.

7. Define a *file*.

8. Distinguish between *temporary* and *permanent* files.

9. List some considerations in designing a file.

10. Describe *fixed-length records*.

11. Name the three most commonly used methods of data set organization.

12. Tape files are usually associated with which of the methods referred to in Exercise 11?

PROBLEMS 1. List a suitable type of record structure and file organization for each of the following applications:

Application	Record Structure	File Organization
Accounts payable file		
Student locator file		
Employee payroll file		
Perpetual inventory file		
Bank depositor file		

2. Design a suitable form to serve as a file of fixed assets. Each record should indicate original cost, date of purchase, cost of permanent improvements, accumulated depreciation to date, date sold or disposed of, amount received on disposition, and method and rate of computing depreciation.

3. Design a sequential data set containing variable-length blocked records of the personal and academic history of each student in your class. Include header, detail, and trailer records.

CHAPTER 6

REPORTS

6.1

**The Function
of Reports**

A report is a formal presentation of summary information, prepared by a person or group of persons and distributed to other persons within a system, usually on a designated date or after a specified interval of time. The accuracy of reports to management is particularly crucial, for managers are not stationed at points of action or transaction in business systems, and most of the major decision-making processes take place several ranks above the operations and clerical personnel.

Reports reflect the actions and progress of a system, and so are aids in management decision-making. If, for example, one of the items in the report in Fig. 6.1 showed a serious decline in sales across the entire sales territory, this event, captured and documented in summary form, could be used as a basis for dropping that item from inventory.

Reports should be simple in format. Unnecessary words should be eliminated. Statistical information should be presented in a manner that facilitates comparative analysis. For example, a company's present balance sheet will always be compared with previous balance sheets.

ABC DRUG AND COSMETICS COMPANY				
SALES ANALYSIS REPORT				
BY CUSTOMER				
CUSTOMER NAME	ITEM NUMBER	SALES	RETURNS	NET SALES
Link Fence Co.	1238	23 60		
	6942		45 91	
	1006	141 80		
	1485	295 03		
		460 43	45 91	414 52
Lee's TV	1006	30 45		
	3692		16 80	
	4811		212 30	
	5630	15 20		
	5630	25 00		
		70 65	229 10	158 45 CR

FIGURE 6.1.

Figure 6.1 shows a typical *sales analysis report*, which in large systems is usually prepared by the office of the sales manager and distributed to other department managers. Reports like this provide timely and periodic feedback. The accuracy of this report is vital to those responsible for purchasing, inventory control, and computing salesmen's commissions.

The *income statement* and the *balance sheet* in Figs. 6.2 and 6.3, respectively, are reports that can be used as decision-making tools by investors contemplating the purchase of stocks in a business system.

Inventory reports reflect the control exercised over a system's resources, as Fig. 6.4 indicates.

6.2

Writing Reports

Creating a report is a cost to a system. To keep these costs to a minimum, a standardized format should be used so that the

VARDON ELECTRICAL SUPPLIES

Income Statement

For Year Ended December 31, 1969

Revenue From Sales:			
Sales		$164,674	
Less: Sales returns and allowances	$ 4,250		
Sales discount	2,414	6,664	
Net sales			$158,010
Cost of merchandise sold:			
Merchandise inventory, January 1, 1969 . . .		$18,800	
Purchases	$105,020		
Less: Purchases returns and allow. $3740			
Purchases discount 2957	6,697		
Net purchase		98,323	
Merchandise available for sale		$117,123	
Less merchandise inventory Dec. 31, 1969		19,300	
Cost of Merchandise Sold:			97,823
Gross profit on sales			$60,187
Operating Expenses:			
Selling Expenses:			
Sales salaries	$ 15,762		
Sales commissions	8,531		
Advertising expense	3,680		
Depreciation expense–store–equip. . .	2,100		
Delivery expense	2,063		
Store supplies expense	1,680		
Insurance expense–selling	1,520		
Misc. general expense	1,824		
Total selling expenses		$ 37,160	
General Expenses:			
Office salaries	$ 6,224		
Taxes expense	2,862		
Depreciation expense–office–equip. . . .	1,440		
Depreciation expense--building	1,800		
Office supplies expense	1,340		
Insurance expense–general	1,396		
Misc. general expense	1,793		
Total general expenses		16,855	
Total operating expenses			54,015
Net income from operations			$ 6,172
Other income:			
Rent income		2,100	
Other expense:			
Interest expense		1,580	520
Net income			$ 6,692

FIGURE 6.2.

VARDON ELECTRICAL SUPPLIES

Balance Sheet

December 31, 1969

ASSETS

Current Assets:

Cash	$10,775	
Accounts receivable-schedule 1	10,000	
Merchandise inventory.	19,300	
Store supplies	1,790	
Office supplies	1,440	
Prepaid insurance	1,904	
Total current assets		$45,209

Plant Assets:

Store equipment	$13,100		
Less accumulated depreciation	6,800	6,300	
Office equipment	4,500		
Less accumulated depreciation	2,120	2,380	
Building.	$29,100		
Less accumulated depreciation	5,300	23,800	
Land		4,100	
Total plant assets			$36,580

Total Assets		$81,789

LIABILITIES

Current Liabilities:

Accounts payable-Schedule 2.	$10,370	
Mortgage payable (current portion)	2,100	
Commissions payable	1,664	
Salaries payable	1,312	
Total current liabilities		$15,446

Long-term Liabilities:

Mortgage payable (final maturity in 1977)		9,200

Total Liabilities		$24,646

CAPITAL

Joseph Vardon, capital–Exhibit C	57,143

Total Liabilities and Capital	$81,789

FIGURE 6.3.

R11.2   TOLEDO-2   STOREROOM CONTROL REPORT DATE 02/04/70   PAGE 1

	STOREROOM ACCOUNT	REQUISITION VALUE	INVOICE VALUE	ADJUSTMENTS VALUE	PHYSICAL VARIANCE VALUE	INVENTORY VALUE	REQUISITION COUNT
OLD	4201	23,876.14		68,248.71–	2,453.27–	685,368.70	
CHANGE	4201	6,016.56		18,213.93		12,197.37	1,163
NEW	4201	29,892.70		50,034.78–	2,453.27–	697,566.07	
OLD	4210			27,269.51		224,174.28	
CHANGE	4210						
NEW	4210			27,269.51		224,174.28	
OLD	4250			3,681.74–		125,337.03	
CHANGE	4250						
NEW	4250			3,681.74–		125,337.03	
OLD	4260	627.82				11,050.43	
CHANGE	4260	206.06				206.06–	101
NEW	4260	833.88				10,844.37	
OLD	4280					3,545.25	
CHANGE	4280						
NEW	4280					3,545.25	
OLD	4290	24,830.13	8,374.02	161.84		273,531.08	
CHANGE	4290	24,764.31	8,374.02	161.84		16,228.45–	337
NEW	4290	49,594.44	16,748.04	323.68		257,302.63	
OLD	PLANT 2	49,334.09	8,374.02	44,499.10–	2,453.27–	1,323.006.77	
CHANGE		30,986.93	8,374.02	18,375.77		4,237.14–	
NEW		80,321.02	16,748.04	26,123.33–	2,453.27–	1,318,769.63	

EXHIBIT A01-IF (Rev. 2/10/70)

FIGURE 6.4.

report writer does not require time to create new formats and the recipient of the report can quickly locate and recognize information pertinent to his job functions.

Don'ts

Avoid jargon or esoteric terms that, like slang, possess meaning for only a small group of persons.

Avoid use of the first person ("I" and "we"). Reports should not be personalized even when addressed to persons of equal rank in the system.

Avoid over-refined or intricate sentences that make the report sound like a legal document; avoid emotional language and florid terminology.

Do's

Prepare an outline listing the salient points to be made.

Document references to any background or supporting materials.

Use action verbs in narratives. They bring life and directness to a report and improve readability.

Wherever possible, use a table or a graph to emphasize a point. Managers and company officers are familiar with this kind of concentration of data and usually are able to analyze and comprehend them more quickly than long narratives on the same subject. Keep the report short. Cut out redundancies and superfluous adjectives and adverbs.

If the report is in narrative form and must require many pages to complete, tables, graphs, exhibits, schedules, charts, etc. may be appended at the end. In this manner they may be used as a reference for the main points. If the report is short, illustrative material might be inserted where appropriate, in the interest of ease in analysis.

In writing reports or memos that contain costs, the savings, or any other financial benefits to the system should be stressed. If disadvantages or possible drawbacks exist, the report writer should point them out before someone else does. If the report is a proposal containing a choice between alternatives, then costs and other benefits can be shown to justify the selection of the alternatives.

6.3

Control of Reports
Unnecessary duplication of information and paperwork may be avoided if the creation and distribution of reports are properly controlled. Controlling reports involves answering the same questions discussed earlier regarding forms control (Chap. 4).

Why is this report needed? Can this information be located in other reports, forms, records, etc.?

What kind of information is needed? financial? marketing? research? labor? government controls? etc.

Where does this required information exist in the system?

Who prepares the report? *Who receives* it?

If this is a periodic report, such as a progress report on new projects, *when* are the due dates? Or is this a one-time-only memo? If so, are there special forms available that provide a reporting function for this same information?

6.4

Storage of Reports

Retention of such information as balance sheets, sales analysis, etc., is important to policymakers in a system. After a report has been read (and if necessary, responded to), it should not clutter up the working areas of its recipients. A centrally located library or storage area can provide a quick reference service to those persons that need access to any historical information contained in reports.

Report Coding

Organization of the library (or report storage area) should be based on an indexing system that functions much like the Library of Congress numbering system does for public libraries. In one typical system the prefix letter indicates the destination (division or department), and the number following the prefix letter indicates the management level to which the report is addressed. (If reports have two or more destinations, two or more prefix letters and management level numbers are used.) This part of the report code is followed by a dash and six-digit number: the first two digits indicate the subject of the report, the next digit the frequency with which the report is issued, and the last three digits the number of copies to be distributed.

If necessary an R may be annexed to the low-order digit to indicate restricted information. The report writer may be identified by his name and title.

DEPARTMENT CODES

A - Accounting
B - Billing
D - Data Processing
E - Engineering
I - Inventory
L - Personnel
M - Manufacturing
P - Purchasing
S - Sales

MANAGEMENT LEVEL CODES

(assuming 3 levels in this case)
1. First level
2. Second level
3. Third level
4. First and Second level
5. First and Third level
6. Second and Third level
7. All three levels

REPORT FREQUENCY CODES

0 - A one-time report
1 - Daily
2 - Weekly
3 - Bi-weekly
4 - Semi-monthly
5 - Monthly
6 - Quarterly
7 - Semi-annually
8 - Annually
9 - Irregular

Thus given a report coded

M3-465005
J. WILSON, MGR. Materials Distribution Center

the breakdown of the code is;

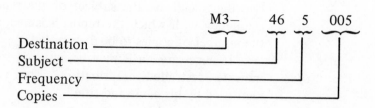

Destination
Subject
Frequency
Copies

REPORT SUBJECT CODES

00-09 PERSONNEL	10-19 FINANCIAL
00 Promotion	10 Payroll
01 Insurance	11 Balance sheet
02 Union	12 Income statement
03 Education	13 Trial balance
04 Sex	14 Cost analysis
05 Marital status	15 Budget
06 Dependents	16 Stocks
07 Department rosters	17 Taxes
08 Unused	18 Insurance
09 Unused	19 Unused

21-29 EQUIPMENT	30-39 MANUFACTURING
20 Safety	30 Fabrication
21 Depreciation	31 Tools
22 Design	32 Assemblies
23 Machinery	33 Quality control
24 Re-tooling	34 Testing
25 Transportation	35 Processing
26 Maintanence	36 Research and Dev.
27 Location	37 Unused
28 Unused	38 Unused
29 Unused	39 Unused

40-49 INVENTORY/MATERIALS	50-59 ADMINISTRATION
40 Raw materials	50 Policies
41 Parts	51 Control/feedback
42 Quantities-on-hand	52 Authority
43 Costs	53 Accountability
44 Office supplies	54 Education
45 Inspection/testing	55 Recruitment
46 Forecasts	56 Unused
47 Unused	57 Unused
48 Unused	58 Unused
49 Unused	59 Unused

FIGURE 6.5.

109

and this is a report by J. Wilson, manager of the warehouse, addressed to third-level managers in manufacturing. The subject of the report is forecasts, the report is issued monthly, and five copies are distributed.

Report Distribution Charts

The distribution of a report can be graphically indicated by a *report distribution chart*; the distribution of the copies (including the original and carbons or duplicates) of the report discussed above is shown in Fig. 6.6. The asterisk on the chart indicates the department to which the original copy of the report is addressed.

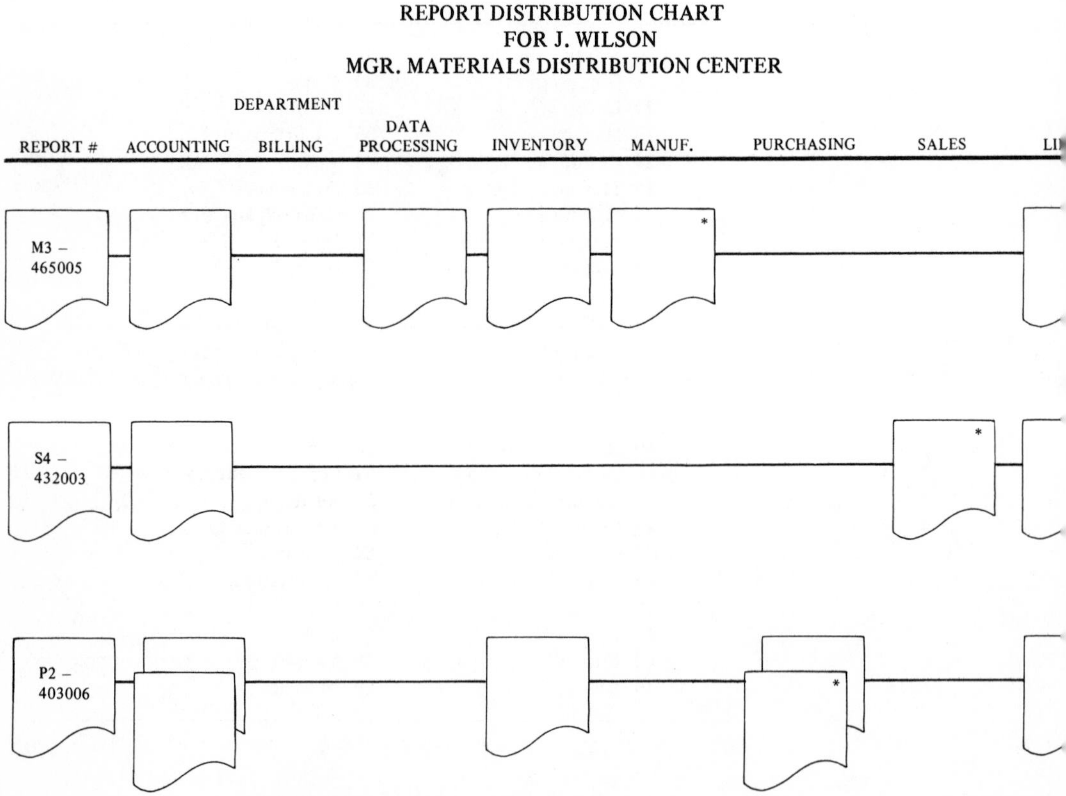

REPORT DISTRIBUTION CHART
FOR J. WILSON
MGR. MATERIALS DISTRIBUTION CENTER

REPORT #	ACCOUNTING	BILLING	DEPARTMENT DATA PROCESSING	INVENTORY	MANUF.	PURCHASING	SALES	LI
M3 – 465005					*			
S4 – 432003							*	
P2 – 403006						*		

FIGURE 6.6.

110

EXERCISES 1. List the reasons reports are prepared and disseminated among members of management.

2. Explain why the following items in Fig. 6.2 are presented in separate sections:
   (a) Net sales $158,010
   (b) Total selling expenses $37,160
   (c) Net income from operations $6,172

3. What is the purpose of dividing Fig. 6.3 into sections such as Current assets, Current liabilities, etc?

4. Briefly state the criteria for creating a report.

5. In formulating report control, what questions need to be answered?

6. Using the coding system of Fig. 6.5, give one example of report coding and explain the meanings of all letters and numbers used.

PROBLEMS 1. The Excello Corporation markets three different products in three market areas. The three products, known as W, X, and Y, all have approximately the same potential sales demand but each requires a somewhat different product knowledge with product X being the easiest for the salesmen to understand. The estimated net profit is $10 per unit for products W and Y and $8 for product X.

In each region there are three salesmen, one of whom acts as regional sales manager coordinating the activities of the other salesmen, supervising clerical work and training, helping to open new accounts, and making some calls himself as time allows. Salesman E has only been with the company for two months; all the other salesmen have each had over 18 months' experience.

The report of monthly sales activities depicted in Fig. 6.7 was given to the Vice-President for Sales. After examining the report for a few minutes, he called you in and requested you to prepare a more meaningful report.

Required: Prepare a revised sales report. Write brief comments concerning the possible causes of performance levels your revised report reveals.

2. The monthly income statement in Fig. 6.8 is submitted to the sales department for its information.

Required: Revise and make any necessary corrections and improvements. Your report should only contain information pertinent to the sales department.

SALESMAN	REGION	PRODUCT	UNITS
A-mgr	1	W	125
A-mgr	1	X	150
A-mgr	1	Y	175
B	1	W	100
B	1	X	200
B	1	Y	125
C	1	W	150
C	1	X	175
C	1	Y	125
			1325
D-mgr	2	W	125
D-mgr	2	X	100
D-mgr	2	Y	125
E	2	W	175
E	2	X	125
E	2	Y	175
F	2	W	200
F	2	X	75
F	2	Y	225
			1325
G-mgr	3	W	150
G-mgr	3	X	125
G-mgr	3	Y	100
H	3	W	175
H	3	X	200
H	3	Y	200
I	3	W	175
I	3	X	225
I	3	Y	250
			1600

FIGURE 6.7. Sales report

3. List five reports that you could expect a manufacturing firm to prepare regularly. Using the report coding charts in the text (Fig. 6.5), assign appropriate code numbers to each report. Design a report distribution chart (See Fig. 6.6) and fill in what you consider to be the proper distribution of the forms you listed.

(Cents Omitted)

Sales			$195,400
Less: Sales returns and allowances		$ 4,100	
Bad debts		2,350	
Sales discounts		1,770	8,220
Net sales			187,180
Cost of Goods Sold:			
Merchandise inventory, beginning		46,000	
Purchases	$91,000		
Add: Freight in	1,640		
	92,640		
Less: Purchase returns and allowances . .	$3,800		
Purchases discounts	1,200	5,000	87,640
			133,640
Less: Merchandise inventory, ending		50,000	83,640
Gross margin on sales			103,540
Selling Expenses:			
Salesmen's salaries		22,000	
Office salaries		20,000	
Delivery expense		8,100	
Freight out		9,200	
Warehouse supplies used		1,490	
Depreciation of delivery equipment		500	
Depreciation of warehouse equipment		480	
Sundry selling expense		3,750	65,520
General and Administrative Expenses:			
Advertising		3,900	
Payroll taxes		3,375	
Property taxes		3,710	
Postage and express		1,600	
Office supplies used		775	
Insurance expense		2,790	
Depreciation of building		2,900	
Depreciation of office furniture and fixtures		410	
Sundry general expense		2,800	22,260	87,780
Net income from operations			15,760

FIGURE 6.8.

CHAPTER 7

DOCUMENTATION

7.1

Documentation

A document is a written or printed paper conveying information and relied upon as the basis or proof of an event or an item. Documents are an aid to understanding an existing system and in describing a new system. A document should provide management and others with references to authoritative supporting information about a system under consideration.

This chapter deals with three types of documentation:

1. *Systems documentation*—documents that provide an overview of a system
2. *Activity documentation*—documents that describe an activity within the system
3. *Procedural documentation*—documents that describe the procedural aspects of a system or of an activity

7.2

Systems Documentation

A total system can be described in a very general manner using the organization chart, the systems model, and the systems flowchart.

115

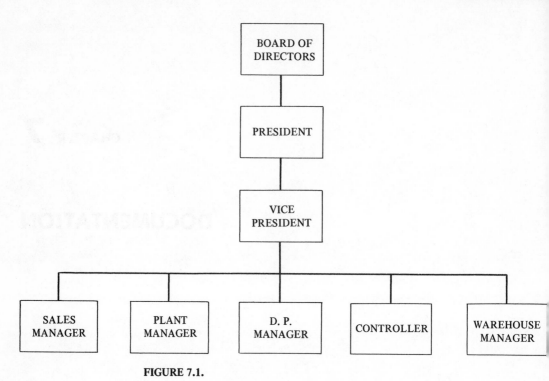

FIGURE 7.1.

Organization Charts and Systems Models

The organization chart and the systems model, both discussed in Chapter 2, are very useful in graphically describing the nature and scope of a business system. *Organization charts* (see Fig. 7.1) provide an overview of the relationships among all systems personnel, including lines of authority. *Systems models* (Fig. 7.2) generalize the relationships of the personnel, equipment, and procedures that make up a total system.

Systems Flowcharts

Systems flowcharts graphically represent the sequence of activities and flow of information in a system.

Consider a payroll system consisting of many activities:

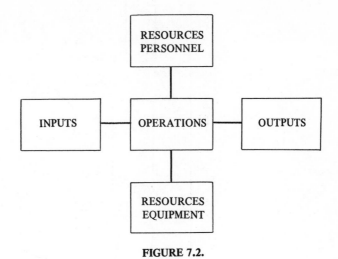

FIGURE 7.2.

Time cards are collected.

Weekly hours and rates are keypunched into a file of punched cards.

These punched cards are used to update each employee's master record on a computer's disk pack.

A payroll journal is printed by the computer indicating each employee's deductions and year-to-date balances.

Checks are prepared for each employee and for the various payroll deductions, such as union dues, savings plans, taxes, etc.

Although several varied activities are involved in a payroll system we can bring out the major activities in a general block diagram (see Fig. 7.3).

After the major operations have been blocked-out, the smaller steps that describe in detail the sequence of activities taken to prepare the weekly payroll can then be identified in a systems flowchart.

The symbols shown in the template in Fig. 7.4 are standardized, conforming to revised flowchart symbols found in the "Draft Recommendation on Flowchart symbols for Information Processing" of the ISO or International Organization for

FIGURE 7.3.

FIGURE 7.4.

Standardization. They are also consistent with the fewer standards adopted by U.S.A.S.I. or U.S.A. Standards Institute.

The template contains symbols that can be used for systems flowcharts as well as computer program flowcharts.

All templates should be used *face up* to maintain a consistent appearance of symbols, and lines should be drawn using a pencil or ballpoint pen (to avoid ink blotting).

Refer to Fig. 7.4. Each of the symbols indicates a specific function such as a decision, an input/output operation, an arithmetic process, and so on. The annotations found within the symbols describe the type of operation, a specific decision, and so on. The flow lines connect the symbols and indicate the sequence of activities.

Figure 7.5 contains a simple flowchart of the payroll system we have just discussed and will serve to illustrate the use of some of these symbols. The flow of information in a systems flowchart is by convention from top to bottom and from left to right. Exceptions are indicated by arrowheads as in Fig. 7.5, where the linkages from the employee master file to the processing block and from the processing block to offline storage are both in opposition to the usual direction.

7.3

**Activity
Documentation**

Systems activities can be described through resource sheets, activity sheets, input-output sheets, and file sheets.

The life of a business system is generally characterized by routine processing, operations, management, and modifications to meet new requirements. To meet new requirements and make modifications where necessary within the system, a comprehensive description of the existing system and its present operations must be available. Such a description forms the basis of analysis by determining how well the system is meeting present demands upon it, and can further serve as one of the tools by which modifications can be planned.

To reduce the complexity of a business as much as possible, all of the business system's current *resources, activities, operations, inputs, outputs,* and *files* should be identified. The following documents, although highly generalized, serve to orient the beginning student to more detailed analyses of an ongoing system.

An organization chart in Fig. 7.6 can assist in the preparation

119

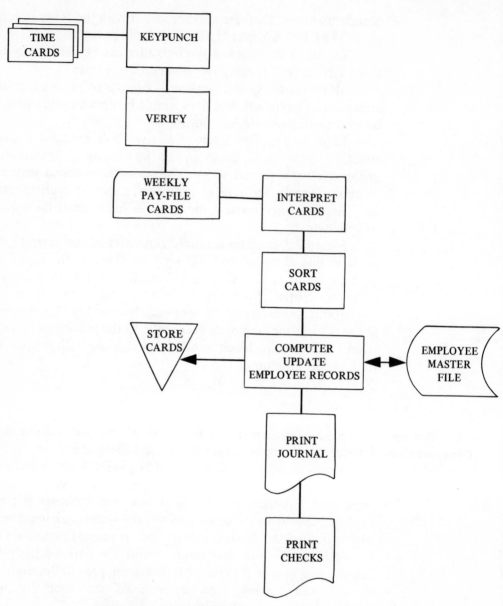

FIGURE 7.5. System flowchart.

of a *personnel resource sheet* (Fig. 7.7), which indicates employee titles, job functions, and costs to the system. A similar form (Fig. 7.8) displays the systems equipment together with functions and costs.

120

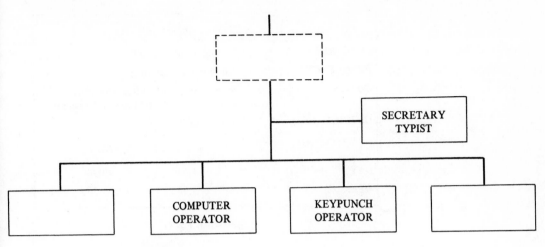

FIGURE 7.6.

RESOURCE SHEET PERSONNEL

ITEM	FUNCTION	COST YEARLY
Keypunch operator	Create punched card files Keypunch computer programs	$5,000.00
Secretary typist	Dictation/typing	$6,200.00
Computer operator	Run computer programs, set up card read/punch and printer for production jobs	$6,000.00

FIGURE 7.7.

RESOURCE SHEET EQUIPMENT

ITEM	FUNCTION	COST
Keypunch	Keypunch cards	$65.00 per month
Computer	Process and prepare reports	$2,000.00 per month

FIGURE 7.8.

```
┌─────────────────────────────────────────────────────────────┐
│                      ACTIVITY SHEET                          │
│                                                              │
│   FUNCTION            Posting to the Journal                 │
│   FREQUENCY           1,000 transactions daily               │
│   INPUTS              Sales orders, work orders, invoices,   │
│                       credit memos (for returns), cash receipts │
│   OUTPUT              The Journal                            │
│                                                              │
│                         AVERAGE        PEAK                  │
│                                                              │
│   DAY                    1,000         1,090                 │
│   WEEK                   5,000         5,450                 │
└─────────────────────────────────────────────────────────────┘
```

FIGURE 7.9.

On an *activity sheet* (Fig. 7.9), the activities of a business system are identified in terms of the inputs and outputs involved; averages and peak loads are also noted. The separate operations required for performing an activity—for example, "Posting to the Journal" in the activity sheet of Fig. 7.9—can be written into an *operation sheet*. The latter, which displays in detail the person or machine that performs each operation, is discussed in Sec. 7.4, "Procedural Documentation."

The *input/output sheet* (Fig. 7.10) is a summary form that displays requirements of inputs and outputs.

INPUT/OUTPUT SHEET

NAME	FREQUENCY	FILE/FORM	I/O*	SOURCE/DESTINATION
Sales vouchers	500/week	Form S-332061	Input	Over the counter sales
Work orders	1750/month	Form W-482061	Input	Maintenance shop
Sales analysis report	1/month	File A/R Report S-226041	Output	To all dept. managers

*means input or output.

FIGURE 7.10.

The *file sheet* (Fig. 7.11) may display such information regarding a file as its name and/or number, location, retention

FILE SHEET

NAME Accounts Receivable   NUMBER AR-435   RETENTION DATE 02/23/71

RESTRICTIONS None   LOCATION Disk pack AR-8

CONTENTS   All active account receivable, credit ratings, balances due, dates of last
payment.

PROGRAMS USED TO PROCESS FILE # AR-435:

1. Billing
2. Adjusted trial balance
3. Income statement
4. Balance Sheet

FIGURE 7.11.

date, a brief description of its contents, any restrictions on its use, and, if used by a computer, the programs that process the file.

7.4

Procedural Documentation

This type of document may provide in detail:

1. the sequence of steps in an activity;
2. the graphic description of the logic or reasoning required to solve a problem;
3. a narrative of a particular job; or
4. a formal job description.

Operations sheets are procedural documents in that they describe, step-by-step, the events needed to complete an activity— for example, Fig. 7.12, which describes the operations required in the activity described on the activity sheet in Fig. 7.9.

It is not necessary to list every individual move or act for each activity. The sheet in Fig. 7.12, for example, omits such trivia as "place A/R punched cards in a run tray," or "place the AR-8 disk pack on drive 192."

In the interest of brevity, only those specific operations that contribute to a clear picture of an activity should appear on the operation sheet.

OPERATION SHEET

INPUT/OUTPUT	OPERATION	RESOURCES
Sales orders, work orders, invoices, credit memos, cash receipts	Count sales slips, work orders, invoices and credit memos	Clerks
	Add up cash receipts	Clerks
	Enter cash amount in Cash Receipts Journal	Bookkeeper/ Cash Rec. Journal
	Deposit cash in bank	Bonded messenger
	Keypunch accounts receivable cards from transaction slips	Keypunch operator/ keypunch machine
	Deliver punched cards to computer center	Messenger
	Run A/R program, posting to the Journal	Computer operator/ computer
	Remove computer output from printer	Computer operator
	Deliver Journal pages to Accounts Receivable Dept.	Messenger

FIGURE 7.12.

Procedural Flowcharts

Procedural flowcharts and decision tables provide graphic descriptions of the logic required to solve a problem or prepare a computer program. *Procedural flowcharts* are a very convenient method of illustrating routine decision-making tasks. Consider an inventory system for which a choice from among several alternative paths of action must be made depending on the number of items in an inventory bin.

In the procedural flowchart of Fig. 7.13, we have *looped back* to read the next request for part ABC using two different methods:

1. a flowline and arrowhead; and
2. the connector symbol.

124

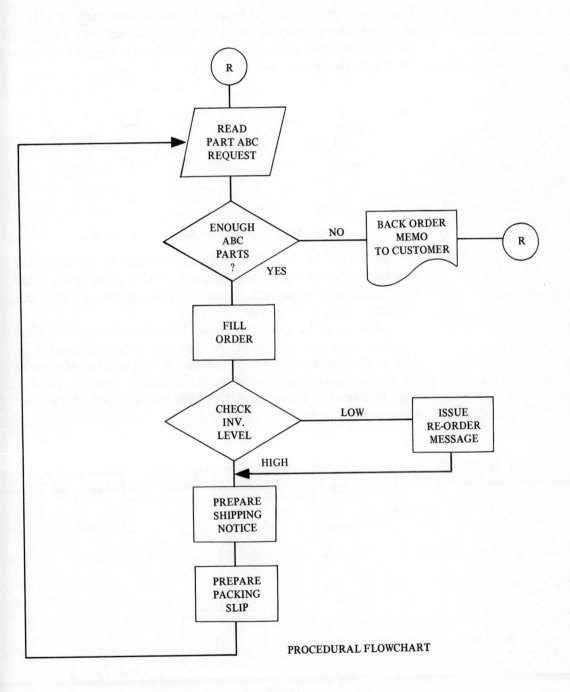

PROCEDURAL FLOWCHART

FIGURE 7.13.

125

The *connector symbol* and its accompanying flowline may appear in various ways: *entry* connectors provide a way into a routine; *branch* connectors provide a way of leaving a routine or skipping over to another part of the program (see Fig. 7.14).

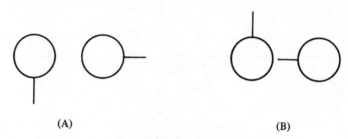

(A)   (B)

FIGURE 7.14. (a) Entry connectors; (b) Branch connectors.

In Fig. 7.13, the first (diamond-shaped) *decision symbol* specifies a test for a sufficient amount of ABC parts: if there are insufficient remaining ABC parts to fill the order, a back-order procedure must be followed.

After an order has been filled, the second decision symbol specifies a test for a re-order level, or the minimum number of ABC parts that can be kept in this bin: if this number of parts in the bin is lower than a predetermined level, a re-order message must be issued; if higher than the predetermined level, no re-order message will be given.

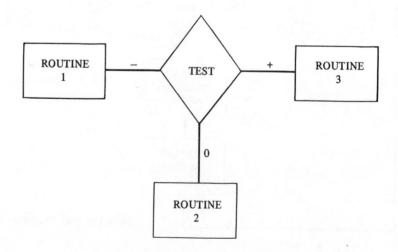

FIGURE 7.15. Procedural flowchart.

126

The decision symbol provides alternative paths for the flow of information, which depend upon the condition being tested. For each of the two decision symbols in Fig. 7.13, one of two alternatives is possible. Note that the shape of the decision symbol makes three alternative paths possible. thus if we wished to test a number and go to a procedure routine depending on whether the number were a positive, negative, or zero amount, the flow of information could be drawn as in Fig. 7.15.

Decision Tables

When the logic of a problem becomes complex, a *decision table* provides a more compact illustration than a flowchart. Suppose the inventory problem discussed above required making the following decisions:

1. Does the quantity ordered by a customer exceed his order limit?
2. Is the customer's credit good?
3. Is the quantity-on-hand sufficient to fill the order?

These questions pose certain conditions. Actions will be taken depending upon the answers to these questions.

If the quantity ordered does not exceed the customer's order limit and the quantity-on-hand is sufficient and the customer's credit is good, we certainly want to approve the order.

If any one of these conditions is not met—in other words, if the answer to any one of these questions is "no"—then other actions must be taken: if the quantity ordered exceeds the customer's order limit or the customer's credit is not good, the order is rejected; if the quantity-on-hand is insufficient, we must then follow special back-order procedures.

All of these decisions can be presented in a tabular form more compact than a flowchart and easier to grasp than a narrative. The conditions and actions in our particular inventory problem can be structured as shown in Fig. 7.16. Whether conditions are or are not met is indicated by a "Y" or "N" respectively, in Fig. 7.17. Actions taken accordingly are indicated by "X's."

The relationship of the Y's, N's, and X's to each other are called *rules*. Each rule contains conditions and actions resulting

127

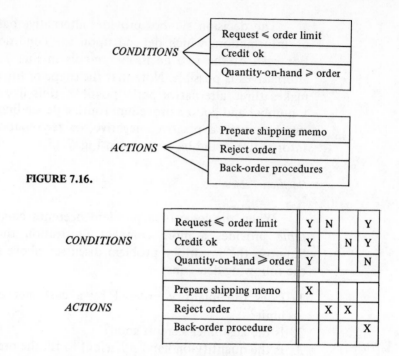

FIGURE 7.16.

CONDITIONS

Request $\leqslant$ order limit	Y	N		Y
Credit ok	Y		N	Y
Quantity-on-hand $\geqslant$ order	Y			N

ACTIONS

Prepare shipping memo	X			
Reject order		X	X	
Back-order procedure				X

FIGURE 7.17.

from a decision. Rules are considered one at a time, and only one rule can be satisfied at any one time.

Three Y's in one column represent the rule that three conditions must be met before an order is approved. Placing the N's in adjacent columns represents the rule that either one of two conditions (or both) can be met and the order will be rejected.

There are more possible rules in Fig. 7.17. In fact, there are 2^n possible rules, where n is the number of conditions. However, 2^n possible rules are usually superfluous, and it is, therefore, unnecessary to list all possible events in a decision table.

Job Narratives

Job narratives describe the sequence of activities required to accomplish specific tasks.

Consider the activities of a maintenance serviceman for an appliance company in a large city. His work day begins when he pulls his truck into a fueling bay. After fueling has been completed he radios that he is ready to accept calls on his route. When a customer on his route calls the central switchboard to have his refrigerator repaired, for example, the request is handed to the dispatcher, who radios the truck the problem information and customer address. The service repairman drives to his assignment. On arrival he logs on a standard report form the time he arrived and his mileage. He repairs the refrigerator, replacing parts as required. Using the same standard form, he makes entries for the new parts he used, the time of job completion, and the labor costs for the hours he worked. After the customer signs the report form, the repairman returns to the truck and radios his dispatcher that he is ready to accept the next assignment.

These operations and the sequence in which they are to be performed must be precisely stated, and any exceptions to the normal routine—such as a breakdown of the truck, an appliance that is not covered by a service contract, or an invalid street address—must be identified.

Describing these activities so that they are easily visualized and simple to follow is frequently accomplished by writing them out in narrative form in a company manual of procedures to be followed at each point of action. A brief and general description of how these procedures might appear is as follows:

SERVICE REPAIRMAN—*Narrative of Procedures*

1. 8:00 A.M.—Bring truck into a fuel bay.
2. After fueling, inform the radio dispatcher that the truck is ready to proceed on repair calls.
3. The dispatcher will radio the assignment by stating the customer's name and address, and the type of appliance to be repaired.
4. Verify this information and enter it on a Repair Report Form.
5. Proceed to the home of the customer and enter the time of arrival and truck's mileage on the Repair Report Form.
6. Repair the appliance and enter costs for labor based on the hourly rate and the costs for replaced parts, if any.
7. Have the customer sign the Repair Report Form.

8. Return to the truck; radio the dispatcher that the assignment has been completed and give him your present location. Be ready for next assignment.

Job Descriptions

Formal job descriptions are required especially when describing the duties of persons of managerial rank. The following is a typical job description.

WESTERN STATE COLLEGE

Position Description

TITLE: *Director of Data Processing*

REPORTS TO: *President*

1. *QUALIFICATIONS:*

   A. Educational Background: A Bachelor of Science in Accounting or related field. Master's Degree preferred.

   B. Experience: Five years in data processing in an educational institution, two years of which should be in programming and one year in systems analysis and design.

   C. Special Skills: Assembler language programming in depth. Knowledge of COBOL, RPG, PL/1 and Fortran programming. Ability to operate computer and all unit record equipment.

2. *GENERAL FUNCTIONS:*

   Schedule the job flow for instructional programs, faculty, administrative and service programs. Design new systems as feasible and required by college business activities.

3. *SPECIFIC RESPONSIBILITIES:*

   A. Be familiar with the logic, flowcharts and all pertinent documentation for administrative and instructional applications.
      1. on the systems level
      2. on the activity level
      3. on the procedural level

   B. Share the responsibility with all users for the integrity of their files and the validity of their computer outputs.

130

C. Maintain a continuous function of planning for college needs, i.e.
   1. immediate needs
   2. short-range needs
   3. long-range needs

D. Establish controls to insure that the expectations of plans can be measured against results through the use of acceptable standards, bench marks, and check points.

E. Design the configuration of new hardware based upon changing instructional needs, and new faculty, administrative and service activities. Determine the effects on facilities of new computer hardware.

F. Prepare an analysis of all costs for his area of responsibility: personnel costs, hardware costs, materials and supplies costs (equipment purchase/lease costs).

G. Maintain inventory control over supplies needed for instructional and administrative computer programs.

H. Direct the training of personnel to keep up-to-date in a still rapidly changing technology.

4. *RELATIONSHIP:*

A. This position reports to the President.

B. Reporting to this position:
   1. programmers
   2. keypunch supervisor
   3. computer operations supervisor

7.5

Documentation of Computer Programs

Program documentation is useful procedural documentation to anyone who must audit an automated system. When computers were first introduced into such commercial installations as banks and insurance companies, very few people understood how such items as a trial balance or an income statement were prepared by the computer. Very often the programmer knew little or nothing about accounting procedures, while the accountant knew little or nothing about programming. Such program documentation as flowcharts, printer spacing charts, layout forms, and problem statements were the only common means of communication these persons had with each other.

Computer programs are often stored as a deck of punched cards which should be identified by writing the program name in felt pen across the first card of the program. The first and last cards of each program should also be so identified; this is usually accomplished by writing "F/C" over the front of the first card and "L/C" over the back of the last card. Tabs should be used to identify and separate punched-card programs residing in storage drawers. (See Fig. 5.8 in Chapter 5).

Programs belonging to the same subsystem should be stored together.

The written documentation for each program, i.e., computer listings, flowcharts, decision tables, etc., should be kept together neatly in a binder, and binders containing program documentation from the same system of programs should be placed *together* on shelves in file cabinets or desk drawers.

Occasionally programs that have been running well for months or even several years are suddenly affected by combinations of events unforeseen by the programmer. These unforeseen events can create "bugs" or invalid output. Such "bugs" may even arise long after the original programmer has left for another job. Thus the need for good computer program documentation is clear.

Because programming documentation is important but highly specialized, this topic is discussed fully in Appendix B.

All of the documents we have been discussing in this chapter, when properly prepared make evident not only the nature of systems activities, but the goals of these activities as well. Documents force the systems analyst to view equipment, personnel, and procedures in dynamic terms, not in the static terms too often found in company manuals.

Systems documentation communicates a formal description of the input and output requirements of a business system and its personnel, equipment, and procedures. Systems documents include organization charts, systems models, and systems flowcharts.

Activity documentation displays the systems resources, activities, inputs and outputs, and files, and should be used to *augment* narratives, organization charts, flowcharts, and decision tables, *not* to replace them. Resource and activity sheets magnify the elements in a system in much the same way that photographic enlargements clarify a small portion of a complex map.

132

Procedural documentation, represented by job descriptions, job narratives, operation sheets, procedural flowcharts, and decision tables, provides a description of the flow of information or sequence of activities.

Documents assist in planning modifications for an existing system, in improving work methods, or in the conversion to or redesigning of an entirely new system.

Analysis of relationships between different types of documents can help determine whether, and to what degree, a system's resources and activities are meeting the goals that management has set. For example, the combined use of the organization chart and the personnel resources sheet can be used to analyze the use of employees: the organization chart displays their deployment throughout the system, while the personnel resource sheet indicates the type of work these people perform and the cost of their work.

Another helpful relationship is the one between the systems flowchart, which illustrates the flow and effect of transactions in a system, and the activity sheet, which indicates the frequency of each transaction, its inputs and outputs, as well as its peak and normal times.

Using the activity sheet in combination with the operation sheet reveals inputs and outputs, as well as the resources, man or machine, used in each step of the work processes that make up an activity.

The input-output sheet can be used to expand relationships among activity sheets, operation sheets, and file sheets.

EXERCISES

1. Describe a document and its uses.

2. What are the three types of business systems documentation?

3. What is a template and how is it used?

4. How are activities described in the documentation process?

5. What does a resource sheet display?

6. What does an activity sheet display?

7. Why is an operation sheet considered a procedural document?

8. (a) Draw the decision symbol.

(b) In terms of flow of information, what does the decision symbol provide for?

9. What is the advantage of a decision table over a flowchart?

10. Summarize in one paragraph the object of systems documentation.

PROBLEMS   1. *Sales Forecast*

Sales information for a systems study directed at improving the compilation of sales forecasts is gathered in the following way:

i. sales forecasts are submitted by each salesman;

ii. cards are punched with the reported sales information;

iii. the cards are sorted by salesman number, and a sales forecast report is prepared;

iv. the cards are sorted by product code, and a sales forecast-by-product report is prepared.

Required: Prepare a systems flowchart displaying the above method of forecasting.

2. *Customer Request*

The following procedural information relates to alternatives in filling customer orders for products A and B:

i. If a customer places an order for A and if A is available, fill the order with A and subtract the quantity from the A inventory.

ii. If a customer places an order for A and if A is not available but B is, and if the customer is willing to take B as a substitute, fill the order with B and subtract the quantity from the B inventory.

iii. If a customer places an order for A and if A is not available, and if the customer is unwilling to take B as a substitute, issue a back-order for A.

iv, v and vi. Same conditions as i, ii and iii, for a customer who places an order for B.

Required: Prepare a decision table to cover the above alternatives.

3. *Perpetual Inventory*

The perpetual inventory system in company X uses individual inventory cards for each item in inventory. As raw materials and supplies are received, the receiving report is forwarded to an inventory control clerk, who posts the amount received to the appropriate card. When supplies are issued to a department, the signed stores requisition is forwarded to a clerk, who posts the amount issued as a reduction on the appropriate inventory control card. The same procedure is followed for raw material, which requires a material requisition form authorized with the proper signature. The daily total transactions average 600 with a peak of 630.

Required: Design and fill in an activity sheet for the above activity.

CHAPTER 8

NATURE AND SCOPE OF THE ELECTRONIC DATA PROCESSING INSTALLATION

8.1

Introduction

The primary function of an electronic data processing installation is service. Whether a computer center is a part of a larger organization or a separate business enterprise in itself, it exists to collect, process, and maintain information about a business and generate reports to business management.

8.2

The Data Base

Refer to Fig. 2.14. A business system is a collection of integrated subsystems as we have illustrated earlier in this text. To keep up-to-date with the activities of these subsystems, management needs fast, dependable, and timely information about payroll, sales-order and customer-billing procedures, inventory control, quality control, trial balance, income statements, balance sheets, depreciation schedules, financial planning, budgetary control, control of manufacturing operations, and the production of goods.

One of the best methods of retrieval of information about

subsystems is through the use of a *data base*—the total collection of all the files containing detailed information on the activities of a business. The data base provides an immediate source of facts needed to develop company reports and statements, and is also used to answer relevant questions about the status of employees, customers, creditors, production, services, equipment, and materials.

Before a computer center can create a viable data base, several factors must be considered:

Data Collection

What information is required for the data base?

Can the raw data found on such forms as employment applications, invoices, packing slips, etc. be reduced to include only those facts needed to process reports and statements to management?

Data Volume

How large are the files?

How many records are in each file?

How does volume affect processing time?

Frequency of Processing

How often are the files processed?

Are there peak times for processing?

When do these peak times occur?

Complexity of Processing

How much information is available in a record?

Can records be broken down so that only pertinent data can be accessed and processed when required?

Is it more efficient to work with one large file or with several smaller, related files?

Type of Input

What is the source of the data to be processed? punched cards? magnetic tape? magnetic disk?

Can data be easily found on any subject that management is concerned with?

What kind of data is to be processed? numeric? alphabetic?

Can identical data be located in several files?

Type of Output

Is the output in the form of a report or statement to be used by management? Or will the output be stored in the data base to be used at a later time?

How many copies of the output are required?

What is the medium for output? paper forms? punched cards? magnetic tape? magnetic disk?

Type of Processing

What is the most economical method of processing the data base?

Which files may be processed only by the computer?

Which files can be processed by a Sorter? by an Interpreter? by a Reproducer? by a Collator? by an Accounting Machine?

Where there are large volume files, can computer programs be written that read and process only that part of a record that is required in a report? Can specific facts be retrieved from the data base and displayed on a videotube or keyboard terminal?

How will an audit trail (see p. 217) be performed in an automated system where data cannot be seen as they are being manipulated or altered?

8.3

File Maintenance

An important function of the data processing installation is the maintenance of the files in the data base (maintenance of computer hardware is performed by the computer manufacturer). Under high-speed computer systems it is mandatory that files in the data base be kept up-to-date and properly labeled, and that the records contain valid information.

File maintenance functions include: integrity of files, sorting, record changes, file update, and creation of back-up files.

Integrity of Files

Invalid data will yield invalid output. Checking routines must be written into every computer program to avoid mistakes that could be disastrous. Such routines should insure positive answers to such questions as:

Have the programmers written computer programs to check the validity of such data as hours and rates before payroll checks are run off on the computer?

Have programmers provided for every possible event, i.e., keypunch errors in the data, blank cards in a file of records, invalid identification numbers, invalid disk addresses and so on?

Accuracy is crucial. Errors can be perpetuated throughout a system. Improperly prepared input records can lead to costly interruptions in processing and may even postpone the running of a job for several hours, thus requiring additional computer time

140

for rerunning the program and possibly doubling computer costs.

Each user of a computer system—the inventory department, the payroll department, accounts receivable, etc.—shares responsibility for the integrity of the data in its files (the validity of input and the accuracy of outputs) with the data processing personnel who keypunch and process these data.

To illustrate this imagine a payroll time sheet that did not contain all of the hours worked by an employee. If this incomplete information is keypunched into the employee's payroll record, invalid computer output such as a negative net pay (after deductions) could occur in computer output when the checks are being run. The payroll department has the responsibility to prepare accurate time sheets and the programmer must incorporate into the check program a routine to identify and appropriately handle such events as negative amounts for net pay.

Sorting Records

Errors in EDP operations *can* be reduced. For example, it is never wise to assume that sequential records will always be in proper order. Sorting records in ascending or descending order by identification number is frequently advisable before processing sequential files in order to avoid computer interrupts on out-of-sequence records. Sorting can be performed on the *Sorter* (see Appendix A) or by computer programs provided by the manufacturers.

Making Record Changes

Refer to Figs. 8.1, 8.2, and 8.3.

Customers change addresses, employees gain promotions, equipment is modified, and so on—such changes require appropriate changes in file records. After the information indicating changes has been prepared and arranged in order, the records to be changed are removed from the file, new records incorporating the information on changes created and inserted in the file, and the outdated records destroyed.

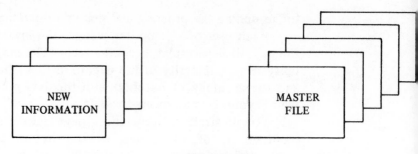

FIGURE 8.1.

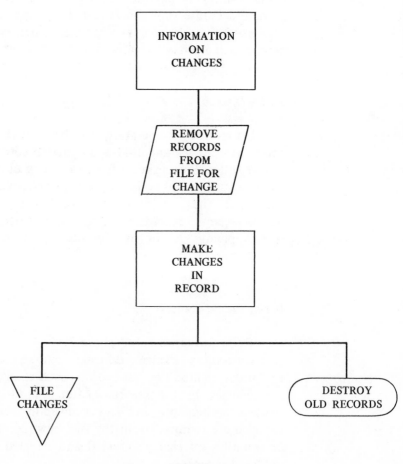

FIGURE 8.2.

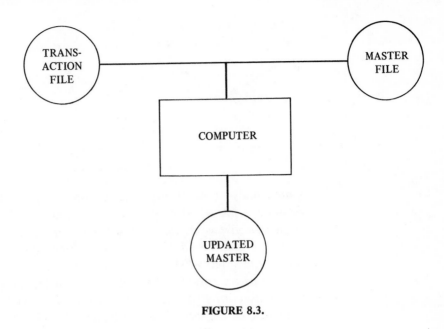

FIGURE 8.3.

Updating Files

Active customer accounts are commonly billed monthly. However, before an account can be billed, a transaction file containing customer records of purchases and returns must be used to update the master accounts receivable file. The updated master file then becomes the new input data for the billing department.

Creating Back-up Files

The loss of magnetic-tape or magnetic-disk files can be minimized in advance by creating duplicate files: The time required is far shorter and the cost less expensive than the time and effort that would be expended in recreating a lost file. Back-up tape, disk, and even card files for an EDP installation can be stored in another part of the building or even in another building. (See Note on page 157.)

As an example, consider an accounts receivable subsystem, in

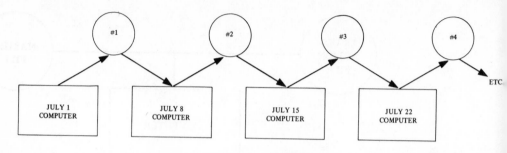

FIGURE 8.4.

which daily transactions require continuous updating of records. Assume that at the end of each week a duplicate accounts receivable file is created for back-up purposes (see Fig. 8.4). (The files—the numbered circles in Fig. 8.4—may be card, magnetic-tape, or magnetic-disk files.)

Thus on July 1, a master file is created in which are entered the transactions for the first week of July. On July 8, file #1 is used to create a second, new file, and file #1 is placed in an offline storage area or library and held as back-up for file #2 in the event file #2 is damaged or destroyed.

On July 15, the file created on July 8 becomes a back-up file for file #3. As of the latest date, two back-up files now exist.

On July 22, file #1 is erased (or, if on punched cards, discarded). On this date, file #2 becomes the new file #1, file #3 the new file #2, and file #4 the new file #3.

By creating duplicate accounts receivable files in this manner and retaining them each for three weeks, two files will always be available as back-up against loss or damage.

8.4

Program Maintenance

The personnel of a data processing installation are accountable to management for the efficient operations of the computer center and for insuring that computer programs perform as intended. Thus, not only the data base, but also the associated computer programs must be properly maintained. Existing computer programs must be modified according to changes in tax tables, new procedures in inventory, new information required in reports, new state and federal regulations, etc. Older computer programs may even require complete rewriting in the event new

computer-language compilers or new computer hardware are
adopted.

8.5

Planning   An important function of the data processing installation
involves studying, planning, and designing new applications to be
put on the computer. Only a few years ago no widely accepted
procedures existed for planning new projects in the automation of
business activities, and managers generally created their own
methods. Planning requires the scheduling of facilities and
manpower. Efficient operation requires planning and scheduling
activities in a manner that balances both cost and time without
making excessive demands on available manpower, equipment, or
facilities.

Crucial to planning are decisions that permit both men and
machines to do what they can each do best. Refer to Fig. 8.5.

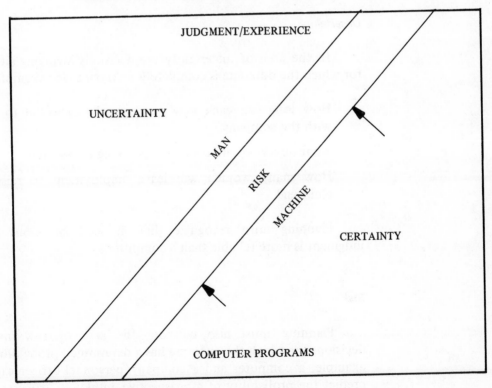

FIGURE 8.5.

Certainty

The area of certainty involves actions and decisions which lead to specific predictable outcomes. Typically, these include repetitive activities—printing payroll checks, posting transactions to a journal, and such simple decisions as:

Has year-to-date pay exceeded taxable FICA wages? If so, make no more deductions for FICA.

Is the transaction a sale and a debit amount, or a return and a credit amount? If a sale, add to sales total, if a return, add to returns total and so on.

The planning and design of any computer system should recognize that such repetitive activities can be performed by the computer faster and much more accurately than by man.

Uncertainty

In the area of uncertainty are decisions involving situations for which the outcome is completely unknown—for example:

How long can each new employee be expected to remain with the company?

What directions are competitors taking in research?

How many women will leave employment to raise their children?

Planning must recognize that in such situations human judgment is more reliable than a computer's.

Risk

Planning must also consider the area of risk involving decisions for which the outcome has a determined probability. For example, a computer and a company personnel officer can each predict the probability of a prospective employee's success, given enough information on the applicant's education and work

146

experience. However, only the personnel officer can evaluate an applicant's interest in the job offered him.

The arrows in Fig. 8.5 represent the goals of the data processing installation—that is, the optimum use of the computer to reduce risk and uncertainty in the business system.

8.6

Organizational Structure

Data processing installations are usually functional structures comprising two basic sections: (1) operations, and (2) programming and systems planning. This separation into two sub-structures reflects important distinctions. For one, systems planning and programming personnel do not usually work under the same pressures of deadlines that operations area personnel are often faced with. Furthermore, systems planning and programming personnel require more extensive training, and possess skills different from those in the operations area.

The organizational structure of a given data processing installation reflects the size of the organization it serves. Typically, the leading professional, perhaps the data processing manager (see Sec. 8.7), reports directly to an officer of the company. In some companies this individual reports to the controller, in others he may be on the same level as the controller and report to an assistant vice-president. Other data processing personnel frequently report to people who have had similar training and/or experience. This type of structure has some similarities to F. W. Taylor's functional organization discussed in Chapter 1.

Figure 8.6 is an organization chart for a small data processing installation. Figure 8.7 is an organization chart for a data processing installation serving a larger company and thus exhibiting a greater degree of specialization in work activities.

8.7

Data Processing Personnel

The following are brief descriptions of the nature and scope of basic positions in data processing operations, programming, and systems.

147

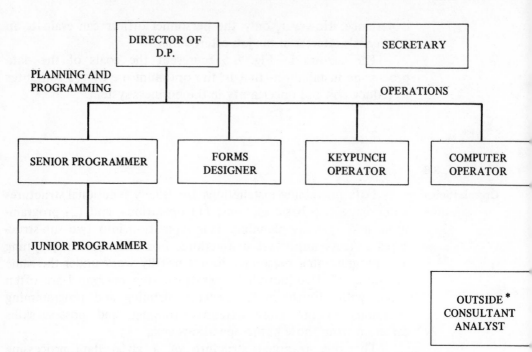

*The impartial assistance of an outside consultant is sometimes useful to a small installation.

FIGURE 8.6. General organization structure for data processing installations.

Data Processing Manager

The data processing manager is the administrative and technical head of a company's entire data processing activities. He supervises all systems analysis, equipment selection, programming and operations.

He is responsible for:

1. forecasting costs of equipment and activities;
2. recommending new uses for computer hardware;
3. selecting new hardware and having obsolete equipment removed; and
4. developing training schedules to continue the education of his staff.

He is usually accountable to general management or to a company officer for the efficiency and progress of his department.

148

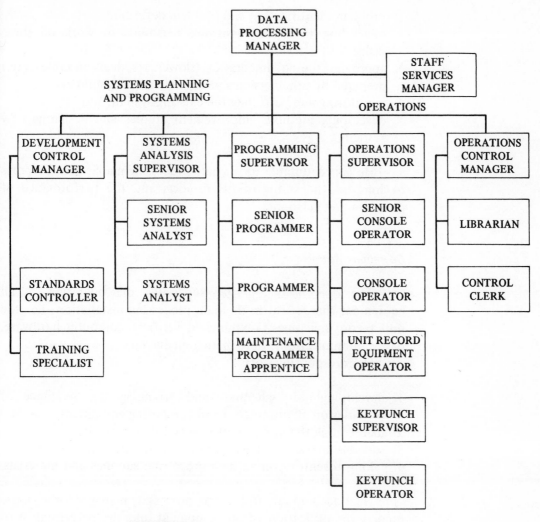

FIGURE 8.7.

Systems Analyst

A systems analyst is an analytical and technical assistant to the data processing manager; he identifies and directs the solution of his company's systems problems (see systems study chart, Sec. 9.7).

He is responsible for:

149

1. problem identification and problem definition;
2. scheduling tasks and assigning personnel to work on these tasks;
3. approving the documentation (flowcharts, decision tables, etc.) prepared by other systems personnel and programmers;
4. monitoring and patrolling the existing system; and
5. developing methods improvement studies and designing new systems.

He is accountable to the data processing manager and reports to him on the status of his projects and the performance of programming personnel.

Operations Manager

The *operations manager* supervises the operation of all equipment (hardware) in the data processing installation—i.e., the unit record machines, keypunches, verifiers, computer hardware, data communications, time-sharing media, etc.

He is responsible for:

1. developing job schedules and arranging the sequence of activities on all unit record and computing equipment;
2. maintaining the integrity of files and their records;
3. supervising the maintenance of disk and tape libraries; and
4. taking inventory on all data processing supplies and materials.

He is accountable to the data processing manager for accurate reports on utilization of all equipment and the performance of operations personnel.

Programmer

Programmers participate with systems analysts in analyzing problems and developing the logical flow of steps involved in the approach to the problem solution.

A programmer is responsible for:

1. developing flowcharts of computer programs (often with the review of the systems analyst);
2. selecting computer language to be used in particular programs;
3. selecting the system configuration to be used for particular programs;
4. coding computer programs;
5. preparing all program documentation—i.e., flowcharts, decision tables, and the file of correspondence and memos pertinent to particular problems, etc.;
6. testing for all possible events in his programs;
7. the interface between each new program and other existing programs; and
8. maintaining existing computer programs.

He is accountable to the systems analyst for the performance of his programs.

Computer (Console) Operator

A *computer operator* operates the computing equipment through a console or control panel and prepares the computer hardware for the execution of a program.

He is responsible for:

1. initializing or preparing the console and the rest of the computer configuration to receive computer programs;
2. setting up the necessary forms and punched cards, paper tape, magnetic tape, or magnetic disks to properly execute the program;
3. logging the inclusive times that jobs are on the computer; and
4. performing required actions upon the configuration during program execution and taking any corrective actions as defined in the operator's manuals.

He is accountable to the operations supervisor for the completion of reports before they leave the data processing installation and for notifying the computer manufacturer of any equipment malfunctions during program execution.

Keypunch Operators

Keypunch operators keypunch and verify keypunched data.

They are responsible for preparing punched cards according to instructions supplied by the programmer or systems analyst.

They are accountable to the operations manager (or a keypunch supervisor) for keypunching and filing source documents.

8.8

Personnel Training   A principal characteristic of computers is change. Change to faster internal processing speeds, faster input/output speeds, greater degrees of miniaturization, more refined microfilming techniques, new audio response units, and so on. Keeping personnel abreast of these advances requires continuous education.

Academic Education

Two-year community colleges, business schools, and some four-year colleges have begun to recognize these needs and have developed curricula that not only provide students with marketable skills in data processing, but also bring up to date the knowledge of those already in the field. Such curricula include courses in computer programming, business systems, data processing mathematics, and, in some schools, one or more years of accounting.

Such curricula are generally characterized by frequent changes in courses and course content. Typically, one year's graduates have studied substantially different courses than have the classes two or three years before them, even though they all hold the same diploma.

Manufacturers' Training Classes

Manufacturers of computer hardware maintain their own training programs, not only to keep their own personnel

152

up-to-date on new developments in technology, but to train their customers' personnel as well.

Courses manufacturers offer their employees may include Boolean algebra, numerical analysis, number theory, principles of accounting, in addition to programming and systems design.

Figure 8.8 shows a schedule of courses offered to users of computer equipment. Courses offered by manufacturers cannot ordinarily be used for college credit. They reflect at an early stage the many changes constantly taking place in the forward edge of this technology.

In-House Training Program

Many industrial and commercial enterprises develop their own data processing training programs. (Many businesses working in unique areas have no other alternative if appropriate courses are not offered in academic institutions or elsewhere.) Employees who demonstrate sufficient aptitude and interest are usually encouraged to take these courses concerned with that part of the total system which is the immediate concern of the individual.

In-house training programs enhance the career development of an employee and this leads to the ultimate benefit of the total system.

Because of the rapidly changing computer technology, periodic training schedules must be developed by the data processing manager and adhered to by the personnel in his installation.

Data Processing as a Profession

Data processing is a profession in the fullest sense. Webster defines a profession as a calling requiring specialized knowledge and often long and intensive academic preparation.

In addition to its specialized knowledge and long and intensive academic preparation, the data processing profession has other characteristics shared by all other professions. The most important function of any profession is its *service* to others, and we have emphasized this earlier in this chapter. Two other very important characteristics of a profession are:

	DAYS	LOCATION	DATE	FEE

FUNDAMENTALS OF PROGRAMMING —
F3601 Prerequisite: Basic Computer
Systems P.I. or Computer Systems
Fundamentals P.I. For new programmers
only.

	5	ROC	11/02	140.00
	5	BUF	02/08	140.00

ASSEMBLER LANGUAGE—K3600
COBOL PROGRAMMING FUNDA-
MENTALS—M3600
COBOL PROGRAM WRITING—M3601
COBOL PROGRAMMING TECH-
NIQUES—M3602
BASIC PL/I CODING—P3650
The above are all Programmed Instruction
Courses and each is prerequisite to attend-
ance at a corresponding Coding Workshop.

		P.I.		13.20
See the Course Selection Guide				
Course Price List for form numbers				8.60
on P.I. texts.				7.40
				6.70
				26.40

S/360 ASSEMBLER CODING WORK-
SHOP—K3601 Prerequisites: S/360
Introduction and Assembler P.I.:
Fundamentals of Programming required
for new programmers. DOS of OS Data
Management Coding is a necessary follow-
on course. This is a wrap-up class and
K3600 P.I. is an absolute necessity.

	3	SYR	10/05	100.00
	3	BUF	11/09	100.00
	3	ROC	02/01	100.00

S/360 COBOL CODING WORKSHOP—
M3609 Prerequisite: S/360 Introduction
and the Cobol P.I.'s; Fundamentals of
Programming required for new
programmers. This is a wrap-up course
and the M3600 P.I. is an absolute *must*.

	3	SYR	10/12	100.00
	3	ROC	11/23	100.00
	3	BUF	01/13	100.00

S/360 INTERMEDIATE PROGRAMMING
TECHNIQUES—COBOL (E0323)
Prerequisite: S/360 Cobol Coding Workshop (M3609) and six months' experience
writing in Cobol.

	5	SYR	11/16	350.00
	5	ROC	01/25	350.00

S/360 PL/I CODING WORK-
SHOP—P3653 Prerequisite: S/360
Introduction and Basic PL/I Coding
P.I. (P3650).

	3	SYR	12/07	110.00
	3	SYR	03/08	110.00

BASIC PL/I ADDITIONAL CODING
TECHNIQUES—P3652 Prerequisite:
Three months' experience coding PL/I.

		P.I.		9.00

S/360 PL/I (F) CODING WORKSHOP—
P3668 Prerequisite: Basic PL/I Coding
P.I. (P3650). Student should take System/
360 PL/I (F) Coding P.I. (P3667) after he
completes this workshop.

	5	ROC	10/26	290.00
	5	ROC	01/18	290.00

FIGURE 8.8.

Autonomy: freedom to set its own standards and select its own people through such tests as the programmer's aptitude test.

Authority: freedom to determine the computer languages to be used in problem-solving and to plan designs for and controls over new business systems and procedures.

The computer center is the nerve center of any modern business enterprise. Therefore it is the responsibility of the director of the computer center to recruit talented but dependable people and to report to management on the activities of his staff, the limits of the hardware and the capability of his personnel and equipment as well as to provide a reliable information service for decision-making.

A viable data base containing the vital facts in related and updated files can be created by experienced programmers and analysts who know their company. Yet one of the problems that has plagued the data processing installation is the frequent turnover of personnel. Because of the high degree of talent required and the highly competitive salaries, good programmers and systems analysts are not only difficult to find, they are often easily lured away to other installations.

Talented data processing personnel who know their business system as well as its computer system can make a greater contribution to management and earn greater financial rewards than the restless individual who is searching for the challenges of larger and more complex computer hardware.

EXERCISES   1. What is the primary function of an EDP installation?

2. List some considerations in creating a data base.

3. List some aspects of file maintenance.

4. In terms of planning an EDP installation, describe the nature of activities that (a) men perform best; and (b) machines perform best.

5. What is the reason for such frequent changes in college courses in data processing?

6. Why do computer manufacturers maintain their own education programs?

7. Can a data processing manager be described as a professional? Give reasons for your answer.

PROBLEMS   **1.** The city manager in a small Midwestern county seat is contemplating the installation of a computer center to assist such county services and offices as:

> The County Attorney
> The Welfare Agencies
> The County Medical Director
> The County Clerk
> The County Controller

Required: Draw an organization chart for a small staff of data processing personnel to run such a computer center.

2. *Required: In your own words, describe the functions and responsibilities of the positions marked with an asterisk in Fig. 8.9.*

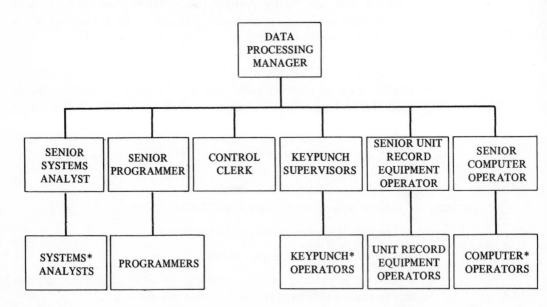

FIGURE 8.9. Organization chart for a medium-size data processing installation.

156

3. *The El Datarato Corporation*

In the accounts receivable department of the El Datarato Corp., the transaction file and the master file are each sequenced in ascending numerical order on a field called ID, which enters into the following events:

Purchase or return when master ID equals Transaction ID

New account when master ID is greater than Transaction ID

Inactive master when master ID is less than Transaction ID

Required: Prepare a procedural flowchart showing the necessary operations for updating the accounts receivable and include satisfactory routines for the events listed above.

NOTE   The problems that threaten Data Processing Center security are fire, natural catastrophe, magnets, riot/vandalism/theft, static electricity (silk clothing), impact (dropping disks and tapes), power surges, and electric storms. In view of these security problems, the following procedures should be followed.

Procedures for Operations

All cards packed firmly in storage trays, all disk packs and tape reels in storage locations.

All cabinets should be locked at the end of each day.

Keypunches and computer cleared of work materials at the end of each day.

All punched cards, continuous forms, tape reels, disk packs and other materials stored when not in use.

Procedures for the Security of Computer Programs and Files

All program listings photocopied and stored off-site.

Object decks copied on tape.

All source decks copied on tape.

All files copied on tape.

All back-up files and programs must be kept up-to-date.

All back-up files are kept off-site.

Restrictions

Only persons accompanied by an authorized company employee are permitted in the computer center.

CHAPTER 9

THE ROLE OF
THE SYSTEMS ANALYST

9.1

Systems Analysis and Systems Analysts

The *systems analyst* is a company employee or independent consultant who studies and analyzes a system in order to develop proposals toward improvements. His major concerns are the flow of information and decision-making in a business organization. The systems analyst assists in the coordination of the work of other departments or divisions of a company. He gathers facts, analyzes existing procedures and defines problems. He must be enthusiastic about his type of work and have the ability to deal with people on all levels within the company.

The increasing importance of the systems analyst reflects the trend towards professionalism in business. At the turn of the century, nepotism was a strong factor in the granting of authority, as fathers handed over the management of business affairs to their sons. World War II accelerated the development of analytical techniques for solving operational problems, and thereafter these techniques were gradually adopted for use in attacking business problems. Today, most companies realize good salesmen or good technicians do not necessarily make the best managers. Promoting a certain worker to foreman or a certain salesman to vice-president sometimes places the wrong people in positions that require the coordination of many activities. Such promotions sometimes cost a company good salesmen and technicians and burden them with poor managers.

In today's business, however, not even competent management is sufficient, by itself, to guarantee total efficiency of the system. Consider the component parts of a small business firm, expressed as subsystems integrated into a total system (Fig. 9.1). One of the most difficult jobs in this or any other business system is making all the subsystems work well together. Levels of management which help improve the effectiveness of each individual subsystem contribute greatly to the efficiency of the total system, and the analysis and improvement of the total system is best performed by persons who specialize in this work. It is easy to see how apt the term "systems analyst" really is.

Because the electronic data processing installation plays a central role in much of the decision-making and information flow in many companies, the activities of the systems analyst are often closely associated with the computer center although he is not necessarily an expert in computer technology or programming. In any event, in an electronic data processing environment, the work of the systems analyst is more challenging and demanding than ever before.

Because his work cuts across departmental and divisional boundaries, the systems analyst and his staff work best when not subject to the authority of a manager or officer responsible for a single department or division of work other than systems and procedures.

9.2

Self-Evaluation   The job functions of the systems analyst in today's business structures (whether or not he is also a manager) demonstrate the overall shift in emphasis from *driving* people to do a day's work to *guiding* people in the performance of their jobs. Because he guides others, the systems analyst must frequently evaluate his own actions, particularly before evaluating other personnel and procedures. He must be able to manage himself before he manages the affairs of his company.

160

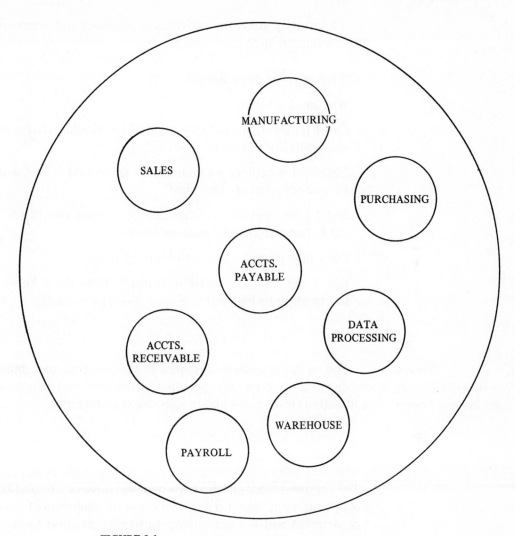

FIGURE 9.1.

His self-evaluation begins with the reason for his own employment, which is to help his company operate more efficiently:

Internally—by eliminating unnecessary activities and cutting wasteful overhead costs; and

Externally—in the market, by helping to produce better goods and services.

161

To properly guide the activities of machines and personnel he must ask himself such questions as:

What must be done today?

Who must do it?

Can I perform this activity myself? Or should I delegate this responsibility to others?

Should this activity be eliminated? Or should it be changed? Or performed at another time?

Did I lose time trouble-shooting or putting out "fires"? or did I successfully anticipate problems?

Did I take proper steps to prevent difficulties?

Did I get the information I need? How do I know the information to be true?

9.3

Personal Qualifications of the Systems Analyst

The systems analyst occupies a key position in a business operation, and thus his personal attributes and educational qualifications must meet highly selective requirements.

Personal Attributes

1. The systems analyst is expected to possess an ability to cooperate with managers, officers, and the members of his own department and the personality to remain on good terms with employees in all departments;
2. leadership qualities which permit him to get at least part of his job done through the efforts of others;
3. initiative—in planning projects that will keep his company on the forward edge of its business life. His initiative must be tempered by both imagination and objectivity;
4. an ability to communicate his ideas clearly and convincingly, both in speech and in writing;
5. a loyalty to his company encompassing respect for the confidential nature of much of the information he works with; and

162

6. an open mind regarding the ideas of others, and a determination to improve his own skills.

Educational Qualifications

The education of systems analyst comprises various factors:

1. Formal education today being more than ever the rule rather than the exception, a systems analyst usually holds an associate's or a bachelor's degree—sometimes a master's degree in business administration, accounting, mathematics, computer science, or some other allied field.
2. Specifically, his academic background should include courses in some or most of the following disciplines: bookkeeping, accounting, forms design, records management, systems design and analysis, operations research, statistics, and probability theory.
3. He should take part in either in-house or executive training programs that orient him to the nature and purpose of his company's activities.
4. He should participate in conferences and meetings concerned with his type of work, including lectures by authorities in his field.
5. He should join appropriate professional organizations and attend their periodic meetings for reviewing those new and modified techniques applicable to his own installation.

9.4

The Approach to Systems Tasks

The nature and scope of the systems analyst's work involve:

1. the development of new projects and applications for computer programs;
2. the integration of business subsystems;
3. the study and design of computer hardware configurations;
4. the implementation of work measurements as a means of comparing performance with standards and goals set by management;

163

5. the preparation of budget forecasts as they apply to his own department.

The activities listed above may be directed at maintaining an existing system, correcting a specific problem, introducing new applications, or designing an entirely new system. The approach to most of these *systems tasks,* as indicated by the block diagram of Fig. 9.2, is divided into four major parts or *modules*:

1. preliminary study;
2. problem analysis and information gathering;
3. planning and control;
4. systems design and implementation.

FIGURE 9.2.

9.5

The Preliminary
Study   The first step in any systems task is conducting a preliminary study which requires:

1. securing necessary cooperation from all department or division managers concerned;
2. acquiring the necessary documents for use as references;
3. identifying those activities of the business which are directly or potentially affected; and
4. selecting a team for conducting the analysis.

Securing Cooperation

The cooperation of affected department or division managers must be guaranteed at the very outset of any systems study. Managers can open lines of communication downward in preparation for subsequent information-gathering through interviews, questionnaires, direct observations, etc. The attitudes of personnel who are made aware of their manager's approval for a study are more likely to be positive and helpful. Furthermore, a cooperative manager can point out specific problems to the analyst, who may consequently direct his attention and energies more profitably.

Acquiring Documents

All documents, organization charts, systems flowcharts, company manuals, job descriptions, activity sheets, operation sheets, file sheets, resource sheets, input/output sheets, computer program documentation, etc.—must be identified and collected for use as references pertinent to the system under consideration.

Identifying the Activities of the Business:

A business is identified by most persons by its product or service. For example, a bus line provides transportation, a dress factory manufactures womens' clothing, a food distributor sells food to retail merchants, and so on. However, the systems analyst must identify the activities of a business as they are described in such documents as the activity sheets, systems flowcharts, company manuals, and any other pertinent data available.

Assembling a Study Team

The size and composition of a study team are functions of the purpose and scope of the analysis. Analysis of a large-scale business system may require analysts with advanced mathematical skills, economists, engineers, and production control experts, whereas the study of a small business may require only the talents of two or three versatile analysts.

The *team leader* is responsible for coordinating the analysis and is usually someone with a demonstrated ability in planning and administration, who can motivate other team members to complete assignments on time while never losing sight of management's objectives.

Additional members should bring a variety of skills and personal attributes to the study.

The members of the team should include persons who are familiar with the system as it presently functions, who have skills in operations research, PERT (see Chapter 14), simulation, systems design, accounting, and computer programming if the subject of the analysis is an EDP installation or system. People who operate any equipment should also be represented on any systems study team. Their confidence is important in dispelling fears of job insecurity among other workers.

The analyst's theoretical view of the system does not always include everyday operating problems. Operations personnel can also point out many practical considerations that might easily escape the analyst's attention.

The system must be sold. Therefore, someone skilled in human relations or motivational techniques should be included on the study team. Although it is often stated that selling begins with design, a good salesman is often necessary to convince management of the worth of a new system.

9.6

Problem Analysis

The systems analyst shares one common experience with modern businessmen, medieval merchants, and ancient traders alike: *problem-solving*. Because a business system consists of persons, equipment, and procedures, a problem can involve:

personnel attitudes, intelligence, training, retraining, costs, or availability;

equipment maintenance, obsolescence, complexity, cost, depreciation, delivery dates, automation, output;

procedural efficiency, duplication, complexity, documentation, or understanding.

Problems can be anticipated when:

personnel go on strike, become sick or injured, or fall back on old habits instead of learning new procedures;

equipment decreases in value due to changes in technology, wear over long periods of use, or increasing maintenance costs;

procedures break down because they are inefficient, not easily understood, difficult, or dangerous to carry out.

Many problems are unforeseen, such as those involving:

an employee's illness or personal difficulties;

competitive groups producing and marketing new or more attractive goods and services;

a procedure that did not provide for an unexpected combination of events, such as a rush on an item for which no inventory back-order procedures were established.

Laying proper groundwork for business problem-solving requires:

1. *recognizing* any problem in the existing system—a "problem" could be frequent cancellation of orders;
2. *identifying* the defect in the system that is causing the problem—the production of obsolete equipment, a bottleneck in sales orders, an overstacked inventory, etc.;
3. *defining* the problem including an analytical, step-by-step exposition of the procedures and actions of personnel and equipment involved.

167

Problem Segmentation

In mathematics and many other disciplines, *understanding* a problem usually represents 50 per cent of the progress toward its solution. Because this is nearly always true of problems in business systems, the concept of problem analysis deserves emphasis.

Competent analysts usually have no difficulty identifying and defining the defects in a business system. Yet the significance of some events or conditions may be overlooked if the nature and scope of their effects on the system are not clearly manifested. Occasionally, difficulties that arise in a system are not simply isolated problems, but symptoms of more serious, underlying trouble. Thus intelligent investigation of such a trivial routine event as a customer complaint concerning the delivery of a home appliance might reveal serious and wide-ranging problems in any number of areas, from inventory to invoicing, or from crating and shipping to customer-billing.

Thus dwindling sales is not only a problem in itself, but may also indicate a defect further back in the business system: observing that sales are dropping off, is simply *recognizing* that a problem exists, not defining it. Careful analysis of the sales-order, inventory, and customer billing subsystems might result in *identifying* the defect as a backlog in processing salesorders, or an understocked inventory, or both. If we assume for the sake of our discussion that the problem is definitely a backlog in processing sales-orders, then defining the problem in detail requires breaking it down into smaller parts by examining the procedures used in processing sales-orders.

In the systems flowchart depicting these procedures (Fig. 9.3), it is clear that the processing time for sales-orders is wastefully drawn out by passing through the hands of two managers and one officer of the company, who in turn must themselves devote too much time to such routine chores. Because of the complicated route that each order must follow, a backlog in processing is inevitable.

Problem segmentation facilitates the approach to the solution of this problem. Note that two major steps are involved in order approval: (1) verification, and (2) credit checks. In our sample problem, proposed changes might include limiting the verification of orders to a clerk and having the customer credit limits checked

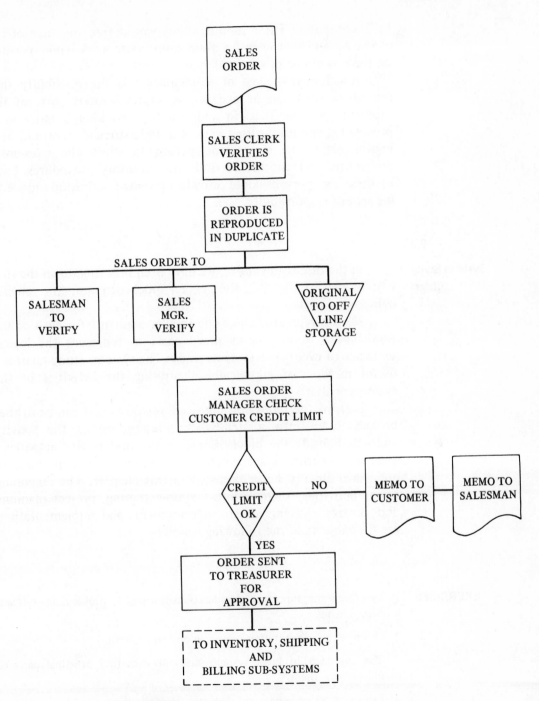

FIGURE 9.3.

by a computer. These modifications would free the time of the executive and managers for more appropriate work while speeding up the processing of sales-orders.

Another advantage of segmentation is the possibility that several persons can be assigned to attack various parts of the problem. Assume that, in addition to a backlog in sales-order processing, the inventories were also understocked. It would be a logical action to assign one person to study the sales-order procedures and another to study the inventory procedures. Each of these two persons could provide a problem definition unique to his area of responsibility.

9.7

Systems Study Charts
In the discussion above, we have been breaking down the first two blocks of Fig. 9.2, the general block diagram, into smaller component parts.

We can represent all of the smaller segments for each of the four blocks in a *systems study chart* to represent the logical sequence of events in a systems study. The systems study chart is a useful method of graphically illustrating the activities of the systems analyst.

Each of the blocks on the systems study chart can be further broken down into a step-by-step description of the activity annotated inside the block. Some of the preliminary activities—such as securing management cooperation, problem analysis, etc.—have already been discussed in this chapter. The remaining major activities, such as information-gathering, project planning and control, systems design, development, and implementation, are the subjects of the following chapters.

EXERCISES
1. Describe some important considerations involved in problem analysis and problem-solving.

2. Describe the segmentation process in problem-solving.

3. The approach to most systems tasks involves four principal parts or modules. Name them.

4. List some desirable personal characteristics for a systems analyst.

170

THE SYSTEMS STUDY CHART

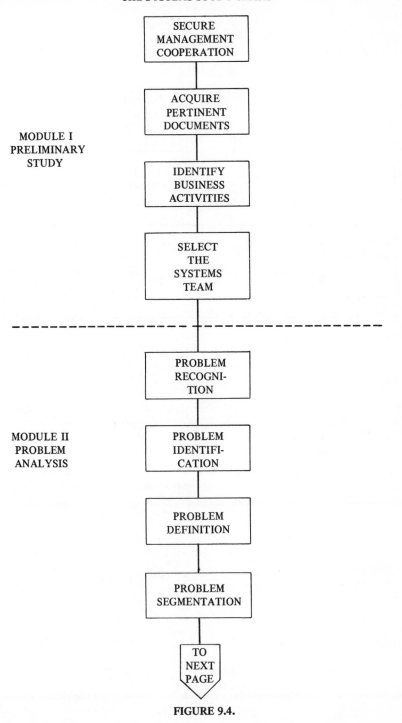

FIGURE 9.4.

171

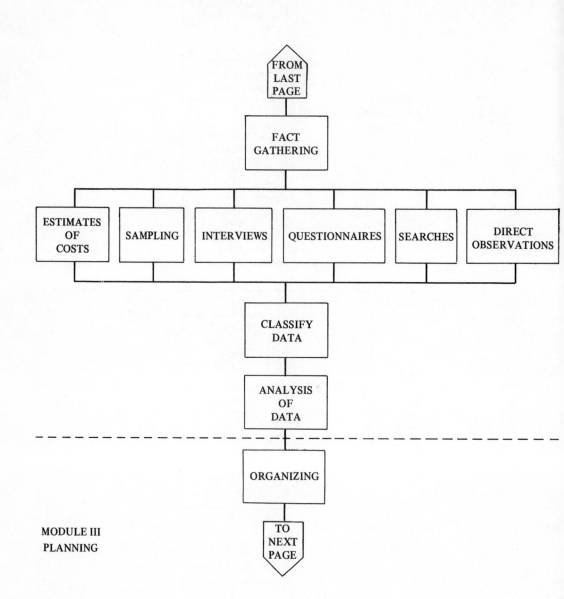

FIGURE 9.4. (Continued)

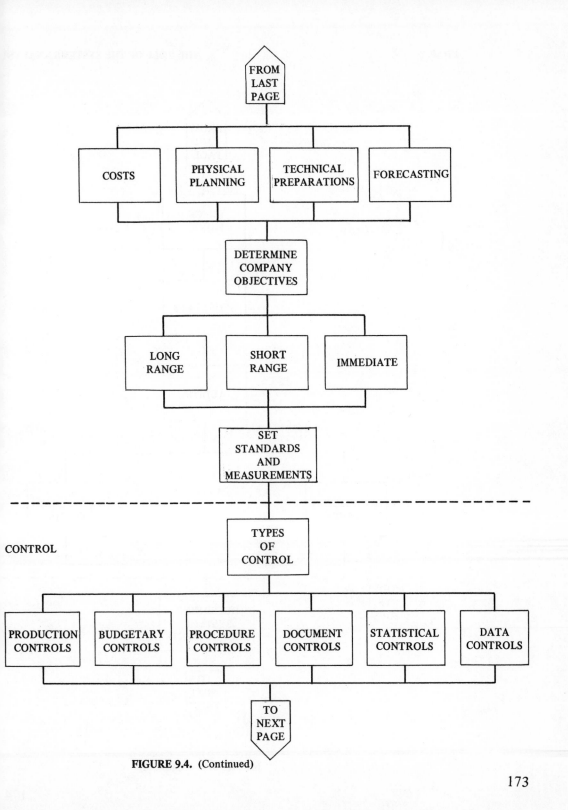

FIGURE 9.4. (Continued)

173

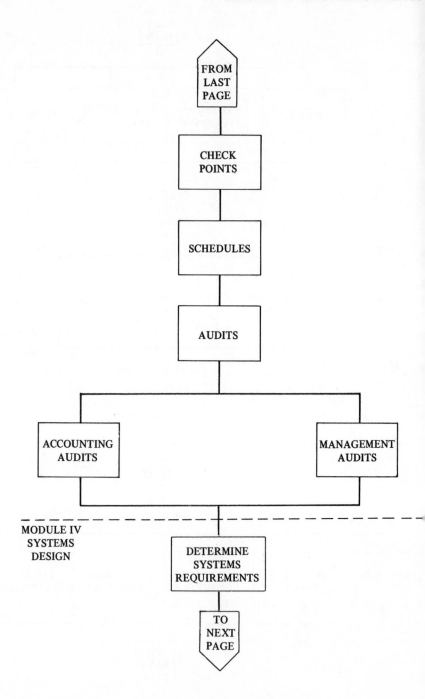

FIGURE 9.4. (Continued)

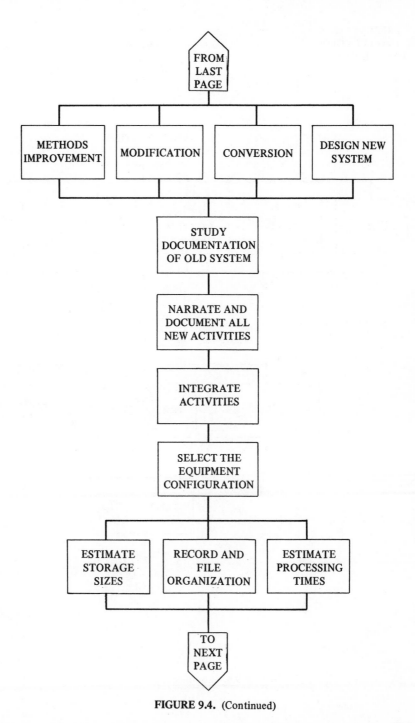

FIGURE 9.4. (Continued)

PRESENTATION,
INSTALLATION,
IMPLEMENTATION

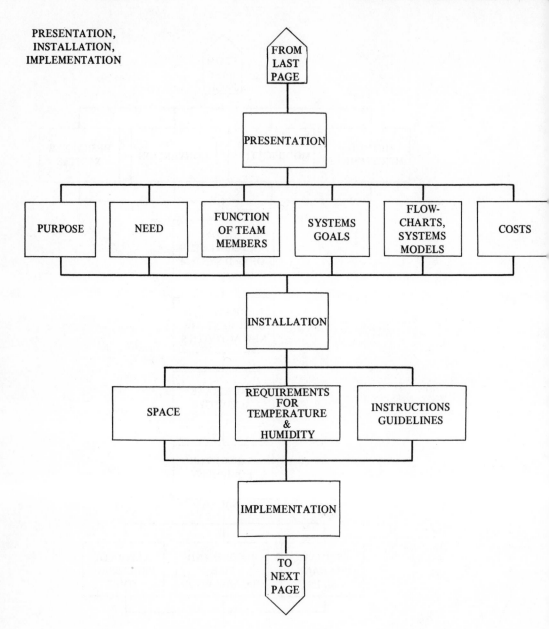

FIGURE 9.4. (Continued)

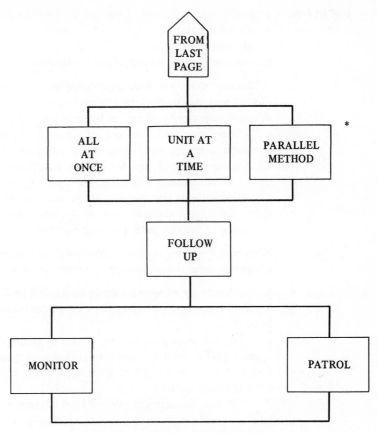

*A choice of one of these methods is usually made.

FIGURE 9.4. (Continued)

5. Why might programming experience be helpful work experience for someone who wishes to become a systems analyst?

6. What kind of educational preparation do you regard as required of all business systems analysts?

7. What sort of personnel should comprise systems study team?

8. What is the first step in making a preliminary study?

9. After a systems defect has been recognized, the defect must be _____ and the problem _____. (Complete the sentence by inserting the proper terms.)

PROBLEMS   1. Redraw the flowchart of Fig. 9.3 showing the following two segments:
   (i) verification
   (ii) credit check
and remove the two managers and the treasurer from these activities.

2. Assume that you have been assigned the responsibility of studying a process and making final recommendations for the computerization of a set of activities presently processed by hand methods.

   The scope and premises of your study must be approved by the computer planning committee. Their approval of the scope and premises upon which you will base your study constitutes authorization for you to review all documents and gather information on all pertinent activities by whatever methods you feel acceptable and relevant to the situation at hand. After you have completed your study, your final recommendations will be forwarded to the computer planning committee for its action.

Required: Prepare a flowchart displaying the various steps you intend to take in implementing the systems study process described.

3. The hierarchy of systems study could well be divided into three different levels: (1) strategic planning; (2) management control; and (3) operational control.

   On the strategic planning level the board of directors and the top operating officers (such as the president of a company) would be interested in such systems as overall labor planning. This would have to be integrated with other planning systems.

   On the management control level concern would be centered on such factors as labor turnover, labor cost accounting, labor productivity, employee safety and welfare, and payroll processing.

   On the operational control level, using payroll processing as an example, specific concerns would be timekeeping, authorization of overtime, wage or rate identification and verification, employee identification for accuracy, etc.

Required: Draw a block diagram to illustrate the hierarchy of a systems study of a labor planning system as described above. Identify the level of planning as being either strategic planning, management control, or operational control.

CHAPTER 10

INFORMATION-GATHERING

10.1

**Planning the
Collection of Facts**

What Is Information?

After a problem has been identified and put forth for a solution, the systems analyst must collect the relevant facts in an orderly and logical manner.

By themselves, however, raw facts do not constitute information. To a systems analyst, information is the knowledge gained through his analysis of problem-oriented facts; his aim in information-gathering is not in amassing volume but in achieving *understanding*. In the words of Dr. Robert Henry Thurston, a prominent professor at Stevens Institute around the time Frederick W. Taylor was there as a student, the first step towards understanding a business system

> "is the careful collection of facts and the patient study of all phenomena in the most accurate possible manner, and so systematically and completely that they shall be readily and conveniently available, and in such shape that their values and their mutual relations shall be most easily detected and quantitatively measured."

The quotation above alludes to facts and a distinction should be noted between facts and data.

A fact is a piece of information presented as having objective reality.

Data are something given as a basis for reasoning or inference, calculating or measuring.

In planning the collection of facts the analyst should ask himself such pertinent questions as:

What data are needed?

Where are these data located?

What should the data do?

How can these data be collected?

What Data Are Needed?

The data needed consists of facts oriented toward the solution of the problem under consideration. For example, if the bank depositor update activity is to be put on the computer, the data needed are facts that will aid in understanding the persons, equipment or materials, policies, procedures, and objectives that apply to the depositor update subsystem, whereas data on vacation pay allowances will probably not be useful.

Pertinent facts may take the form of:

1. numerical data, such as those indicating the costs of an operation, the date a procedure went into effect, and so on;
2. non-numerical data, such as statements concerning policies or procedures in a system; and
3. a combination of numerical and non-numerical data—for example, depositors' names, addresses, and current balances.

All facts should contribute to attaining a perspective on the human resources, materials, equipment, and procedures in a system, in line with our definition of a business *system* on p. 30.

Where Are These Data Located?

A great amount of data can be found in the records and files of a system under consideration—not without difficulties, however. Records in some files are carefully completed, others are not. Documents may be confidential, or restricted, or longer than anticipated. Files may be incomplete, or dispersed throughout a large company. Employee records may be identified by a Social Security number in the personnel department and by a different and unique employee identification number in the payroll department.

In the interest of saving time, it is sometimes desirable to reduce part of the data collected to items that involve dollars and hours if these facts are valid and pertinent to the problem. If files are on punched cards, magnetic tape, or magnetic disk, they can be easily duplicated and sent to the systems analyst. If they are lying in several widely scattered file cabinets, the location of data can be a serious and time-consuming problem.

What Should the Data Do?

Facts are gathered not only to assist in designing new computer hardware configurations, but also to assist systems analysts and company managers in:

1. Describing the purpose, programs, projects, and long- and short-range goals of the business system.
2. evaluating these goals and, if necessary, modifying them;
3. improving work methods by revising old procedures;
4. developing better controls over an existing system, or planning new controls for a proposed system;
5. providing a basis for consideration of alternatives to a present or a proposed course of action; and
6. measuring the performance of personnel and equipment against standards.

Thus information must be as complete as possible, and consequently the analyst should ask questions that are organized and structured toward problem-solving:

Operational questions—What work is performed?...why?...by whom?...by what machines?...how?...in what sequence?

Quantitative questions—What is the volume of work? How much time is required:...in man-hours?...in machine-hours?

Qualitative questions—How much does the work cost:...by material needed?...by man-hours?...by machine-hours? Does this job activity meet:...internal needs (of the system)?...external demands (of the markets)? Does the output meet:...company standards?...the requirements of federal and state regulations?...customer expectations?

The answers to such questions may be found in the company's files, reports, products, services, and in the personal knowledge and experience of its employees. The data provided by these answers is indispensable to the successful solution of any problem.

How Can These Data Be Collected?

Among the media for recording facts are the forms used to collect data on business systems discussed in Chapter 7, including job descriptions, narratives, flowcharts, decision tables and so on.

The systems analyst should not limit himself to these formal documents, however. He should, for example, design whatever additional forms he requires to serve his needs, such as checklists, questionnaires, and interview summaries. He should also examine previous studies, audits, and proposals of similar problems, especially those concerning the same system, and might even divide his problem into several smaller problems, studying each of these one at a time.

Some of the most useful data on an existing system may be taken from:

Estimates of costs

Sampling

Interviews

Questionnaires

A search of organization charts, company manuals, files, records, reports, forms, systems flowcharts, decision tables, work/schedule charts, journals, etc.

Direct observations

Each of the above sources is discussed in the following sections.

10.2

Estimating

Estimates of costs are mandatory when considering modifications of or changes in a system. These estimates must be verified against the budgeted amounts for the various departments in the company. For example, if a maintenance department operates both a repair shop and a home repair service, its budget should be compared to its activity costs—that is, the departmental budget should be compared to:

Costs for inventory—parts used by the maintenance department

Costs for fuel and maintenance of the trucks used for home repairs

Costs for wages and salaries paid (which may be included among inventory costs)

Alternative uses for the money

10.3

Sampling

From a relatively few observations of personnel, machines, outputs, or related events, many inferences can be made on a total operation. Such a *sampling* may either be random or conducted according to some special method of selection—for example, a check of one out of every ten sales orders, of 13 per cent of a machine's output, of one week's batch of purchase orders, of employees whose last names begin with B and T, of the activities of a computer operator from 3-4 P.M. daily, and so on. Sampling constitutes a time-saving method of inspection by reducing observation time and minimizing interruptions of normal work activities. It is a reasonable technique, useful for measuring

183

high-volume output and complex operations, or situations where no formalized or summarized data exists.

If every part of a system could be observed and measured, the results could be regarded as certain; but this is nearly always impractical. The cost of employing specialists to observe the output of every machine and worker would be prohibitive. Even more unrealistic is the 100 per cent testing of consumable items.

If the life expectancy of light bulbs were being measured, testing every bulb until it burned out would mean no products could be sold. Testing the life span of a sample of one out of 25 light bulbs is a more reasonable approach.

The amount of sampling to be done must always be weighed against the degree of certainty desired. Where sampling is crucial to problem-solving, it is usually advisable to employ a statistician to assist the systems analyst.

10.4

Interviews

An interview is a formal consultation for the specific purpose of obtaining information. One common form in business is the employment interview, conducted to screen and select job applicants.

Before initiating interviews, the systems analyst should secure cooperation and support from top executives who may help him structure his questions by providing a broad picture of the system's present activities and future plans.

Interviews conducted by the systems analyst should be carefully prepared in advance and designed to elicit from the interviewee only those facts based on his personal knowledge and job experience. An outline of the topic under discussion should be prepared, and either memorized or written out and brought to the interview (this approach also helps prevent a rambling and meaningless dialogue)—for example:

INTERVIEW OUTLINE

Date: 9/24/71   *Time*: 2:30 P.M.

Interviewee: Mr. Thompson
                      Warehouse Manager

Topic: Converting manual inventory system to computer system

Specific Points To Be Discussed:

1. Has any methods improvement study been made in the past?
   If so, where are the results of that study?
2. How are orders handled?
3. Where is product-test performed?
4. When are items packaged and shipped?
5. How are back-orders processed?
6. Are company standards presently being met?
7. Are government regulations being followed?

The interviewer should ask pertinent questions and avoid digressions, concentrate on listening (not on talking), and avoid arguments. He should take notes during the interview, which he may later compare with information gathered from questionnaires, samplings, searches, and observations.

Because personal interviews are influenced by individual personalities more than are most other methods of information-gathering, the interviewer should study his interviewees beforehand to determine their attitudes, likes, dislikes, and so on. For example, if an employee is wary because of even a vague threat to his job security, the interviewer can try to win his confidence by conducting the interview as informally as possible.

All interviews should be conducted in a friendly manner. The interviewee's cooperation should be *solicited*, and he should be made to feel part of the total business picture. An interviewer's aggressive or belligerent tone of voice can trigger an interviewee's fear or insecurity and even lead to intentionally inaccurate or incomplete answers. Since the object of the interview is to obtain information helpful in approaching the solution of a problem, employees must be motivated to speak freely and truthfully.

One way of structuring the interview is to first describe the problem, then to raise questions that concentrate on the specific points in the outline. Direct questions which do not give the interviewee leeway for commenting or expressing opinions should be used sparingly. For example, the question, "Can you submit reports on the 15th of every month?" can hardly be expected to bring more than a "Yes" or "No" response, whereas the same point phrased as an open-ended questions such as "What reports must your office submit to fulfill its functions?" will bring more information to the surface and may even provide a basis for additional questions on the same point.

Appointments for interviews should be kept on time, and interviews themselves should never be long, drawn-out affairs, but concluded when the interviewer has covered all of the points on the outline.

To make the most efficient use of time, an interview schedule (see Fig. 10.1) should be drawn up. Such a schedule will help to reduce the number of interviews and identify personnel whose knowledge of the system makes a second interview desirable.

	MR. BROWN	MR. VORWALD	MR. ALLEN	MRS. BRADY	MR. LANG	MR. PITT
DATE	9/22/70	9/22/70	9/23/70	9/23/70	9/24/70	9/24/70
TIME	9:30 a.m.	2:00 p.m.	10:15 a.m.	3:45 p.m.	9:30 a.m.	1:45 p.m.
ROOM	300	402	101	301	Shop A	Shop A
TOPIC	Costs	Accounting programs	New employees	Journals	Standards	Maintenance
DEPT.	Accounting	Data Processing	Personnel	Accounts Payable	Cutting	Cutting
TITLE	Manager	Programmer	Psychologist	Clerk	Foreman	Worker
RETURN	X	X				X

FIGURE 10.1 Interview schedule.

10.5

Questionnaires

The *questionnaire*, a form containing questions and spaces for writing in answers that constitute information, is efficient for obtaining a number of vital facts or opinions from a large group of people. Questionnaires should seek to elicit information about job functions, workloads, reports, records, facts needed by employees to better perform their jobs, and difficulties encountered by employees. (Fig. 10.2).

Questionnaires should be brief and to the point. When questions are numerous or require time-consuming answers, people usually feel annoyed by the interruption in their work. The wording of questions should be precise in order to avoid

```
                      JOB FUNCTIONS
                      QUESTIONNAIRE

1. What operations do you perform?  _____

2. How many job orders are received each day?  _____

3. How many job orders are completed each day?  _____

4. Does machinery receive periodic or preventative maintenance?

   _____

5. Are standards being met?  _____

COMMENTS:
```

FIGURE 10.2.

misunderstandings that lead to inaccurate answers. Statements prejudiced toward either management or labor should be avoided. Frequently it is helpful to include a cover letter explaining the reason for the questionnaire and to provide extra space for unsolicited comments which might yield unexpected data.

Questionnaires should be sent to *key* people who can provide problem-oriented answers—not only officers, managers, and foremen, but clerical and production workers at points of action as well (suggestion boxes are placed in factories and offices on this premise).

The following sample questionnaire is designed to determine additional advantages of automating the activities of a business office.

187

QUESTIONNAIRE

Subject: DATA PROCESSING

Check
Your Dept.   ☐ ACCOUNTING   ☐ SALES

                    ☐ WAREHOUSE   ☐ MAINTENANCE

1. What applications would you like to see in a data processing system?

2. Can data processing personally help you?

                                    before the work flow reaches you

            your area of responsibility

                                    after the work flow has left your area of
                                    responsibility

3. What reports generated by your office are repetitious or otherwise
   suitable for machine application?

4. How many different forms do you fill out each week?

5. Which of these forms do you feel the computer should process?

6. What applications can you audit during their first machine runs?

7. What type of statistical information does your office require?

8. Are you involved with any simple decision-making tasks that are repetitious and might be performed by a computer? What are they?

9. What files does your office require in order to carry out its functions?

10. Would you like a copy of the results of this questionnaire?

10.6

Search

    Searching involves the examination of company organization charts, manuals, files, records, reports, forms, systems flowcharts, decision tables, work/schedule charts, journals, etc.

    Organization charts and company manuals can usually show the analyst the framework of the business structure with which he is working and provide a narrative description of the procedures and activities taking place. Organization charts are a source of data on lines of authority and should be verified by observation, interviews, and so on. Manuals can be used to compare job descriptions and specifications with the work as performed—that is, to determine whether job functions conform to published descriptions, whether written procedures are being carried out (and how efficient they are), whether operations overlap each other, and if management's expectations are being met.

    One way of determining whether the entire company is meeting expectations is through comparison of production work schedules and actual production outputs. Work schedules are also helpful in assessing the effective utilization of the system's resources—its equipment and manpower.

    Information regarding files and records includes their

location and the personnel who work with them. Company files should be examined in conjunction with applicable flowcharts and instructions for accessing and processing those files.

Forms such as purchase orders, sales slips, invoices, and packing slips and reports such as budget reports, sales analysis reports, income statements, and balance sheets all provide facts useful in assessing the objectives, growth, and worth of the business. If the facts to be collected are specific and limited in nature, the search can be narrowed down. For example, if the analyst is working on a billing system, his activity is concentrated on such items as accounts receivable ledgers, credit ratings, and sales analysis reports.

Systems flowcharts, decision tables, and similar documents, whose value has been stressed before, graphically describe the information flow and repetitious decision-making operations within the business system.

Handbooks such as the *Financial Handbook, Accounting Handbook* and the *Production Handbook* contain detailed and factual information about specific areas in business.

Historical information about a specific system may provide reasons for the creation of the company, and back-issues of financial reports can reveal reasons for introducing, expanding, or discontinuing various products or services.

Information regarding competition is also important and can help lead to the development of new products, improvement of procedures, retraining of employees, and so on.

Among other potential sources of information are:

Previous system studies

Company audits

Trade journals

Articles in the *Business Index*

Periodicals and business directories

Publications of the federal government, especially those of the Departments of Agriculture; Health, Education and Welfare; Interior; Commerce; and Labor—all available from the U.S. Government Printing Office, Washington, D.C.

10.7

Direct Observation

The direct observation of people and equipment at work yields information that can be used in conjunction with the results of questionnaires and interviews.

Some systems analysts prefer to make such observations before conducting interviews, so that they can:

1. more easily determine the information they need to obtain from employees;
2. consequently reduce the time spent interviewing and the number of interviews;
3. anticipate cooperative and potentially hostile interviewees, and thus be better equipped to separate facts from opinions.

10.8

Classification and Verification

After all the facts have been collected for a study they must be classified and checked for accuracy, relevancy, completeness, timeliness, and intelligibility.

Classification

The analyst must maintain his own accurate record of his information-gathering activities and prepare his own file system. Records of interviews, questionnaires, samples, and direct observations; flowcharts; files; and estimates should be separated, categorized, and placed in folders or looseleaf binders with a table of contents. An index should be prepared, so that all data may be accessed in an orderly manner.

When investigations are complete the analyst may then refer to his file to summarize his activities in narrative form.

Verification

All information gathered must be checked for the following attributes:

Accuracy—Accuracy is crucial to understanding the present

system. Human errors and machine malfunctions often persist, and the role of the analyst is to determine, as far as possible, the validity of each item of data he has collected.

Relevancy—The data assembled and classified must all be pertinent to the problem, subsystem, or total system under consideration. Only relevant data can be used to justify or support changes or modifications required to solve a business problem. Current activities must be renarrated or reflowcharted, if necessary, to bring them up to date.

Completeness—If cost factors for a business venture were incomplete, no serious investor could be expected to support it. Likewise, when classifying data, *all* the facts must be included so that the problem can be viewed from every possible angle and solutions approached satisfactorily.

Timeliness—All the facts gathered should be up-to-date. Last year's index on the rise in the cost of living, last month's sales analysis report, or even last week's commodity prices can be useless information depending upon the nature of problem to be solved.

Intelligibility—Data collected should be arranged in a logical order. All facts pertaining to the system or activity under consideration should be grouped together with related vital information and placed prominently, not buried among supporting documents. The writing of the analyst must be concise; decorative adjectives and extravagant use of the first person ("I" and "me") should be avoided.

10.9

Analysis

After all data has been collected, classified, and verified, it must be carefully analyzed before any meaningful information can be taken from it. As we noted at the beginning of this chapter, facts alone do not constitute information. Analysis of the facts should lead to the definition of a problem and distinguish mere symptoms from functional defects or other sources of difficulty.

A principal reason for collecting certain types of data is the need for a comparison between the expectations of management and the actual activities of a business system. Any analysis of the data gathered should attempt to answer such questions as:

Are schedules being adhered to?

Are job functions performed as specified in company manuals?

Are company policies clearly understood by those implementing them?

Are policies administered properly and consistently throughout the system?

Are expectations being met: in production? in the work force? in the machinery? in standards? in costs?

Are organization charts up-to-date?

If no completely documented picture of the relationship among persons, machines, and procedures is available, the systems analyst must create his own documentation, using the materials discussed in Chapter 7.

EXERCISES

1. What questions should an analyst ask himself before gathering facts?

2. When a systems analyst collects facts and information for a study, what expectations may management have for the results of the report?

3. How would the following studies aid management decision-making? What judgment and/or information can be expected?
   (a) A study of the company credit extension procedures, bad debt losses, including comparison with similar firms
   (b) A study of the productivity, operating costs, purchase prices, and quality of output of a new production process compared with present methods
   (c) A study of employee productivity, absenteeism, and turnover as correlated with education and occupation

4. Discuss, in general, where an analyst may find sources of information.

5. What would be your sources of information for a study evaluating the advisability of a new computer?

6. What types of forms does an analyst use to collect data for a study of a business system?

7. Under what circumstances are cost estimates desirable?

8. If you are observing activities, how great a sampling would you consider a necessary minimum to detect, with a reasonable degree of accuracy, each of the following:

(a) the number of errors on invoices where the total number processed daily averages between 500 and 600?

(b) the same as (a), except that the daily average processed is 8-10?

(c) the quality of output of an automatic machine that produces 1,000 units per hour?

9. What basic approach and attitude should an interviewer have?

10. Write a paragraph defining the term *search* as used by the systems analyst in gathering information.

11. Why might a systems analyst prefer to utilize direct observations as a method of gathering information *before* interviewing employees?

12. What attributes should all information gathered ideally possess?

PROBLEMS   1. You have been given the responsibility of studying the adequacy of the methods and procedures used in the sales-order, sales-billing, accounts receivable, credit, and collection section of your firm. The firm is medium-sized, and you are assigned a staff of two other people to assist you in this study.

After spending the afternoon observing the operations of personnel in this section and discussing various procedures with the office manager, you decided to construct questionnaires for use in reviewing operations, corresponding to the component parts of the section. You also decide that each questionnaire will start with general questions to obtain information concerning the overall operation, and then shift to specific question on the various activities in each subsection.

Required: Prepare an outline indicating the kind of general information you intend to gather concerning the overall operation of the sales-order, sales-billings, accounts receivable, credits, and collection system. This information should reveal the overall organization and volume of activity, the organization of personnel and staffing and the competence of staff in training personnel. You are concerned here with the kinds of forms, reports, and policies that are common to the entire area of operation. You should organize this overall view of the organization in three sections: (i) general information, (ii) organization and personnel, and (iii) supplementary information that may contribute to a clear understanding of the area under study. Keep in mind that this document will serve as a guide for your information-gathering activities.

2. Referring to the firm and responsibilities described in Problem 1, above, prepare a questionnaire to serve as a guide in the analysis of the sales-orders and sales-billings subsections. Assuming that this questionnaire will be the basis of a detailed study of the procedures used in sales orders and billings, include questions to reveal the adequacy of procedures as well as the timeliness and quality with which they are prepared.

3. Prepare a detailed table of contents of the sort you would expect to find in a complete business system analysis—i.e., one whose objectives include understanding the present system, determining new system requirements, and designing the new system. This table of contents should reflect all important phases and areas of this study, from examination of the old system through the installation and implementation of the new system.

CHAPTER 11

PLANNING AND CONTROL

11.1

Planning and Change

Module III in Fig. 9.4 implies that planning is a fundamental and continuous function of management. In looking to the future a manager must think before he acts. He must plan ahead to take the best possible advantage of his company's resources in our rapidly changing environment. Such changes may be:

Technological changes caused by advances that make old equipment obsolete

Social changes such as population shifts from urban to suburban areas or new hiring practices that no longer discriminate against minority groups

Economic changes that bring about periods of inflation or recession, an increase or decrease in interest rates, and so on

Political changes that lead to new laws and regulations

Ecological changes that call attention to the necessity of conserving natural resources and protecting the natural environment

Intelligent planning is crucial to the survival and growth of today's business systems. The dictionary definition of *plan* as a "scheme of action" or "procedure" barely implies its full significance to a business manager, for whom planning means that facts pertinent to change must be gathered, assumptions made concerning future operations, activities mapped out, contingencies provided for, and an orderly sequence of events established.

Some questions that a planner must first ask himself are:

What are the objectives of the company?

Has the present system been described and flowcharted?

What improvements are needed?

Have alternative courses of action been studied?

Plans must support and further systems objectives. They must be efficient, reduce or eliminate unproductive work, and achieve desired objectives while justifying their costs and producing a minimum of harmful unexpected side-effects.

11.2

Basic Planning Considerations

In his role as a planner a manager must consider:

The nature of the plan

The organization of the plan

The structure of the plan

The explanation of the plan

The execution of the plan

Nature of the Plan

Business plans may involve the modification of a single activity in a system, a work improvement study to increase the output of personnel and/or machines, a conversion from a manual data processing system to an electronic data processing system or the design of a completely new business system.

198

Organization of the Plan

Planning begins with organization. After pertinent facts have been gathered, all the system's resources—i.e., personnel, equipment, and procedures—must be considered and assessed with a view toward making business operations more efficient.

Before plans can be put into action, the planner (who may be a systems analyst) must arrange these resources so that the best possible relationships exist among them. To find effective patterns for reaching goals, problems must be broken down or segmented, and groups of qualified persons assigned to study these various segments. Authority must be delegated to persons who will lead these groups, and a spirit of teamwork instilled. Integrating these groups and subplans provides the planner with an overview of the direction in which the business system is going.

Other aspects of organizing a plan include estimating the plan's costs, determing its physical requirements, making technical preparations, and forecasting. *Costs* must be estimated to insure that all planned activities are realistic and consistent with the system's financial resources. *Physical requirements* include such factors as equipment, plant sites, buildings, temperatures, humidity, work space, electrical requirements, parking areas, loading docks, and so on. *Technical preparations* include architectural layouts, tested computer programs, and personnel training. *Forecasting* attempts to anticipate:

Changes in market demands

Changes in competing products and services

Changes in technical knowledge

Changes in social climate

Changes in the labor market

Changes in political currents

Structure of the Plan

A plan's structure, which translates goals into actions, includes company policies, procedures, budgets, equipment, personnel, and, perhaps most important of all, communications.

199

Explanation of the Plan

One function of an effective communications network is to insure that company goals, policies, and procedures are understood and uniformly administered throughout the system. The communications media for explaining new plans include memos, departmental meetings, manuals containing new instructions, system flowcharts, and so on.

Execution of the Plan

Management responsibility for the execution of plans includes:

1. overseeing subordinates to make certain that they are carrying out their job functions and keeping all activities goal-directed;
2. instituting controls over execution of the plan—such as checkpoints to verify results against expectations and the standards by which these results may be measured; and
3. auditing and reviewing all progress on the plans, making recommendations for improvements when necessary.

11.3

Developing and Implementing Plans

Managers responsible for planning are expected to:

1. determine company objectives:
   (a) long-range,
   (b) short-range,
   (c) immediate;
2. develop policies and procedures to help meet these objectives;
3. establish standards for products or services;
4. develop methods of measurement to determine whether or not standards are being met;
5. set schedules informing personnel of management's expectations;
6. develop contingency plans anticipating any unforeseen consequences of planning;
7. motivate employees to accept and comply with necessary changes.

200

Company Objectives

Long-range objectives or goals might include:

New product lines

Diversification of products

Specialization in a particularly successful product or service

Decentralization of a business system by separating its divisions by geographic areas—for example, locating manufacturing operations in suburban industrial parks and accounting and sales offices in large cities

Planning for long-range objectives must take into account the equally long-range uncertainty of markets, technology, and competition. Pessimistic and optimistic alternatives must be prepared in advance of the execution of any plan.

Short-range objectives might include:

Retraining or hiring personnel to adapt to changes in technology

Changing a procedure in inventory control

Putting the company payroll system on a computer

Immediate objectives might include:

Flowcharting the present system

Assessing systems resources in terms of capital, labor, and equipment

Scheduling activities needed to implement changes for the future

Policies and Procedures

As part of every plan, policies must be developed as guidelines for maintaining consistency of current and future activities; such a

201

policy might involve, for example, hiring practices that exhibit no biases on account of race, color, religion or age, but only stress talent, education, enthusiasm, and experience.

Procedures must also be developed that provide a sequence of related and orderly steps required to accomplish specific job functions—for example, filing inventory reports in ascending order by part number.

To meet his objectives a manager must develop realistic policies and procedures, put them in writing, making them clear and uniformly disseminated and enforced.

Standards

All plans must establish standards of measurement and operating procedures in order to insure uniformity as well as optimum performance and output. Standardization involves setting forth specific sizes, types, measurements, quantities, times, periods, etc., for a person, procedure or machine. Two special types of standards that business systems are required to meet are contractual (those required by customers), and legal (those required by state and federal laws).

Standards for work performance permit the comparison of results with expectations. A production standard may be in terms of number of units per hour or day; cost standards may require the cost of work performed under a specified dollar amount; statistical standards may require a product to meet specifications such as an average lightbulb life of from 1,000 to 1,050 hours.

Methods of Measurements

Measurements of actual performance must be compared with standards set forth by management (using units of measurement consistent with pre-determined criteria). For example: shop timecards or job cards can be used as a source of information concerning employees' output; sampling the product life of one out of every 100 brake bands can help determine the quality of the product; budgets can be compared to actual costs to determine if cost standards are being met; current sales quotas can be measured against projections of future sales; and so on.

Scheduling

Schedules illustrate time-and-work relationships. They provide a graphic description of the nature of the business, and should be used to motivate employees to reach management's goals.

Contingency Plans

Robert Burns noted years ago that the best-laid plans of men often go astray. In today's world, government regulations and tax rates change, labor may demand higher wages in the middle of a project, the cost of materials can increase, competitors may introduce a product that outperforms one that is about to go into production, and so on. In situations like these priorities may have to be changed.

Good managers possess the sensitivity and flexibility to meet the unexpected, minimizing unsought consequences and shifting when necessary to alternatives that have been prepared to meet and cope with unforeseen events, without excessive costs.

It is a mistake to assume that all of the consequences of any plan will be beneficial ones and that nothing will alter a course of action once it has been fixed. Unforeseen events always occur because change is characteristic of our society. Planning must be strategic, allowing flexibility to deal with the unforeseen. Planning for contingencies means providing a choice of operational patterns that will influence decision-making over the span of time needed to convert management goals into actions.

The planner should use the higher mathematics of statistics and probability theory, the techniques of operations research and simulation as well as PERT networks (see Chapter 14), so that his judgments in selecting alternatives and handling of contingencies can be based upon the best tools available to him.

Inflexible policies, procedures, and attitudes are like obsolete equipment. They have a negative effect on the survival of a system.

Motivation

Personnel should be informed of the objectives of the company so that by helping the company they will help themselves to accomplish goals. In this respect, management sometimes uses the influence of rewards, financial incentives and bonuses, penalties, and sanctions to meet their objectives.

11.4

The Purpose of Controls

Control pervades all human activities. We exercise control upon ourselves when walking upright, speaking clearly, and writing legibly. We know the desired result beforehand and we can guide our own activities according to "standards" for walking upright, speaking clearly, and writing legibly. *Control* in a business system means guiding people and procedures in the directions consistent with the system's objectives, and a good manager attempts to plan only those activities which he can control.

Controls must be understood by the people who will use them, especially those employees whose performance is to be evaluated. Crucial to maintaining control is the application of standards to performance. Managers must constantly compare performance against expectations and apply corrective measures when deviations or exceptions interfere. Feedback resulting from a deviation from standards must be answered by first fixing responsibility for the deviation.

If the error lies with personnel, the objectives of the plan must be re-established in the minds of everyone concerned. Employees must be motivated in a positive manner, and favorable attitudes must be encouraged.

If the exception to the standards is the fault of machinery, then equipment must be modified or replaced.

If the fault lies in procedures, then management must design new work methods.

11.5

Types of Controls

Whatever can be measured—in terms of quality, quantity, time, and cost—can also, theoretically at least, be controlled.

Production Controls

Production Controls attempt to maintain a constant, smooth workflow from raw materials to finished product in the shortest possible time and at the lowest possible cost.

Budgetary Controls

Budgetary Controls help to shape and structure plans. The planner must be aware of demands made for funds, the capital allocated for expenditures, the income anticipated during the period of planning, and ways of reducing costs. A *cost* to a planner is a function of a unit of work, time, space—i.e., costs may be in terms of numbers of automobiles, deliveries per hour, square feet of floorspace, etc.

Procedure Controls

Procedure Controls stress accurate clerical handling of data to develop a means for audit. These audits should be used to locate errors and inconsistencies early enough to correct them before they are perpetuated throughout a system. Procedure controls may also be the means by which government regulations are followed.

Document Controls

Systems flowcharts, decision tables, and narratives of job functions found in manuals, resource sheets, activity sheets, operation sheets, and file sheets are all useful documents which may be used as guidelines for the execution of new plans.

Statistical Controls

Such devices as tables and graphs conveniently display the statistical information for measuring the accomplishments of

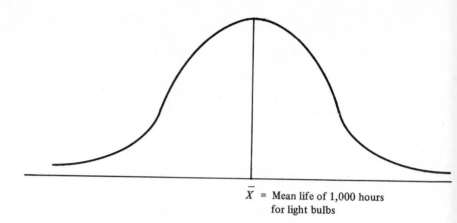

$\overline{X}$ = Mean life of 1,000 hours
for light bulbs

FIGURE 11.1.

plans. For example, in the graph in Fig. 11.1 those lightbulbs whose lifetime is shorter than 1,000 hours (the portion to the left of the mean) are inferior, and should not be sold to customers, while those whose lifetime is longer than 1,000 hours (to the right of the mean) are too costly to produce in a competitive market.

In Fig. 11.2, for another example, the two heavy lines represent tolerances planned for a certain machine tool, while the wavy line indicates measured performance. At points A and B, the deviations are too great to be accepted; at point C the deviation might be too small to be investigated.

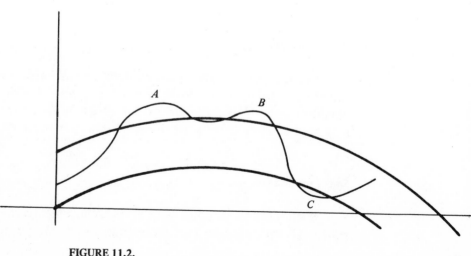

FIGURE 11.2.

11.6

Data Controls   Checks must be made on inputs and outputs to make sure that only valid data is to be processed. Examples of data controls are prenumbered forms such as sequentially numbered payroll checks, and periodic sampling of computer output. Other commonly used data controls are discussed below.

Record Counts

If a count of all the records in a file appears at the end of a file, this number can be verified against a computer count of the records while that file is being processed. Such a *record count* insures that all records in a file have been processed.

Sequence Check

A *sequence check* is simply a verification that records are being processed in sequence—e.g., in ascending or descending numerical order, or in alphabetical order.

Proof Figures

Proof figures provide a unique number for each record in a file. For example, in a file of salaried employees whose biweekly pay is constant for one year, to be certain that all deductions have been properly taken, we could add them up as shown in Fig. 11.3, yielding the *proof figure* 35.48. Thus at any time during the preparation of checks an individual's proof figure computes improperly, an invalid deduction can be assumed.

−	+	−	+	−	
STATE TAX	FED. TAX	FICA	HEALTH INSURANCE	UNITED FUND	PROOF NUMBER
13.28	63.04	21.88	12.60	5.00	35.48
−(13.28) +	(63.04) −	(21.88) +	(12.60) −	(5.00) =	35.48

FIGURE 11.3.

207

Crossfooting

Updating master files often involves computations on data in individual records. *Crossfooting* is a technique used in checking these computations. For example, suppose that it is necessary to form a total of all the X's, a total for all the Y's, and a total for all the Z's, as well as a grand total of the three fields in Fig. 11.4 (shown in tabular form in Fig. 11.5). To verify these computations, the programmer might instruct the computer to take crossfooted totals, as shown in Table 2 (Fig. 11.6). The number 450 represents the grand total achieved by both processes of addition. If the total in Table 1 did not agree with the total in Table 2, the programmer would have to audit this segment of his program to locate any possible mistake.

Hash Totals

A control total of a number of records in a file may be taken in the following manner. Identification numbers seldom change but an error in updating a master file might result in the omission of few records. Using identification numbers, a *hash total* could be forced by "adding" such alphanumeric characters (numeric, alphabetic, and special characters) as 240W+Y103+3A31. The *"hash" total* is a result of the individual computer's ADD operation and has no special numerical meaning. Nevertheless, the result—which might be V2R3—functions as a control total and must be tested for each time the file is processed. Control total found in header or trailer records can be compared with the total obtained from "hashing" or adding in every item number after the file has been updated and/or processed.

Check Digits

All computer INPUTS must be valid. Nevertheless, keypunch operators, clerks, bookkeepers, accountants, managers, salesmen, and customers occasionally alter and transpose numbers inadvertently. One method of verifying identification numbers (such as a payroll or account numbers) is to use a *check digit* attached to the

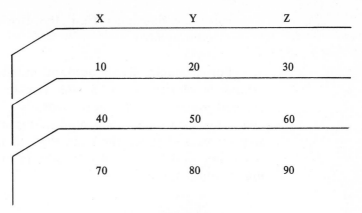

FIGURE 11.4.

TABLE 1

VERTICAL ADDITION

X	Y	Z			
10	20	30		120	
40	50	60	and	150	
+70	+80	+90		180	
120	150	180		450	GRAND TOTAL

FIGURE 11.5.

TABLE 2

HORIZONTAL ADDITION

X	+	Y	+	Z			
10		20		30	=	60	
40		50		60	=	150	
70		80		90	=	240	
120		150		180		450	GRAND TOTAL

FIGURE 11.6.

identification number. Credit cards frequently employ check digits. In the "modulo n check method," the check digit is calculated as follows:

Let n = any number.

Divide the account number by n.

209

Place the remainder from the division to the right of this account number.

For example, if an account number is 23612 and n is arbitrarily chosen to be 5, the remainder = 2; thus the full account number, with check digit, is 236122. Every time the computer reads an account number it is instructed to perform the step above and verify the sixth digit to the right as the correct remainder, which is stored internally in the record of the account under consideration.

11.7

Planning/Control
Flowchart

Figure 11.7 is a graphic description of the planning and control function of management, and includes the following features:

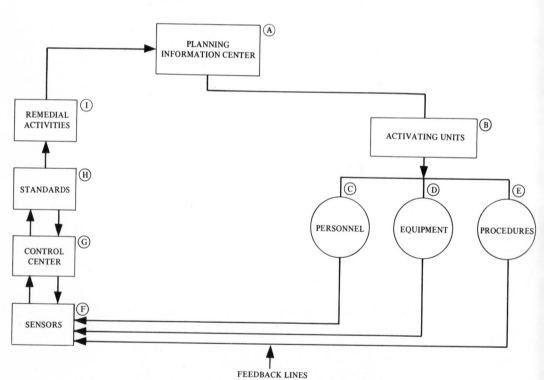

FIGURE 11.7. Planning and control flow diagram.

A. The *planning information center* initiates the objectives of the plan and all the necessary specifications on the old system and the proposed system.

B. *Activating units* are new forms, flowcharts, instructions, policy statements, incentive bonuses, retraining programs, communications, etc.

C. *Personnel*—their education, experience, attitudes, and abilities.

D. *Equipment*—all the materials needed to implement the new business activities.

E. *Procedures*—the detailed, orderly, step-by-step job methods needed to perform the new business activity.

(Blocks C, D, and E are the principal areas under consideration and will be tested and measured against the expectations of management.)

F. *Sensors* are measuring units (much like a thermometer in the thermostat)—and are either *budgetary* (to measure actual costs), *mechanical* (to measure actual specifications and performance of new products), or *supervisory personnel* (to measure the work performance of other persons).

G. The function of the *control center,* which usually consists of a systems analyst and/or managers involved in the new activities, is to measure the output of blocks C, D, and E against standards (block H).

H. *Standards* are set by management for costs, time, production, etc.

I. *Corrective actions* are taken after feedback indicates deviations from or exceptions to standards.

(The feedback lines in the closed loop diagram, Fig. 11.7, are a basic characteristic of control.)

11.8

Checkpoints   In a business system, good control does not always mean complete control. Because monitoring every activity, machine, and person would be too costly, *checkpoints* are frequently set up. For example, imagine planning a payroll system to be put on a

211

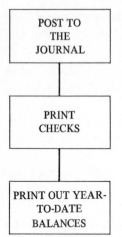

FIGURE 11.8.

computer, involving three reports to be run off every two week
Assume that the blocks in Fig. 11.8 represent the propose
computer programs, and that they are to be run in the sequenc
shown. Thus rates of pay, hours worked, and deductions must b
posted to the payroll journal before the checks can be printed; an
the year-to-date balances report can only be run off after check
have been printed.

Each of these programs contains many instructions for th
computer to perform, and the computer center personnel mu:
carry out several operations in order to run each job.

Checkpoint 1: Under the old system, payroll clerks posted t
the journal the biweekly hours, rates, and deductions, along wit
employees' name and employee numbers. Standards here are th
correct gross pay, deductions, and net pay, and valid employe
number and name. By checking the output or journal in the ne
EDP system at this point—i.e., verifying a sample of output again:
parallel output in the old system—it is possible to measure th
accuracy of results in the first computer program. (See Fig. 11.9a

Checkpoint 2: Checkpoint 2 provides a point for verifyin
not only gross pay, deductions, and net pay, but also the gener:
format for printing the checks and comparing the output again:
the parallel segments in the old system. (See Fig. 11.9b.)

Checkpoint 3: This checkpoint provides a point for verifyin
computer output for year-to-date totals in net pay and deductior
as well as any other required summary data. Here, as elsewhere, :
is the function of the analyst (or management) and th
programmer to know when standards are or are not being met. I
an error occurs at any one of the checkpoints, the programme
must take corrective actions. (See Fig. 11.9c.)

11.9

**Developing
Standards**

There are several methods of establishing standards fc
machine and/or human output. For example, the *motion stud*
segments job function into elementary motions—those motior
that can be broken down no further into simpler motions (e.g
lifting, reaching, grasping, etc.). In a motion study the rhythm c
movement, coordination, distance travelled, and sequence c
operations are analyzed with the aim of reducing movemen

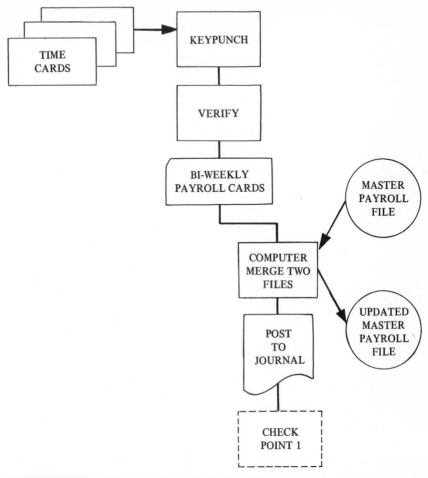

FIGURE 11.9a.

maximizing coordination, shortening distances, improving the sequence of operations, and eliminating wasted effort.

The *time study* analyzes motions in terms of elapsed time. Elementary motions or work-unit cycles are clocked, usually with a stopwatch. After times are measured, including delays and work stoppages, the average time for each work-unit cycle is computed. This average time then becomes the *standard* for the work-unit cycle under consideration.

In some shops, the work-unit cycles take place so quickly that intelligible studies and accurate measurements require filming

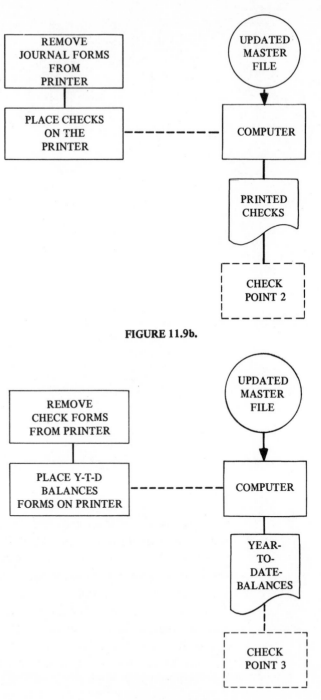

FIGURE 11.9b.

FIGURE 11.9c.

the worker in composite with a clock, calibrated in hundredths of a second, and a slow-motion movie camera.

Both time and motion studies cannot yield valid results without the cooperation of the workers and their unions, otherwise workers might deliberately slow down work-unit cycles when they are being timed in order to lower the standards they will be expected to meet.

11.10

Schedules–Gantt Charts

Determining what activities must be done and estimating when the activity will be accomplished can be described graphically in schedules. Schedules are attempts to control the relationships that exist between time and work and invest plans with a sense of urgency.

Time/work schedules can be graphically illustrated or plotted on a horizontal scale in chart form, and perhaps the most familiar work/time or work/progress chart is the *Gantt chart*. This type of chart was developed by H.L. Gantt, about the time of World War I, and represents one of the earliest tools of "scientific" management.

Figure 11.10 illustrates a Gantt chart in which the items of production are steering columns, brake bands, and odometers. The number in the upper-left-hand corner of each block represents the planned or expected number of units for that day, while the number in the right-hand portion represents the actual number of units completed on that day. The

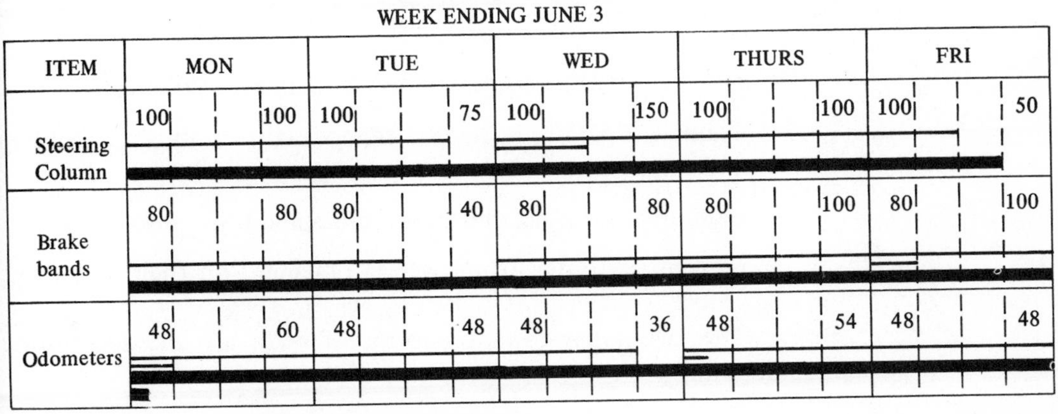

WEEK ENDING JUNE 3

ITEM	MON		TUE		WED		THURS		FRI	
Steering Column	100	100	100	75	100	150	100	100	100	50
Brake bands	80	80	80	40	80	80	80	100	80	100
Odometers	48	60	48	48	48	36	48	54	48	48

FIGURE 11.10. Gantt chart.

215

thin lines represent actual units completed daily, as indicated by their length; heavy lines represent cumulative amounts of units completed weekly. Thus if one day's production is equated with one inch on the chart, then inspection reveals that for steering columns the heavy line is ¼", or 25 units short of the week's planned production.

In addition, for the week ending June 3, the goals for brake bands were met, and the goals for odometers were exceeded by 6 units. These determinations can be made either by using simple arithmetic and subtracting actual units from expected units, or by measurement of the bar lines.

By setting production units in terms of costs, Gantt charts can also be used to express relationships between time and money as well as time and work. Alternatively, if it were necessary to convert time into dollars, the unit cost of an item is the only additional information required. Thus if the cost for making each brake band is $6.50, then 400 × 6.50 = $2,600.00 is the cost of making brake bands for the week ending June 3.

We could have just as easily measured output in terms of *persons* instead of *items* in Fig. 11.10 by listing employee names in the left-hand column and indicating work units produced daily by each *individual*.

Gantt charts are useful tools for control because they graphically describe performance in a manner that is easy to grasp and summarize.

11.11

Audits   Audits are conducted to:

insure correct use of the system's financial resources

evaluate operations in accordance with established policies and procedures

discourage criminal abuse of monies and other resources

prevent personnel from passing judgment on their own work

The two most common forms of audit are the accounting audit and the management audit.

Accounting Audits

Double-entry bookkeeping methods comprise a convenient tool of financial control. For example, if office supplies are purchased from a vendor, recording the transaction as shown in Fig. 11.11 not only provides a chronological record of this and other transactions and eliminates the need for lengthy explanations of routine financial events, but also indicates that business transactions always affect at least two accounts, increasing one and decreasing the other.

DATE	DESCRIPTION	DEBIT	CREDIT
4/8/70	Office supplies	500.00	
	Accts. pay.		500.00

FIGURE 11.11.

Periodic examinations, or *accounting audits*, should be made of all accounting records, reports, and statements, not only to make certain that they are properly maintained but also to determine whether actual costs are meeting or exceeding the planned costs. Management's knowledge that records, reports, and other statements are accurate assures them that they have a reliable frame of reference for controlling a new system.

One particular form of accounting audit is the *audit trail*, which begins with the initial recording of a transaction and then is traced through all its processing steps, possibly including effects on other transactions or records. Audit trails end in the final output resulting from that transaction or in its final residence in an updated file.

Even when the "trail" becomes a magnetic one—one leading the investigator through magnetic tapes or disks, or into the storage units of a computer—it can be traced by specialists who have both programming and accounting skills.

217

Management Audits

A *management audit* may be described as a periodic evaluation of managerial planning and control, based on some prescribed norm for the successful operations of a business system. Such an assessment of management reviews the past and present as well as future plans.

Management audits are also frequently performed by an independent organization, which bases its evaluations on such factors as

financial stability

policies pursued

production efficiency

sales volumes

economic growth

EXERCISES   1. What sorts of changes in the environment may necessitate business to alter its methods or goals?

2. What questions should planners ask themselves before gathering facts pertinent to change?

3. (a) After the nature of the plan has been determined, what is the first step in the planning process?
(b) What system resources are used in this first step?
(c) Name four separate categories of this first step?

4. Briefly discuss the nature of the objectives a planner must determine.

5. What do *policies* and *procedures* mean as used in planning?

6. Define *standards* as used in planning products or services.

7. Describe management's responsibility in the execution of a plan.

8. Write a short paragraph explaining what is meant by "control over activities" in the planning process.

9. Write a brief definition of five types of controls.

10. Explain what is meant by *data control*.

11. Referring to Fig. 11.7 briefly explain the function of:
    (a) blocks C, D, and E
    (b) the block labeled "Sensors"
    (c) the block labeled "Control Center"

12. Why is it desirable to provide checkpoints in a system?

13. Which features of a Gantt chart make it advantageous for indicating performance in relation to quotas?

14. What is meant by a *management audit*?

PROBLEMS   1. The officers and management of a medium-sized manufacturing concern are having considerable discussion over whether they should offer a wider variety of products in the marketplace than they do at present.

The Vice-President in charge of Marketing has expressed his desire to expand the number of products the company offers. His major justification is that "We should produce and offer to customers whatever they desire; otherwise," he argues, "other companies will offer these products and weaken our competitive position."

The Vice-President in charge of Manufacturing argues that "We should stay with the present number of products, or even eliminate some which do not generate high volume," pointing out that only through volume production of a small number of products can he be expected to maintain reasonable production costs. In other words, increasing the number of different products produced and sold will, in his view, increase cost of production.

The Treasurer of the firm indicates that he would merely like to know *what* the final decision is going to be so that he can arrange financing. From his vantage point, changing over a production line may involve the purchase of new machinery, which, depending on seasonal fluctuations, may require the company to borrow substantial amounts of money on inventories or accounts receivable. While he acknowledges that by expanding its line of products the company may experience significant growth and greater profits, on the other hand he acknowledges that an expanded line might require additional equipment, larger facilities, greater investments and inventories, and higher costs. His major concern, however, is not which decision is finally made, but *when* it will be made—so that he can adequately prepare financing for whichever alternative is chosen.

The Chief Engineer of the company tends to agree with the Vice-President of Manufacturing, adding that if changes are to be made, he must know about them well before the start of production because of the difficulties of designing and changing the production line.

The President of the company asks you to outline a plan for getting the top executives together in planning production for the next year.

Required:
(a) *State the nature of the plan and the form it should take.*
(b) *What kind of participation should you expect of each executive?*
(c) *Diagram the steps of the plan that you propose.*

2.

PART I

The Injecto Corp. is about to start production of a new fuel-injection system. The Marketing Department has been accepting orders promising the first delivery by August 15. An analysis of the orders for the first month indicate the following weekly shipment dates must be met:

August 15	1,000 units
22	2,000 units
29	3,000 units
Sept. 6	3,000 units

It is anticipated that one week of production lead time will be sufficient to meet the above shipment dates.

The injector is produced in two different departments. Department A assembles the pumping section; Department B assembles the housing and mounting brackets on the pumping unit, completing the product.

The Production Manager has stated that to meet deadlines Department A must finish its work one week before Department B is scheduled to complete the pumps.

Required: Outline a Gantt chart (see Sec. 11.10) of the required production schedules for Departments A and B.

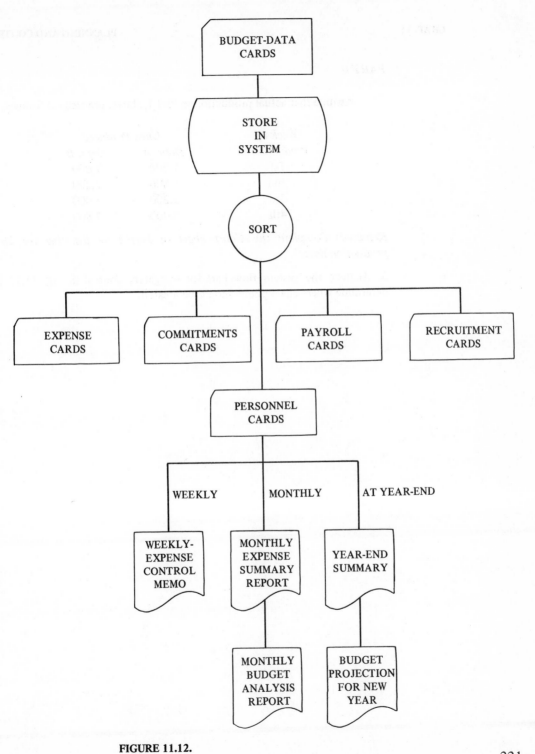

FIGURE 11.12.

PART II

Assume that actual production in Part I, above, proceeds as follows:

Week of Production	Units Produced	
	Dept. A	*Dept. B*
1st	1,200	1,000
2nd	1,800	2,200
3rd	3,200	3,000
4th	3,000	2,800

Required: Complete the Gantt chart of Part I by inserting the abov production data.

3. Analyze the system flowchart for budgetary control in Fig. 11.12 an determine where checkpoints should be located.

CHAPTER 12

SYSTEMS DESIGN CONCEPTS

12.1

Determining Systems Requirements

The basic steps in systems design are:

1. an analysis of the *existing systems* in order to understand the relationships among their resources, activities, operations, inputs/outputs, and files; and
2. a study of management's plans and goals with the view of *determining the requirements* of the new system.

Analysis of existing systems has been discussed in previous chapters. To determine what management wants the new system to accomplish, the systems analyst must ask such questions as:

What new outputs are desired?

What kind of equipment is management willing to utilize to improve the system?

How are new procedures to be implemented?

Who will man the system?

By what date should the system be operational?

What controls are to be put into effect?

Are there any special exceptions to normal procedures?

After the activities and accompanying operations of the new system are thoroughly understood, the personnel and equipment have been proposed for several alternative solutions, and a careful analysis has been made of all requirements and alternative solutions, a choice is made of the best possible design, which may take the form of:

1. a *methods improvement study* to determine ways of increasing efficiency;
2. a simple *change* or *modification* in something as minor as a single activity;
3. a *conversion* from manual methods to machine methods; or
4. a completely *new* business *system*.

12.2

Methods Improvement Studies

A *method* is a general or established way or order of doing anything; in business systems this includes the expenditure of time, money, and energies. *Methods improvement studies* are concerned with:

Adapting methods to new technologies

Simplifying work by eliminating tasks which do not contribute to production or services

Effecting more economical utilization of persons, procedures, equipment, space, time, and motion

Consider the design for a sequence of tasks in the manufacture of electric motors. In Fig. 12.1, all copper wire is manufactured before any armatures are wound, and electro magnets are all constructed before the motor housing is assembled. In Fig. 12.2, these consecutive tasks are *overlapped*. Because the time line for the process in Fig. 12.2 is considerably shorter than the time line in Fig. 12.1, clearly Fig. 12.2 represents an improvement in the method of performing these tasks.

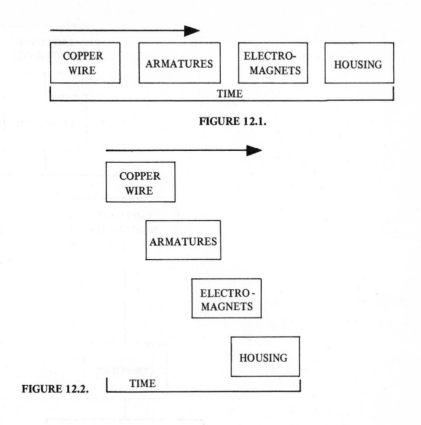

FIGURE 12.1.

FIGURE 12.2.

12.3

Modification

   Modification in a business system can mean change in equipment, personnel, or procedures.

   As an illustration, let us consider the modification of a single activity. Suppose that each time a quarterly FICA report is prepared, an entire employee master payroll file on punched cards is processed by the computer, and that at the beginning of the second quarter some employees have left and thus are no longer on the company payroll. Only those persons employed in the second quarter who received taxable FICA wages should appear on this 941a or quarterly FICA report. However, *all* employees who have worked in any period during a given year should appear on that year's W-2 report.

   Figure 12.3 shows the systems flowchart of the procedure for processing the 941a report and the W-2 forms. The payroll system in Fig. 12.4 shows a change or modification designed to avoid the problem of excessive computer time costs. Here the computer will

225

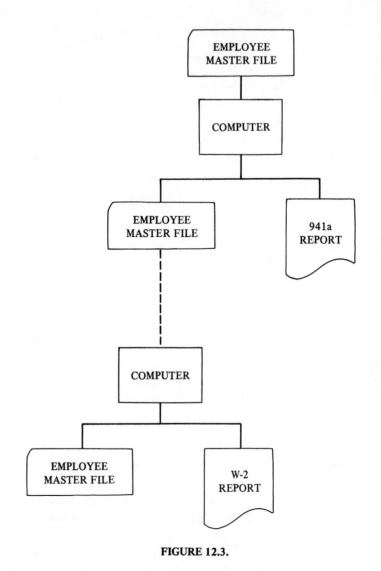

FIGURE 12.3.

read and process *only active employee records* for each 941a
report. In preparing the W-2 report, inactive employee records are
merged with active employee records before processing.

Note that all modifications in the activity performed to
produce the 941a and the W-2 reports should be incorporated into
all supporting documents—i.e., activity sheets, operation sheets,
resource sheets, input/output sheets, and file sheets.

226

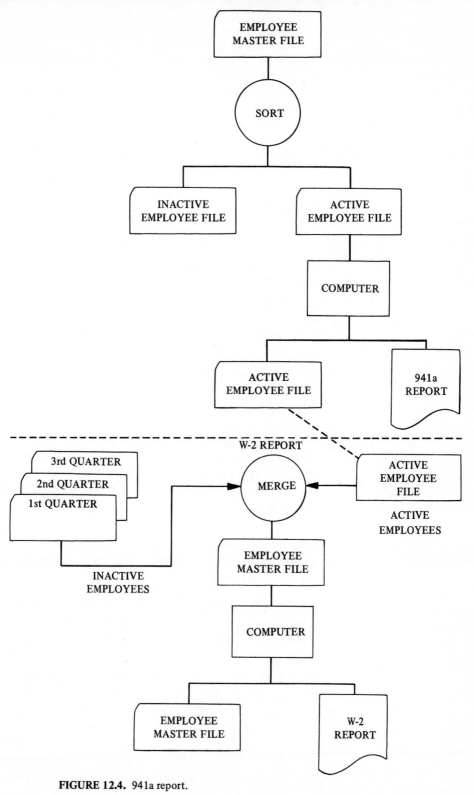

FIGURE 12.4. 941a report.

227

12.4

Conversion

To convert means to change into another form or state, *conversion* in data processing systems means an orderly change from old methods to new methods. The scope of any particular conversion depends upon steps taken earlier in the planning and control phase of the systems study.

Among the factors that should be considered for conversion are:

1. *Effects on present and planned facilities:*
   Is more space needed for new hardware?
   Are electrical, heating, and humidity requirements different?
   Are raised floors needed?
2. *Effects on personnel:*
   Are additional employees needed to carry out operations and/or man new equipment?
   Must present employees be retrained?
3. *Effects on costs:*
   What additional costs are involved . . .
     for leasing new equipment? . . .
     for installation of new equipment? . . .
     for training personnel? . . .
     for operating new equipment?
   What are the comparable costs of the old system and the new system?
   How much more (or less) expensive will the new system be?
4. *Effects on outputs:*
   How can results expected of the new system be compared to the (known) results of the old system?

Documents pertinent to any conversion are discussed in Chapter 7, and used in the following illustration.

Suppose a home appliance manufacturer wishes to convert his data processing activities from unit record equipment to a computer system (see Appendix A for descriptions of data processing hardware). In addition to some of his present applications, he wishes the computer to provide him with a sales analysis report. In this section we shall consider the existing system; Sec. 12.5 describes the conversion of the activities in this system to the new system, including the modification of one activity and the design of two completely new activities.

Information Gathered on the Present System

Narrative: The manufacturer supplies many small retail outlets throughout the country. Orders for new appliances are written on forms similar to the one shown in Fig. 12.5 and forwarded to the central business office. If an appliance is returned, a similar form is filled out and stamped "RETURN."

Each business day orders and returns are batched together and brought to the keypunch operators to be keypunched into cards similar to the one shown in Fig. 12.6. One card is punched for each line on the order form.

Note the following arrangement of fields on the cards:

FIELD NAME	CARD COLUMNS
Store Number	1-4
Return Code	5
Salesman Number	6-8
Item Number	9-13
Quantity	14-16
Item Description	17-34
Unit Price	60-64
Price	70-74
Date Processed	75-80

Returns are differentiated from orders by an X-punch or special "RETURN" code in column 5.

To save keypunch time, the date and item descriptions are not punched in. Instead, the date is created from a punched card each business day and the item description information is found in a master deck of item description cards. There is one item description master card for each of 500 different appliances sold in outlet stores (Fig. 12.7).

After a batch of sales orders and returns has been keypunched, cards are assembled as shown in Fig. 12.8. Return cards are selected out on the sorter, placed behind the order cards, and listed with dollar and quantity totals on the accounting machine. This list ("LIST-1"—Fig. 12.9) is proofread and checked against the original source documents (Fig. 12.5) to make certain that all cards have been punched correctly. Any cards not in agreement with the data on the original order or return form must be repunched, and the entire batch listed again.

229

SALES ORDER   0001

0-23612

BILL TO   Elba Appliance Co.   STORE #   1360

                                                 SLSMAN #   461

                                                 DATE   3/17/71

                                                 SHIP VIA   X   Truck

                                                                      Rail

                                                                      Customer

QTY	ITEM #	DESCRIPTION	COLOR/ FINISH	UNIT PRICE	PRICE
10	1468	Refrigerator	Brown	200.00	2000.00
30	3291	Stove	Brown	310.00	9300.00
15	6485	Air conditioner	Tan	175.25	2628.75
21	0059	Television	Walnut	425.00	8925.00
				TOTAL	22853.75
				TAX	914.15
					23767.90

FIGURE 12.5.

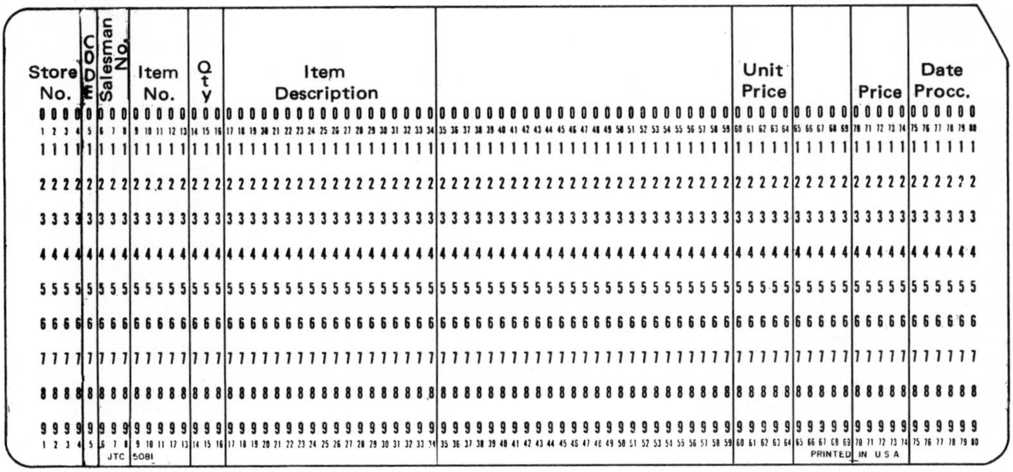

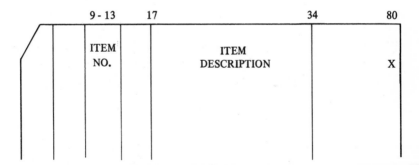

FIGURE 12.6.

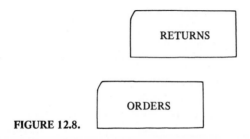

FIGURE 12.7.

FIGURE 12.8.

LIST-1

STORE #	SLSMAN #	ITEM #	UNIT PRICE	PRICE	QTY
1360	461	1468	200.00	600.00	3
1360	461	3291	310.00	23250.00	75
2461	463	6485	175.25	3680.25	21
7800	500	0059	425.00	42500.00	100
5861	049	3040	150.00	1200.00	8
1004	325	6401	120.25	240.50	2
1004	325	7009	210.00	630.00	3
3742	112	4185	250.95	250.95	1
			1841.45	72351.70	213*
7800	500	0059	425.00	8500.00CR	20
1360	461	3291	310.00	2480.00CR	8
3742	112	4185	250.95	1756.65CR	7
1004	325	7009	210.00	630.00CR	3
5861	049	3040	150.00	150.00CR	1
			1345.95	13516.65	39CR*

*Notice the CR symbol used to indicate RETURNS, the asterisk indicates total amounts.

FIGURE 12.9.

Since the original orders and returns are keypunched in the order they are received, at this point they must be sorted in ascending numerical order by item number. After both orders and returns are sorted, cards are interspersed and make up a sequenced transaction deck, which must be collated with the master deck of item description cards. When a master card and transaction cards show the same item number, the master card is placed in front of its corresponding transaction cards. Unmatched masters and unmatched transactions are selected out into separate stacks in the collator (Fig. 12.10). Unmatched masters indicate no orders or returns for that item. Unmatched transactions indicate that an invalid item number appears on the order or return form, and the situation must be reported to the sales manager.

The matched masters and their accompanying transaction

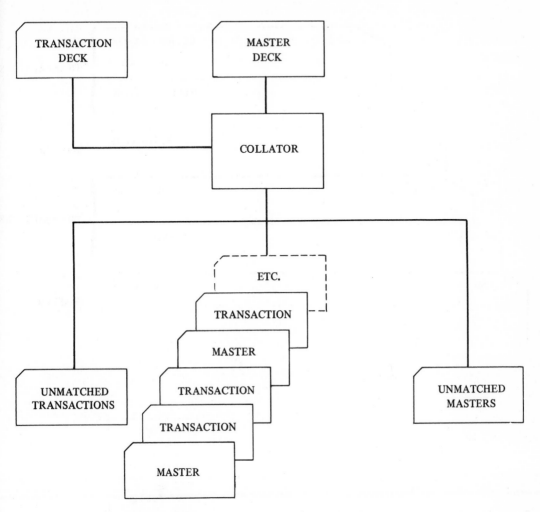

FIGURE 12.10

cards are now ready for interspersed gangpunching on the reproducer, which in this case (see Appendix A) simply involves punching the item description into only those cards with identical item numbers (Fig. 12.11).

After the item description has been interspersed-gangpunched into the appropriate transaction cards, the entire deck is placed on the sorter (Fig. 12.12) and the item master cards are selected out (item master cards have an X-punch in card column 80—see Fig. 12.7). The item master deck is now placed on the sorter together

233

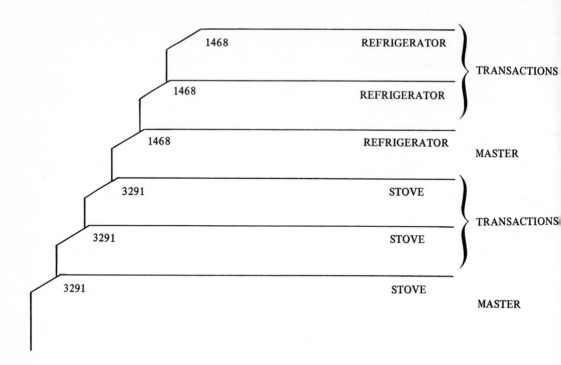

1468	REFRIGERATOR	} TRANSACTIONS
1468	REFRIGERATOR	
1468	REFRIGERATOR	MASTER
3291	STOVE	} TRANSACTIONS
3291	STOVE	
3291	STOVE	MASTER

FIGURE 12.11.

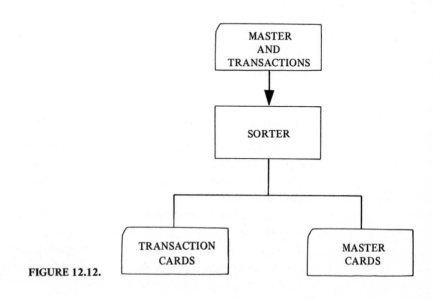

FIGURE 12.12.

with those unmatched item master cards in the collator and sorted into ascending numerical order by item number. When the cards in the item master deck are back in sequential order, this file is returned to its storage location.

A card containing the current date in the appropriate card columns is now placed in front of the transaction cards (Fig. 12.13), and these cards are run through the reproducer once more and the date gangpunched into every card in the transaction file. All transaction cards must then be placed in the interpreter, where the item number and date are printed out.

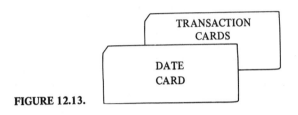

FIGURE 12.13.

Finally, another listing ("LIST-2") is made on the accounting machine and these totals are checked against "LIST-1" (Fig. 12.9). If not all totals agree, a card has been lost in processing and must be located or repunched and the listing run off again. When totals agree, this activity is completed for the day.

The documents in Figs. 12.14 through 12.22, which support the preceding narrative and bring out the relationships among the persons, equipment, and procedures found in the activity of recording sales orders and returns, should be carefully studied; they are crucial to understanding the conversion of the system under discussion.

12.5

Designing the New System

Assume now that, concerning the system in Sec. 12.4, all information-gathering activities have been performed, that the

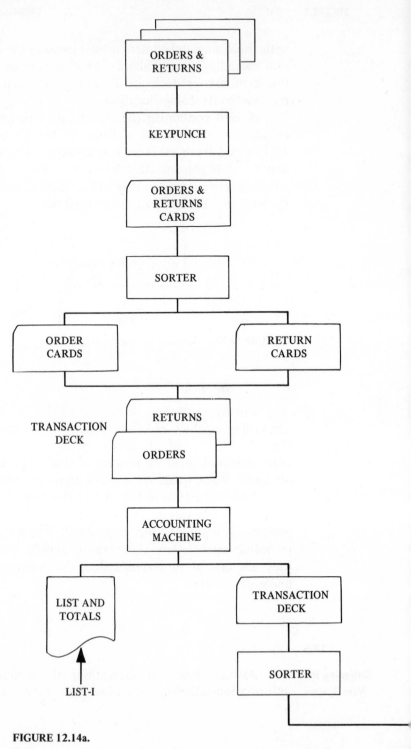

FIGURE 12.14a.

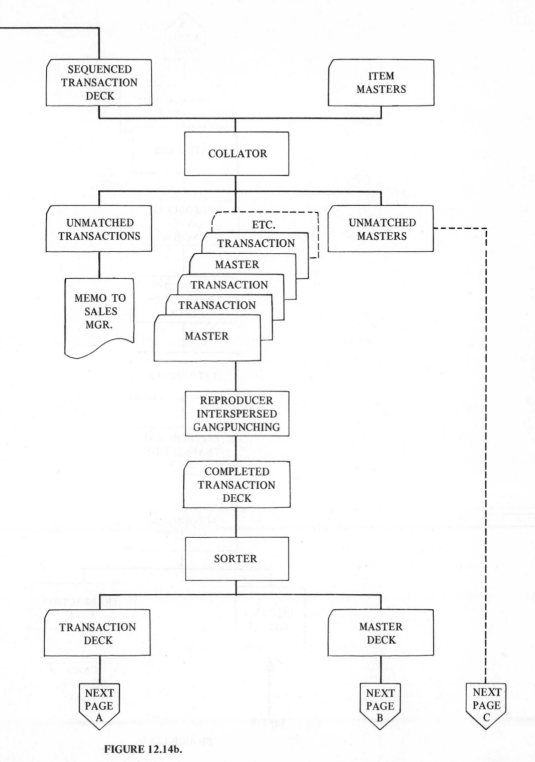

FIGURE 12.14b.

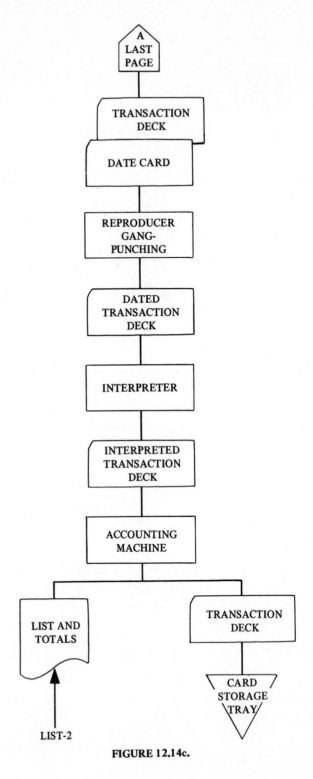

FIGURE 12.14c.

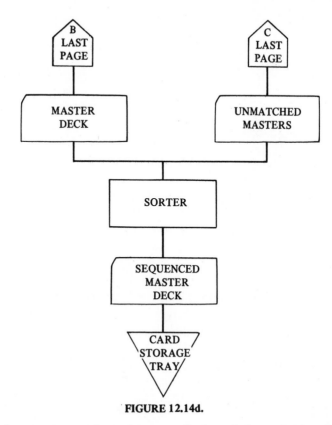

FIGURE 12.14d.

plans of management have been studied, and the requirements of the new system have been determined to include:

Activity	*Frequency*
1. Record all orders and returns	Daily
2. Prepare a sales analysis report for the volume of items sold	Weekly
3. Prepare inputs for the customer billing system	Monthly

Note that the new requirements still include the recording of all orders and returns. However, this first activity is now to be converted from a unit record machine operation to a computer operation. The two new activities are planned and designed by the analyst.

All three activities may be regarded as comprising *sales-order subsystem* that is a complete and unique subsystem within the total business system.

The principal tasks in designing the new system are:

1. developing the operations for each activity;
2. illustrating the relationships of persons, procedures, and equipment in all pertinent documentation; and
3. designing the configuration of the new equipment.

Before going on to the conversion of Activity 1 to computer operation, the reader should review all of the documentation for this activity as described earlier for the unit record operations (Figs. 12.14 through 12.22). This documentation is vital not only in understanding this conversion, but also for developing the logical sequence of operations in Activities 2 and 3 and for integrating all three activities. The documentation for Activity 1 *as a computer operation* (Figs. 12.25 through 12.33) should also be thoroughly studied.

RESOURCE SHEET PERSONNEL

ITEM	FUNCTION	COST
3 Keypunch operators	Create punched card files	@ $5,000.00
2 Unit record machine operators	Wire plug boards and operate unit record equipment	@ $6,000.00

FIGURE 12.15.

RESOURCE SHEET EQUIPMENT

ITEM	FUNCTION	RENTAL COST PER MO.
3 Keypunches	Punch cards	$ 65.00 each
Sorter	Sort punched card files, select out item master cards	32.00
Interpreter	Interpret punched cards	80.00
Collator	Collate, merge, match punched cards	76.00
Reproducer	Interspersed gangpunching, gangpunching	58.00
Accounting machine	Prepare listings	216.00
*Punched cards (purchase)	Punched card files	4.00 per 2M

FIGURE 12.16.

UNIT RECORD ROOM

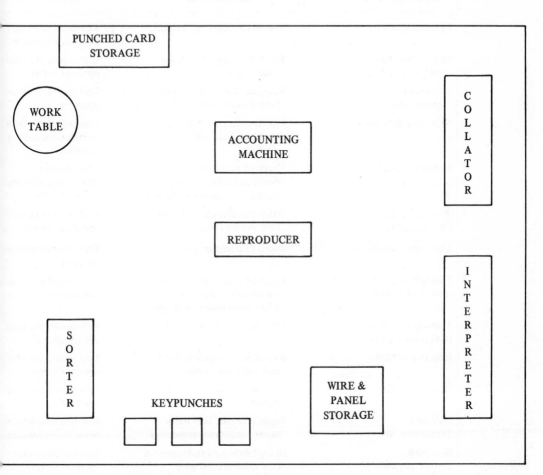

FIGURE 12.17. Showing layout of equipment on the resource sheet equipment.

ACTIVITY SHEET

			AVERAGE	PEAK
FUNCTION	– Record sales orders and returns			
Frequency	– 1200 Transactions daily	DAY	1,200	2,000
Inputs	– Sales order forms, Return forms	WEEK	6,000	10,000
Outputs	– Punched card file of daily orders and			
	returns, listings of orders with dollar			
	totals and quantity totals (List-1)			

FIGURE 12.18.

OPERATION SHEET

INPUT/OUTPUT	OPERATION	RESOURCES
Orders and returns	Keypunch orders and returns	Keypunch operator/ keypunch machine
Transaction deck of punched cards	Sort returns out from trans-action deck	Unit record machine operator/sorter
Order cards and return cards	Manually place return cards behind order cards	Unit record machine operator
All transaction cards	List all orders and returns, total quantities and dollar amounts	Unit record machine operator/accounting machine
Orders and returns, list-1 transaction cards	Verify all transactions Sort transaction cards in ascending sequence by item #	All operators Unit record machine operator/sorter
Transaction file Item master file	Match transaction cards with Item master cards	Unit record machine operator/collator
Unmatched transactions	Memo to salesmanager	Unit record machine operator
Transaction cards Item master cards	Reproduce item description masters into transaction cards (intersperse gang-punching)	Unit record machine operator/reproducer
Transaction cards Item master cards	Sort out item masters	Unit record machine operator/sorter
Item master cards	Re-sequence unmatched and matched item masters	Unit record machine operator/sorter
Item master file	Place item master file in its storage tray	Unit record machine operator
Date card Transaction file	Reproduce date into trans-action cards (gang punching)	Unit record machine operator/reproducer
Date card Transaction file	Discard date card and interpret item numbers and date	Unit record machine operator/interpreter
Transaction file List-2	List all transactions and take totals to verify that file is complete	Unit record machine operator/accounting machine
Transaction file	Place transaction file in storage tray	Unit record machine operator

FIGURE 12.19.

24

INPUT/OUTPUT SHEET

NAME	FREQUENCY	FILE/FORM	I/O	SOURCE/DESTINATION
Orders	1100/day	Form 0-23612	Input	Outlet stores/source
Returns	100/day	Form R-23612	Input	Outlet stores/source
Transaction file	1200/day	File DT/F	Input/ Output	Keypunch/source, file tray/dest.
Item master file	500/day	File IM/F	Input	File tray/dest.
Date card	1/day	–	Input	Discard/dest.
List of transactions	1/day	List-1	Output	All operators
List of transactions	1/day	List-2	Output	Unit record machine operator
Memo	1/day if needed	Form SL-02134	Output	Sales manager/dest.

FIGURE 12.20.

FILE SHEET

NAME   Item master   *NUMBER*   IM/F   *RETENTION DATE*   None

RESTRICTIONS   None   *LOCATION*   Card drawer 112

CONTENTS   All item descriptions and their associated item numbers for every appliance on the market

MACHINES USED TO PROCESS FILE IM/F

    1. Collator
    2. Reproducer
    3. Sorter

FIGURE 12.21.

FILE SHEET

NAME   Transaction File   NUMBER   DT/F   RETENTION DATE 30 Days

RESTRICTIONS None   LOCATION   Card drawer 111

CONTENTS   All orders and returns including item numbers and descriptions,
store numbers, salesman numbers, quantity, unit price, price and
date processed

MACHINES USED TO PROCESS FILE DT/F

1. Keypunch
2. Sorter
3. Accounting machine
4. Collator
5. Reproducer
6. Interpreter

FIGURE 12.22.

ACTIVITY 1—Recording Orders and Returns

Narrative: All orders and returns forms are to be batched
together at the end of each workday. They are to be sent to the
keypunching room at 9:00 A.M. of the following workday, and a
punched card (Fig. 12.6) is to be prepared for each line on the
order form (Fig. 12.5).

Returns are identified by an 11-punch in card column 5

Orders are identified by no punch in card column 5

After the batch has been keypunched, the deck of punched
cards, now referred to as the *daily transaction file,* is placed in the
computer. A computer program reads the cards and separates
orders from returns.

The computer operator removes both orders and return
cards from the card reader, placing the returns cards behind the
order cards in the daily transaction file (Fig. 12.23).

The daily transaction file is placed in the computer's card
reader and a list of all cards with dollar and quantity totals

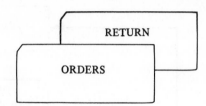

FIGURE 12.23. Daily transaction file.

prepared (see LIST-1, Fig. 12.9). LIST-1 is verified by the keypunch operators and the quantity totals are recorded in the computer logbook by the computer operator.

After all transactions have been verified, the daily transaction file is read and sorted onto a magnetic tape called TAPE-1. Items in the daily transaction file are now sequenced in ascending numerical order.

An item master file found on TAPE-2 and containing item numbers and descriptions is compared to the item numbers on TAPE-1. For each equal comparison found, the item description from TAPE-2 is written into the appropriate record on TAPE-1 (Fig. 12.24). All transactions whose item numbers cannot be located on TAPE-2 must be printed out (LIST-3) and reported to the sales manager, since they indicate an invalid item number. All item masters whose item numbers are not located on TAPE-1 are bypassed or ignored.

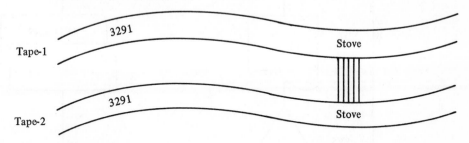

FIGURE 12.24.

Today's date is entered into the computer console by the computer operator and read into each record in the daily transaction file.

The quantities for orders and returns are totaled by the computer, printed on the computer console typewriter, and compared with the quantity entry made earlier by the computer

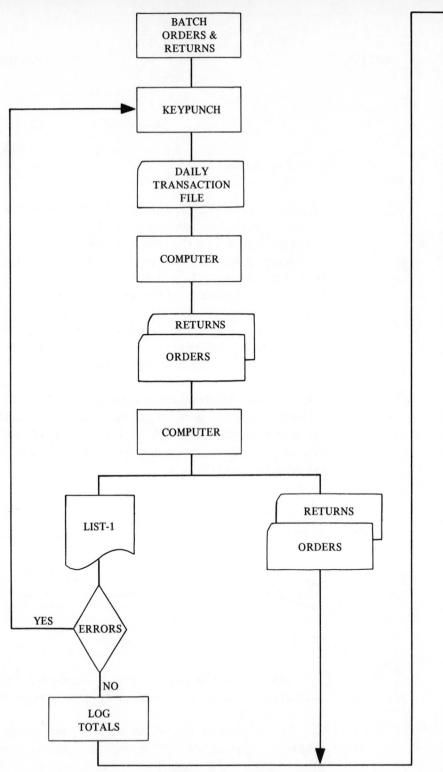

FIGURE 12.25. Flowchart of activity 1.

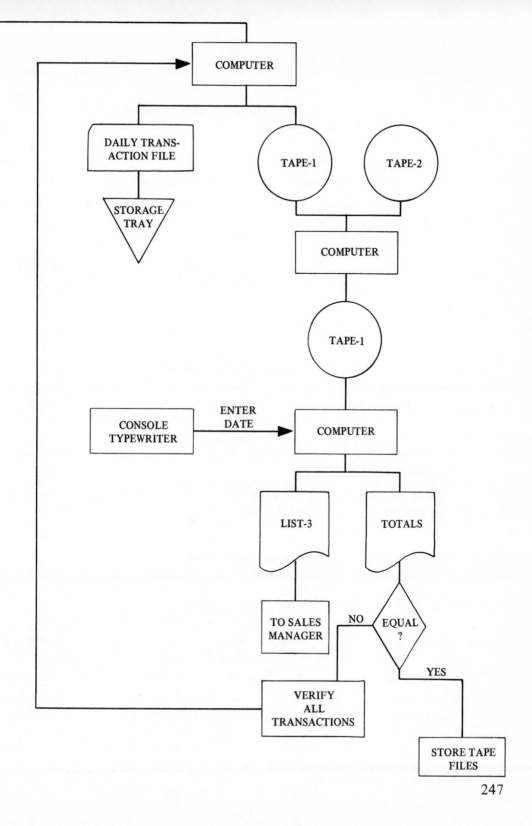

COMPUTER

DAILY TRANS-
ACTION FILE

STORAGE
TRAY

TAPE-1

TAPE-2

COMPUTER

TAPE-1

CONSOLE
TYPEWRITER

ENTER
DATE

COMPUTER

LIST-3

TOTALS

TO SALES
MANAGER

NO

EQUAL
?

YES

VERIFY
ALL
TRANSACTIONS

STORE TAPE
FILES

RESOURCE SHEET PERSONNEL

ITEM	FUNCTION	COST
3 Keypunch operators	Create daily transaction file	@ $5,000.00
1 Computer operator	Operate computer	@ $6,000.00

FIGURE 12.26.

RESOURCE SHEET EQUIPMENT

ITEM	FUNCTION	RENTAL COST PER MO.
3 Keypunches	Punch Cards	$ 65.00 each
Computer System:		
Central proc. unit	Process computer programs	2,670.00
Console typewriter	Print Totals from Tape-1	148.00
4 tape drives	Sorting and updating tape files	1,205.00
Card read/punch	Read in computer programs, daily transaction file on cards	
Printer	Print list-1, report to sales manager (list-3)	750.00
Control units		970.00
*Tape reels	Store daily transaction files and item master files	25.00 each
*Punched cards	Punched card files	4.00 per 2M
**Computer programs	Process sales orders and returns	500.00
*Continuous paper forms	Print reports	3.10 per 1M

*Purchase price
**Non-recurring cost for programmer

FIGURE 12.27.

ACTIVITY SHEET

FUNCTION	Record sales orders and returns.
FREQUENCY	1200 transactions daily.
INPUTS	Sales order forms, return forms, tape-2, tape-1.
OUTPUTS	Daily transaction file on cards, tape-1, list-1, listing of orders with dollar and quantity totals, computer log entry of totals, console typewriter print out of totals, list-3, if needed.

	AVERAGE	PEAK
DAY	1,200	2,000
WEEK	6,000	10,000

FIGURE 12.28.

OPERATION SHEET

INPUT/OUTPUT	*OPERATION*	*RESOURCES*
Batched orders and returns	Keypunch orders and returns	Keypunch operator/ keypunch machine
Daily transaction file	Separate orders from returns	Computer Program/ computer/computer operator
Order and return cards	Manually place return cards behind order cards	Computer operator
All transaction cards	List all orders and returns, total quantities and dollar amounts	Computer program/ computer/computer operator
Orders and returns, list-1	Verify all transactions	Keypunch operators
Computer log book	Log totals	Computer operator
Daily transaction file	Prepare Tape-1	Computer program/ computer/computer operator
Daily transaction file	Store daily transaction file cards	Computer operator

FIGURE 12.29.

249

INPUT/OUTPUT	OPERATION	RESOURCES
Tape-1, tape-2	Update tape-1	Computer program/ computer/computer operator
Console typewriter	Enter today's date	Computer operator
Tape-1, tape-2	Prepare list-3 (unmatched transactions) console totals	Computer program/ computer/computer operator
Computer log	Verify totals against log	Computer operator
Unmatched transaction	List-3 memo to sales manager	Computer operator
Tape-1, tape-2	Store tape files	Computer operator

FIGURE 12.29. Continued

INPUT/OUTPUT SHEET

NAME	FREQUENCY	FILE/FORM	I/O	SOURCE/DESTINATION
Orders	1100/day	Form 0-23612	Input	Outlet stores/source
Returns	100/day	Form R-23612	Input	Outlet stores/source
Daily transaction file (card)	1200/day	File DT/F	Output/ Input	Keypunch/source file tray/ dest.
Item master file (tape)	500/day	Tape-2	Input	Tape library/dest.
List of transactions	1/day	List-1	Output	All operators/dest.
Computer log	1/day	Daily log	Output	Data processing mgr./ dest.
Daily (tape) transaction file	1200/day	Tape-1	Output/ Input	Tape library/dest.
Console totals	1/day		Output	Data processing mgr./ dest.
Memo	1/day if needed	List-3	Output	Salesmanager/dest.

FIGURE 12.30.

FILE SHEET

NAME   Item master   *NUMBER* Tape-2   *RETENTION DATE* Permanent

RESTRICTIONS   None   *LOCATION* Section 511 tape library

CONTENTS   All item descriptions and their associated item numbers for every appliance
                     on the market

RECORD FORMAT

Item No.	Item description

TAPE POSITIONS   1 _____ 5, 6 _____ 23

FILE USE   Computer programs to process sales-order-cycle

FIGURE 12.31

FILE SHEET

NAME   Daily transaction file   NUMBER DT/F   *RETENTION DATE* 30 Days

RESTRICTIONS   None   LOCATION Card drawer 111

CONTENTS   All orders and returns including item numbers and descriptions, store
                     numbers, salesman numbers, quantity, unit price, price and date processed

RECORD FORMAT   See Fig. 12-6

FILE USE   Computer programs to separate orders from returns and prepare Tape-1

FIGURE 12.32.

FILE SHEET

RETENTION
DATE

NAME   Daily Transaction Tape File   NUMBER   Tape-1   30 days

RESTRICTIONS   None   LOCATION   Section 512 tape library

CONTENTS   All data from file number DT/F

RECORD FORMAT

Store No.	Code	Sls No.	Item No.	Qty	Item Description	Unit Price	Price	Date

TAPE POSITIONS 1   4 5 6 8 9 13 14 16 17   34 35 39 40 44 45   50

FILE USE   Computer programs to process sales-order-billing cycle

FIGURE 12.33.

operator in the logbook. This is done to insure that all transactions were written onto TAPE-1. If the totals agree, TAPE-1 and TAPE-2 are stored in the tape library and the deck of punched cards is filed as back-up storage for a period of 30 days.

For activities 2 and 3, only the narratives are supplied. Development of the remaining documentation constitutes Problem 1 at the end of this chapter. All three activities should be integrated and the smooth flow from one activity to the next should be indicated in all documentation. The succeeding narratives should be studied carefully, noting that outputs from one activity may be used as inputs for a following activity.

ACTIVITY 2—Sales Analysis

Narrative: To analyze sales and determine which items are selling better than others, a weekly sales analysis report (Fig. 12.34), showing quantity by item, must be prepared on the first working day of each week.

To prepare this report, the weekly transactions consisting of

252

SALES ANALYSIS REPORT

NUMBER	DESCRIPTION	SALES	RETURNS	NET SALES
0059	Television sets	4670	105	4565*
1468	Refrigerators	539	41	498
3040	Radios	3049	319	2730
3291	Stoves	675	68	607
5185	Antennas	95	18	77
6401	Record players	831	73	758
6485	Air conditions	709	82	627
7009	Tape recorders	245	10	235

*Indicates the item with the greatest net sales

FIGURE 12.34.

five daily transaction files from TAPE-1 must be written onto a work tape called TAPE-3. Orders and returns must be individually sorted on this work tape in ascending numerical order by item number and the report run off. TAPE-3 may be erased after the SALES ANALYSIS report is completed. TAPE-1 is then returned to the tape library.

ACTIVITY 3—Preparing Inputs For Customer Billing

Narrative: The inputs for customer billing are TAPE-1 and the customer master file found on TAPE-4 (see Fig. 12.35). The monthly transactions found on TAPE-1 are to be read onto the work tape (TAPE-3) and sorted in ascending numerical order by customer number. TAPE-3 and TAPE-4 are then to be compared by customer number.

TAPE-4

Customer number	Name	Address	Balance due	Date of last payment

FIGURE 12.35.

253

For each equal comparison on customer number, the PRICE is added algebraically to the balance due field. If the PRICE contains the amount for a return, it is found in the PRICE field as a negative number and algebraic addition will reduce the amount in the balance due field.

After this updating on the balance due field is read onto TAPE-4, TAPE-4 can be used to prepare the bills to be mailed to customers.

Computer Configuration Design

In addition to the foregoing documentation, the systems analyst is also concerned with recommending computer hardware configurations appropriate to the plans of management and the needs of his company. In designing the computer configuration, the systems analyst must know what will be required of machines and what will be required of the people who will man these machines. He must answer such questions as:

What are the required inputs?...the required outputs?

Where may activities be integrated?

How much computer storage is required to process computer programs?

Is a console typewriter necessary?

How are records to be structured?...as fixed?...variable-length?...undefined?

How are files to be organized?...sequentially?...direct?...indexed sequential?

Would tape drives or disk drives be more feasible for processing the system's files? How many tape reels or disk packs are required for storing the files?

How fast must cards be read?...cards be punched?...or lines be printed?

How much computer processing time is required for each activity?

254

What model card/read punch and what model printer should be attached to the system?

What are the educational and training requirements, or other special qualifications, for personnel who will man the equipment?

What are the checkpoints for error detection at the earliest possible stage?

These questions may also be put to consultants employed by vendors of computer equipment so that costs and capabilities can be understood by everyone involved in planning the computer system. Several vendors should be consulted so that competitive prices or rental programs can be submitted to management for their review.

Figure 12.36 shows a rough sketch for a layout of computer hardware that may be used to support the new sales-order system. The components in Fig. 12.36 are listed with their costs in the equipment resource sheet (Fig. 12.27).

Specifications for installation of computer equipment are discussed in the next chapter, and an example of a full proposal is given in Appendix C.

EXERCISES   1. How should a systems analyst initiate a study to determine systems requirements?

2. What are the various forms that a new system design may take?

3. What does an analyst expect to achieve by conducting a methods improvement study?

4. How does methods improvement differ from system modification?

5. Give an example of a procedure conversion.

6. What purpose do resource sheets serve in a systems study?

7. What information would you expect to find on an activity sheet?

8. Describe the purpose of the headings on an input/output sheet.

9. What purpose does the file sheet serve after the system design is complete and the new system is operating?

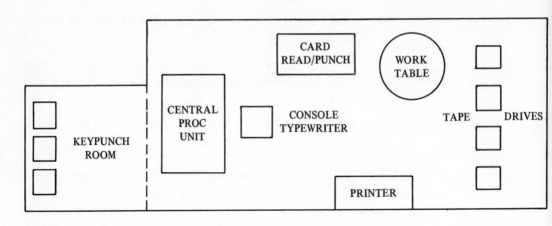

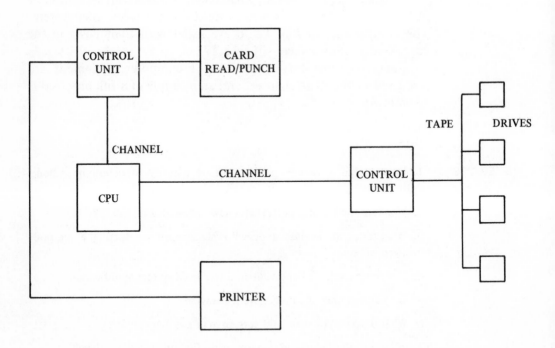

FIGURE 12.36.

10. Who has the greatest need for the operation sheet? Why?

11. What kind of information must the analyst be aware of when he designs a computer configuration?

PROBLEMS   1. Prepare the flowcharts, activity sheets, operation sheets, resource sheets, input/output sheets, and file sheets for Activities 2 and 3 in Sec. 12.5.

2. Assume the daily transaction file is written onto tape and blocked 16 records to a block, with a tape density of 800 characters to an inch, an IRG* of 0.75 inch, and a tape reel containing 2,400 feet, 14.5 feet of which are used for a leader.

(a) How many inches are used for the average daily transaction file? (*Remember:* there are 1,200 transactions as a daily average; refer to Chapter 5 if necessary.)

(b) How many inches are used for records?

(c) How many inches are used for IRG's?

(d) If the tape speed is 100 inches per second, how long will it take to read a daily transaction file?

(e) How many daily transaction files can be written on one tape reel?

*inter-record gap.

CHAPTER 13

PRESENTATION/INSTALLATION/ IMPLEMENTATION

13.1

Introducing New Systems Designs

In Chapter 12 we were concerned with the logic used in business activities and the design of systems. Yet the best-planned system is worthless until it has been sold to management, has been installed, and its applications are running smoothly. Thus turning plans into realities requires effective presentation of the new system, proper installation of equipment, and efficient implementation of all activities and operations.

People often oppose new ideas; in addition, new systems have built-in resistances, such as employee retraining programs and higher overhead costs. Furthermore, familiar work patterns may induce a false sense of security in some people, who regard orderly improvements as constituting a threat to their jobs or some form of trespass into their private domains within the system. The analyst should refuse to be discouraged by any such resistance; rather he must persist, methodically continuing to improve his designs in order to overcome hurdles.

The first person who must be convinced of the worth of any new system is the analyst's immediate superior—usually the data processing manager. To help accomplish this the analyst should put himself in the data processing manager's position by asking himself such questions as: How does he accomplish his tasks? What are his needs? What does he consider important? and so on.

When the analyst's immediate superior is convinced of the value of a new system, a formal presentation must be made to management.

13.2

Presentation   Presentation of the new system may be written up in report form and distributed to officers and appropriate managers, or it may be the subject of a talk. The presentation should include:

1. short introductory narrative describing:
    (a) the purpose of the presentation,
    (b) the need for the systems study,
    (c) the functions of the team members,
    (d) systems goals as they are designed to fulfill management's objectives;
2. flowcharts, narrative descriptions, or systems models of both the old and new systems stressing the benefits of the new system;
3. a summary of cost factors for the new system;
4. installation requirements and implementation schedules briefly described;
5. a summary of the presentation, and a formal request that management take action on the proposal.

Introduction

The *purpose* of any systems presentation is twofold:

1. to win management approval of the new system, its hardware, procedures, personnel, costs, and benefits to the company; and
2. to orient the members of the audience to new systems design and functions, especially in their areas of responsibility.

Discussion of the *need* for the systems study should answer such questions as:

Who requested the study?

Why did they request it?

When did they request it?

The *functions* of the systems study team can be summarized by indicating the various segments of the problem and identifying the team members assigned to them. For example:

Procedures—K. Hawke, team leader
Hardware configuration—R. Roberts
Computer operations—W. Salerno
Computer programming—J. Whalen
Simulation—J. Cookson

Systems Goals depend on the specific needs of the company, and must be geared to producing results that fulfill management's expectations. Goals must also reflect management's plans for improving operations, and stress outputs that management considers desirable. Any list of goals should include statements on efficiency, profits, accuracy, and improved information services for management.

Documents

Systems flowcharts, narrative, or *system models* all provide useful graphic methods of describing the information flow in the new system. While a review of every operation and activity in the new system is unnecessary, such factors as inputs, processing, resources, and outputs should be highlighted in order to impart a general overall understanding. Any comparisons of old and new should stress the system's goals and management's expectations as *benefits*.

Benefits should be mentioned in specific, not general, terms. For example, it can be pointed out that a new system will:

reduce credit-checking time by 3 days

process customer billing in one-quarter of the present time

save $500 monthly in machine rental...and so on

Cost Factors

Cost factors must be very carefully considered in evaluating any new system, particularly one that includes expensive computer hardware. Systems analysts and computer operation personnel, who perhaps too often are inclined to favor complex and challenging equipment, must follow budgetary guidelines just as all other departments do.

Two types of costs must be included in the presentation:

1. Nonrecurring or one-time costs, including those for:
   Systems study
   System conversion
   Operator and programmer retraining
   Preparation of physical facilities
   Records, forms, and reports design
   Implementation costs
2. Recurring costs—for sustaining operations after the new system has been installed, including those for:
   Renting or leasing of new equipment
   Salaries for new personnel
   Supplies—punched cards, tape, etc
   Room or floorspace rental

Installation and Implementation

The presentation should briefly discuss *installation require-ments* in terms of floorspace, rooms, buildings, and the time required to replace the old equipment with the new. *Implementation* of the new activities can be described in schedule form, as shown in Fig. 13.1.

Because any systems presentation is crucial to the reputation of all members of the study team, it must be well prepared. A

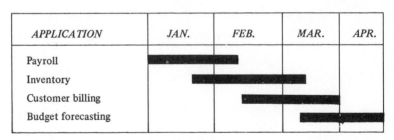

APPLICATION	JAN.	FEB.	MAR.	APR.
Payroll				
Inventory				
Customer billing				
Budget forecasting				

FIGURE 13.1.

check-list should be prepared that includes a list of the topics just discussed.

For Oral Presentations

Audio-visual aids should be employed such as chalk boards, videotapes, flip charts, printed handouts, films, film slides, overhead projectors, etc.

The presentation should be given a title that has an appeal and can be remembered long after the presentation has been made. The person making the presentation should study his audience beforehand, their likes and dislikes, temperaments, and attitudes towards their own job functions in the total system.

The speaker should get to the point quickly and phrase his talk in concise statements; he should avoid side-issues and digressions, redundancies, technical jargon, and overuse of the first person ("I" and "we"); he should freely share credit with others for ideas and concepts.

The speaker should prepare in advance to answer questions and to meet objections offered at the end of his presentation. If the proposal contains defects of which he is aware, he should point them out before any of his listeners does. Arguments should be avoided because they can indicate insecurity.

If objections are strong they should be handled in a cool manner, and suggestions for improvements should be sought.

Lastly, the discussion should be broken off, the presentation reviewed once more by the analyst with a strong emphasis on the benefits of the new system and an indication of the hope of a favorable response from management to accept the recommendations of his team.

13.3

Installation   To derive the full benefits of good systems design, the task c
installing new equipment must conform strictly with manufactu
ers' specifications (particularly in the case of computers). (Se
Figs. 13.2, 13.3, and 13.4.)

Figure 13.2 describes space requirements needed to install
small computer system, the dotted 90° arcs indicate room fo
opening doors on the hardware units that must be opened fo
maintenance.

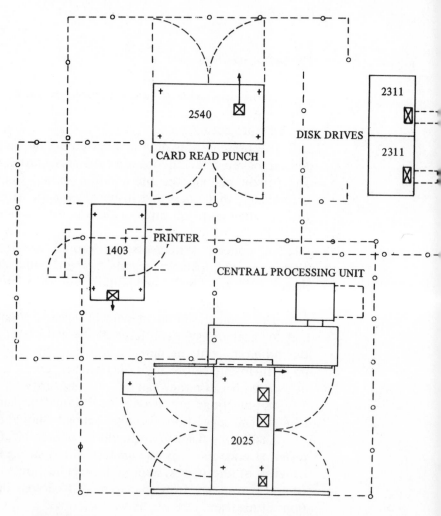

FIGURE 13.2.

Floor construction is another consideration. Computer centers usually have "false" or raised floors (Fig. 13.3) that permit concealment of the various cables needed to connect such hardware units as the central processing unit, printer, card read/punch, and disk and tape drives.

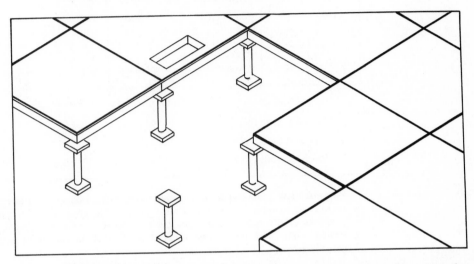

FIGURE 13.3. Free access floor pedestal supported panels. Removable cutouts in panels.

Other installation factors include electrical and weight considerations, as indicated in Fig. 13.4, and temperature and humidity criteria, which can be found in vendors' installation manuals; generally, optimum conditions are 75°F and 50% relative humidity.

Printed instructions, guidelines, and training manuals are essential in orienting personnel to a new system, and the operations manager must be certain that all personnel understand the operations and procedures to be followed.

13.4

Implementation

After a new system's hardware has been installed, the software applications of the new system must be implemented, including the activation of payroll programs, sales-order recording, inventory controls, customer-billing, budget forecasting and so on.

There are three principal methods of implementing the activities of a new system:

265

UNIT	MOD.	DESCRIPTION	BTU/HR	KVA	CONN.	WEIGHT
2030	C2	Processor	11,000	4.1	A	1400
2203	A1	Printer	4,000	1.5		725
2501	Ai	Card Reader	700	0.3		340
1442	5	Card Punch	1,800	0.7		525
		Total	17,500	6.6		

Plug Type	In-Line Connector	Receptacle	Rating
A. Russell & Stoll FS3760	FS3934	FS3754	30A,3ph. 4-wir
B. Russell & Stoll SC7328	SC7428	SC7324	60A,3ph. 4-wir
C. Russell & Stoll FS3750	FS3933	FS3753	30A,1ph. 3-wir

FIGURE 13.4. This system is equipped with radio frequency interference contro circuitry and requires a good wired earth ground or an adequate building ground. Tota resistance of the ground conductor, measured between the receptacle and the buildin ground point, may not exceed three ohms. Conduit is not an adequate means o grounding.

The all-at-once method

The unit-at-a-time method

The parallel method

The All-at-Once Method

This method is feasible if the application to be implemented is simple and the volume of transactions to be processed is low.

If the changeover involves very new or much more complex machinery or computer systems, then unforeseen events or emergencies could be catastrophic. Moreover, if this method is adopted, then workers must be completely convinced of the value of any new production machinery and 100 per cent checked out on its operation and maintenance; thus a period of training before new equipment is installed may be required.

If a changeover requires a new computer system, programs

can be written in advance and pretested on the vendor's own equipment of the same model type, which may also require a period of personnel retraining away from the home installation.

The Unit Method

This is the easiest but often the most costly method of implementing a new system. By this method, one activity at a time, well documented and thoroughly explained, is implemented before proceeding to the next activity, providing for a gradual but tightly controlled conversion.

Where new and expensive equipment is to be installed, the unit approach would be far too costly. Consider, for example, the conversion of the sales-order subsystem in the last chapter (Secs. 12.4 and 12.5), which utilizes several computer programs. It would be prohibitive to install even a moderately priced computer system at $4,000 per month rental, then allow the system to waste time and money while the programmer wrote, debugged, and tested one program at a time. (Such unfortunate circumstances have occurred with appalling costs to business systems or taxpayers.)

The Parallel Method

This represents a reasonable middleground between the unit method and the all-at-once method. The changeover of the payroll system (Sec. 11.8) provides a fair illustration of the parallel method. While the manual system continued to print out employee checks, the new system was being proven out. Checkpoints were set up at the end of three stages. After the new journal, checks, and to-date-balances were all found to be in agreement with their counterparts in the old system, the computerized system was ready for complete implementation.

The parallel method provides a means of verifying results without pressure, because only one activity or subsystem at a time is tested, while the same or "parallel" activity or subsystem is still running under the old procedures.

267

13.5

Follow-Up   After applications have been implemented, the system analyst must provide procedures for monitoring and patrolling th new system.

Hardware must be monitored to make certain that performs as it was designed to. Work stations should be informall patrolled and observed.

Employees should be motivated to perform at their be: under the new procedures. Patrol or follow-up is necessary t prevent personnel from falling back into old work habits c forgetting, ignoring, or misunderstanding their functions under th new system.

Talking to everyone involved with the new system can lead t a consolidation of gains as well as suggest further improvement: Conversations with employees may also reveal to the analyst ne or unexpected problems or yield other relevant information.

EXERCISES   1. Who is the first person the systems analyst must convince of the value of new system?

2. What information should a systems presentation include?

3. How should objections raised in an oral systems presentation be handled

4. List installation requirements mentioned in this chapter.

5. What are the three principal methods of implementing the activities of system?

6. What is the primary disadvantage of the unit-at-a-time method of syste implementation? Why?

7. What do the terms *monitor* and *patrol* mean with reference to a newl implemented system?

PROBLEMS   1. Prepare an oral presentation of the sales-order system described in Chapte 12 (Secs. 12.4 and 12.5). Plan to make use of the blackboard, and prepare:

    i. flipcharts describing the information flow in the system; and

    ii. handouts containing an implementation schedule for the thre activities, and a justification of the recommended method of implementatior

CHAPTER 14

NETWORK SCHEDULES

14.1

The Management Process

Management of a business system may be defined as the process of identifying objectives and employing resources to meet them. The process consists of five steps:

1. establishing and communicating objectives;
2. developing a plan of action;
3. converting the plan into a reasonable schedule given available resources (manpower, money, space, equipment, etc.);
4. evaluating actual progress and costs against schedule and cost estimates; and
5. a recycling of the above steps incorporating changes and additions into a new plan (see Fig. 14.1).

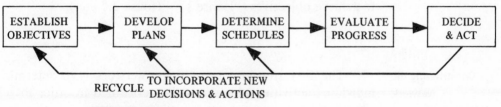

FIGURE 14.1.

As business systems have become more complex, the proce of managing such systems has become more difficult, and busine firms, government agencies, and universities have expended va amounts of money and developing techniques for use in th management process. Of these techniques, two of the mos popular are PERT (Program Evaluation and Review Technique and CPM (Critical Path Method). Both PERT and CPM are base on the concept of using a network as a model for an actual system The basic techniques of network construction and calculations ar the subjects of the following sections.

14.2
The Work Breakdown Structure

If a single network were used to model a complex system, th network itself would be complex. To simplify the modeling of complex system, several networks may be used, each of whic models some component or subsystem. This subdivision of th larger system into more manageable functions may be accom plished by means of a *work breakdown structure*—a graphi representation of the system structure reflecting the organizatio of the system objectives. The structure is developed by proceedin from the definition of the prime objective down throug successive levels of objectives to the lowest level of detail require

Figure 14.2 is a work breakdown structure for a syste whose primary objective is to create a housing development. Thi objective is realized by achieving the secondary objectives "Roads," "Sewers," "Houses," etc. Each of the latter could b further subdivided into its component elements. In Fig. 14.2 however, only the "Houses" component has been furthe subdivided to successively lower levels, until level 4 is reached. A this level, the elements represent manageable units to be modele

At this lowest level, individual networks can easily b constructed to model all the related events and activities require to achieve objectives ("House 1," "House 2," etc.).

14.3
Constructing the Network

The first step in constructing a network is to determine th individual activities which must be performed in order to achiev

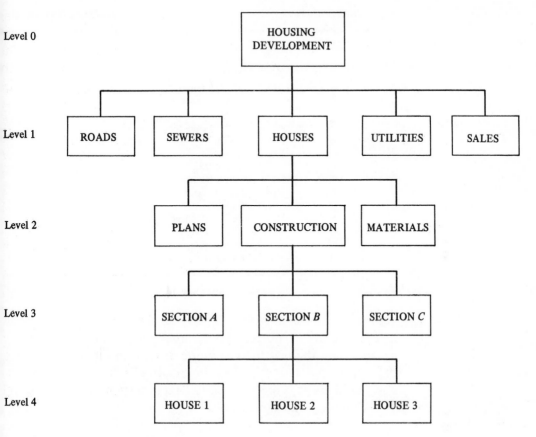

FIGURE 14.2.

the desired objective. Here an *activity* is defined as any operation which requires time and/or resources and which has a definite beginning and end. Figure 14.3 is a list of activities associated with building a house.

Once activities have been determined, a network may be constructed which graphically displays the interrelationships among activities. This graphic representation is sometimes called an *arrow diagram*, and the process of creating the diagram *arrow diagramming*.

In arrow diagramming, each activity is represented by an arrow and has an origin event and a terminal event associated with it, where an *event* denotes the specific starting or ending point for an activity or group of activities and has no expenditure of

IDENTIFICATION		DURATION IN DAYS
A	Lay foundation	5
B	Erect shell	6
C	Roofing	3
D	Rough plumbing	3
E	Rough electrical	2
F	Flooring	4
G	Windows and doors	2
H	Siding	3
I	Grading	1
J	Wallboard	4
K	Finish plumbing	2
L	Paint interior	2
M	Finish floors	3
N	Finish electrical	2
O	Paint exterior	3
P	Landscaping	2
Q	Finishing touches	1

FIGURE 14.3.

resources associated with it. In diagrams, events are represented t
circles and are numbered, the terminal-event number always bei
greater than the origin-event number. Thus in Fig. 14.4, the arro
represents the activity, "Lay Foundation"; 1 and 2 represe
the origin event ("Start of House") and terminal event ("Found
tion Complete"), respectively.

Start of house   Foundation complete

FIGURE 14.4.

In constructing the network, it is frequently more convenie
to start with the final activity and work backward by asking whic
activities must be completed before it can begin. After the
activities have been selected, continue to work backward in t
same way. This approach is called *backward planning*.

In Fig. 14.3, activity Q is the last activity and activities D,
L, M, N, O, and P must be completed before it can start. Figu
14.5 depicts what a network might look like at the initial stage
its construction using backward planning. Event 14 is associate

with the completion of the seven activities that must be completed before activity Q can start. That these activities may be going on concurrently is denoted by the seven arrows ending at 14 .

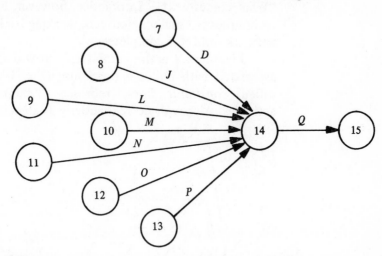

FIGURE 14.5. The event numbers were chosen arbitrarily as the number of events was not known yet.

An alternative approach would be to start with the initial activity and work forward by asking what activities come next. This approach is called *forward planning*.

In Fig. 14.3, activity A is the initial activity and may be followed immediately by activities B and C. Figure 14.6 depicts what the network might look like at the initial stage using forward planning. The two arrows starting at 2 represent activities B and C, which may be performed concurrently and are dependent upon the completion of activity A.

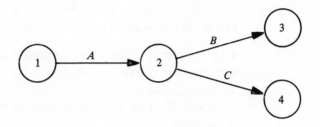

FIGURE 14.6.

273

Backward planning is generally considered more reliabl because it asks the more objective question, "What must hav already occurred?" rather than the more subjective question "What comes next?" In practice, however, a combination of bot techniques is usually employed, working back and forth across th network until it is completed.

Figure 14.7 is the completed arrow diagram for the networ associated with building the house (Fig. 14.3). The dotted line called *constraint lines*, represent "dummy" or "zero-time activities. Although no real activity is associated with going, fror

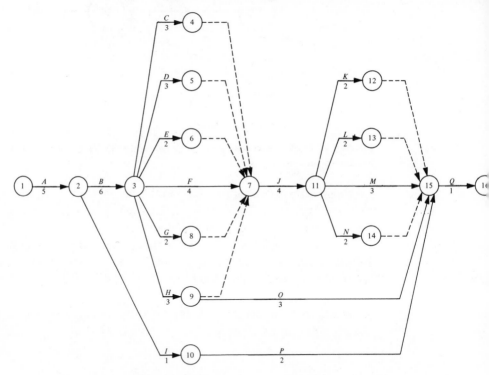

FIGURE 14.7. Network for activities of Fig. 14.3.

4 to 7, activity C must be completed before activity J can start, s this dummy activity is necessary to depict the true relationshi between C and J. Similarly, the constraint line between 12 and 1 denotes a dummy activity that must be completed before activit Q can start.

The network (arrow diagram) is a graphic representation of the sequence in which activities take place. As such it also represents the *plan* of action.

To use the network as a *scheduling* tool requires the addition of time estimates for the activities. Obtaining objective and accurate time estimates is usually quite difficult. However, as a time estimate is associated with an individual activity, its effect on the entire network is minimal. Frequently, on large projects, underestimates are cancelled out by overestimates.

14.4

Network Calculations

We may now use the network of Fig. 14.7, in conjunction with reasonable time estimates for each activity, to perform the calculations necessary to develop a schedule. In Fig. 14.7 observe that activities I and P together only require 3 days to complete. When should they be scheduled? The arrow diagram does not tell when to schedule them, but can be used to determine:

1. Earliest start date (E.S.)
2. Latest start date (L.S.)
3. Earliest completion date (E.C.)
4. Latest completion date (L.C.)

Forward Pass Calculations

"Earliest start dates" and "earliest completion dates" are computed by a *forward pass* through the diagram. First assume some baseline from which to start—either an actual date, such as "May 15th," or some other starting time, such as "day 0." Event 1 in Fig. 14.7 is assumed to have occurred at "day 0." Thus the E.S. for the first activity in Fig. 14.7 is 0 and the E.C. (from the table in Fig. 14.8) is 5.

The E.C. for a given activity is used as the E.S. for the succeeding activity. Having selected a baseline, which becomes the E.S. for the first activity, compute:

$$E.C. = E.S. + Duration$$

275

ACTIVITY	DURATION	E.S.	E.C.	L.S.	L.C.	T.S.	F.S.
A	5	0	5	0	5	0	0
B	6	5	11	5	11	0	0
C	3	11	14	12	15	1	1
D	3	11	14	12	15	1	1
E	2	11	13	13	15	2	2
F	4	11	15	11	15	0	0
G	2	11	13	13	15	2	2
H	3	11	14	12	15	1	0
I	1	5	6	19	20	14	0
J	4	15	19	15	19	0	0
K	2	19	21	20	22	1	1
L	2	19	21	20	22	1	1
M	3	19	22	19	22	0	0
N	2	19	21	20	22	1	1
O	3	14	17	19	22	5	5
P	2	6	8	20	22	14	14
Q	1	22	23	22	23	0	0

FIGURE 14.8.

Thus in Fig. 14.7:

Activity	E.C.	=	E.S.	+	Duration
B	11	=	5	+	6
I	6	=	5	+	1

When the start of an activity is dependent on the completic of more than one preceeding activity, the E.S. is the maximu E.C. of the preceeding activities. For example, to calculate t E.C. and E.S. of J in Fig. 14.7, compute:

Activity	E.C.	=	E.S.	+	Duration
C	14	=	11	+	3
D	14	=	11	+	3
E	13	=	11	+	2
F	15	=	11	+	4
G	13	=	11	+	2
H	14	=	11	+	3

and thus:

	J	19	=	15	+	4

The E.C. for the final activity establishes the expected completion date of the project. This amount—the duration of the project time—is equivalent to the time of the longest sequence of activities in the network. This sequence is called the *critical path*. In Fig. 14.7, the critical path is:

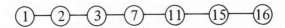

(See Fig. 14.8 for the E.S. and E.C. for each of the activities in Fig. 14.7.)

Backward Pass Calculations

"Latest Start dates" and "Latest Completion dates" are computed by starting with the last activity and working backward (by a *backward pass*) along each path to the baseline or beginning event to find out when the project should be initiated. First assume a scheduled completion date (usually the expected completion date of the project), then calculate:

$$L.S. = L.C. - Duration$$

Thus the L.C. for the last activity in Fig. 14.7 is 23, and the L.S. is 22.

Working backward, the L.S. of an activity is used as the L.C. for the preceding activity. Thus in Fig. 14.7:

Activity	L.S.	=	L.C.	-	Duration
Q	22	=	23	-	1
⑫—⑮	22	=	22	-	0
⑬—⑮	22	=	22	-	0
M	19	=	22	-	3
⑭—⑮	22	=	22	-	0
O	19	=	22	-	3
P	20	=	22	-	2

When several activities are dependent on the completion of one activity, the L.C. of that activity is the *minimum L.S.* of the

succeeding activities. For example, to calculate the L.S. and L.C
for J in Fig. 14.7:

Activity	L.S.	=	L.C.	-	Duration
Q	22	=	23	-	1
(12)——(15)	22	=	22		0
K	20	=	22	-	2
(13)——(15)	22	=	22	-	0
L	20	=	22	-	2
M	19	=	22	-	3
(14)——(15)	22	=	22	-	0
N	20	=	22	-	2

and thus:

| J | 15 | = | 19 | - | 4 |

The L.S. for the first activity establishes the latest date on
which the project must start if the objectives of the network are to
be met. If the L.C. for the last activity was chosen as the expected
completion date calculated from the forward pass, then the L.S.
for the first activity should be the baseline of the forward pass.
(See Fig. 14.8 for the backward pass calculations for Fig. 14.7.)

Slack Calculations

In Fig. 14.8 note that the earliest start date and the latest
start date for any given activity may be, but are not necessarily,
the same. The difference in these dates represents the amount of
flexibility available for the scheduling of that activity, and is called
total slack (T.S.), or *total float* (T.F.). T.S. or T.F. represents the
amount of time the start of an activity can be delayed without
delaying the completion of the project, and can be calculated as:

T.S. = L.C. - E.C.   or   T.S. = L.S. - E.S.

Free slack (F.S.) or float is the flexibility allowed for an
activity when all preceding activities start as early as possible and

all succeeding activities start as early as possible. An activity with free slack may be delayed without rescheduling any other activity.

In performing the calculations for Fig. 14.8, we treated an activity and an immediately succeeding dummy activity as though they were only one activity; in other words:

$$\textcircled{11}\!\!-\!\!\textcircled{12} \quad \text{and} \quad \textcircled{12}\!\!-\!\!\textcircled{15}$$

were considered as one activity, or:

$$\textcircled{11} \quad [\ 12\ ] \quad \textcircled{15}$$

The slack calculations also indicate which activities lie in the critical path. Note that in Fig. 14.8, the activities in the critical path of Fig. 14.7 all have slack of zero.

In the example used in this chapter, the network was relatively simple and the calculations easily done by hand. In most applications of networks, projects are more complex and calculations laborious. The calculations and associated reports are usually done by computer.

It is important to remember that the network and the associated calculations are only tools to be used in developing the schedule. The manager must also consider the availability of resources (manpower, money, space, equipment, etc). This is necessary to avoid setting unrealistic manpower requirements, overuse or underuse of equipment, delays due to undelivered materials, etc.

Once a plan and schedule have been prepared, the network representing them may then be used as a tool to *evaluate progress*. As activities are completed, the network is updated and analyzed. If circumstances warrant, the network may be modified to reflect more accurate time estimates. External influences such as labor strikes may also cause modifications. Changes made in the network are also reflected in corresponding modifications of the *plan* and *schedule*.

In summary—network analysis is a powerful tool for use in each step of the management process cycle (see Fig. 14.9).

ADVANTAGES OF PERT/CPM

1. Forces management to *plan* a project before it begins.
2. Requires an analytical approach to planning.
3. Separates the planning and scheduling functions.
4. Permits the planner to concentrate on the relationship of items of work, without considering their occurrence in time.
5. Allows the planner to develop a more detailed plan, since he is concerned with *how* the work will be performed, not when.
6. Results in a more realistic schedule.
7. Clearly shows dependency relationships between work tasks.
8. Facilitates *control* of a project.
9. Simplifies maintenance of the plan and schedule.
10. Informs management of the current status of the project.
11. Focuses management attention on critical items of work.
12. Gives management the ability to assess consequences of anticipated changes to the plan.
13. Makes it easy to relate other functions of project control to the basic planning and scheduling function.
14. Meets contractual requirements of government, private industry, and customers.

FIGURE 14.9.

EXERCISES
1. What are the five steps in the management process?

2. What is purpose of a work breakdown structure?

3. Define the terms *activity* and *event* as applied to networks. How are they represented in a network?

4. What are two ways of constructing a network?

5. Define *float* and *total float* as applied to network calculations. How are they calculated?

6. Define *critical path* and explain how it is determined.

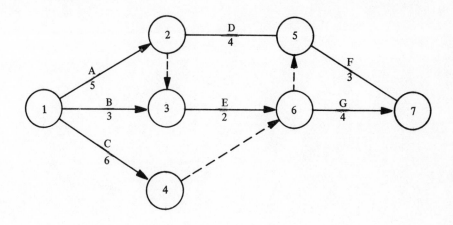

FIGURE 14.10.

PROBLEMS
1. Construct a network for the following:

   Project: Paint House

   Activities: Choose color
   Buy paint
   Mix paint
   Paint house
   Paint trim
   Clean brushes

2. In Fig. 14.10:
   (a) calculate for each activity—
      i. earliest start time,
      ii. earliest complete time,
      iii. latest start time,
      iv. latest complete time,
      v. total slack, and
      vi. float; and
   (b) determine the critical path.

PRINCIPAL DATA PROCESSING
HARDWARE DEVICES

Unit Record Systems	*Computer Systems*
Punched card	Console typewriter
Keypunch	Central processing unit
Sorter	Card reader/punch
Interpreter	Printer
Reproducer	Tape drives
Collator	Disk drives
Accounting machine	

References to specific data processing hardware units occur throughout the text, especially through Chap. 12. This appendix provides brief explanations of the hardware units listed above, so that the student will be better able to understand the functions of those machines found in the data processing centers of business systems.

A.1

Unit Record Systems

The Punched Card

Most *punched cards* (Fig. A.1) contain 80 columns for numeric or alphabetic information as well as for such special characters as the $, #, @, etc.

Numeric information is represented by a numeric punch. Alphabetic information is represented by a combination of numeric and zone punches in the Hollerith Code.

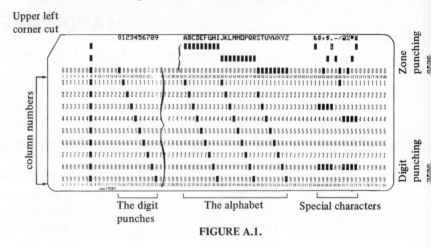

Upper left corner cut

The digit punches

The alphabet

Special characters

FIGURE A.1.

The Keypunch Machine

Punched cards are one of the principal sources of data for computer systems. Operators punch data into cards from source documents (see Fig. 12.5) on *keypunch machines* (also called *card punches*—see Fig. A.2) by depressing appropriate keys in the keyboard.

Keypunch machines can be programmed to skip blank fields or duplicate other fields containing numeric or alphabetic information. Most keypunch machines have a printing unit that will interpret the punched holes at the top of the columns in which the data is punched.

284

FIGURE A.2. IBM 029 Keypunch.

The Sorter

The *sorter* (Fig. A.3) classifies information by arranging punched cards in numerical or alphabetical order. The sorter can also "select-out" those cards with special identification, such as an 11-punch in a predesignated card column.

The Interpreter

The *interpreter* (Fig. A.4) "translates" the punched holes in punched cards into printed characters.

The Reproducer

The *reproducer* performs the functions of reproducing, gangpunching, and interspersed gangpunching:

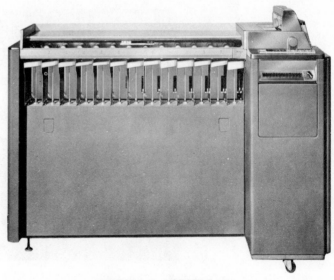

FIGURE A.3. IBM 083 Sorter.

FIGURE A.4. IBM Alphabetic Interpreter.

1. *Reproducing* means transferring data from one deck of punched cards to another, or transferring a part of the information in one deck to another (see Fig. A.5).

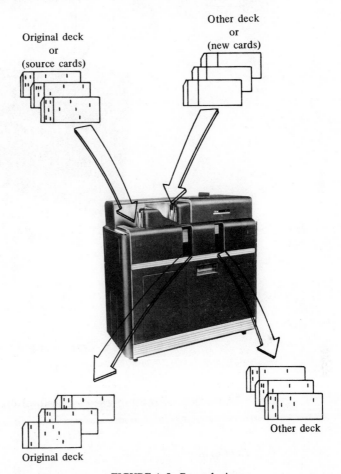

FIGURE A.5. Reproducing.

2. *Gangpunching* means transferring information from one master card to a group of succeeding detail cards (see Fig. A.6).

3. *Interspersed gangpunching* means interspersing several master cards in a deck of detail cards and transferring information from each master to only those detail cards placed behind it. Gangpunching continues until a new master is sensed. No punches are made in the next master, but the information from that master is transferred to succeeding detail cards (see

287

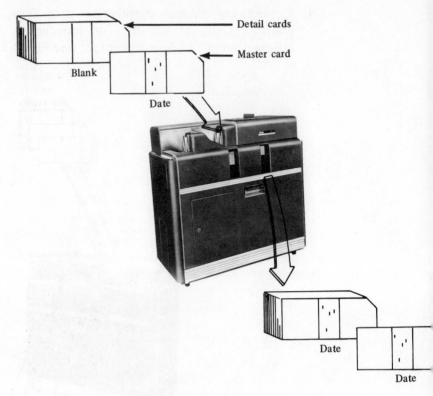

FIGURE A.6. Gangpunching from a master card.

Fig. A.7). The activity described in Sec. 12.4 illustrates th function of interspersed gangpunching.

The Collator

The *collator* (Fig. A.8) performs the functions of sequence checking, merging, matching, and selecting-out:

1. *Sequence-checking* is an operation which verifies the ascendin or descending order of identification numbers found in specific field in a deck of punched cards.
2. *Merging* is an operation that combines two decks of cards t produce one file. (The activity in Sec. 12.4 illustrates thi function of the collator.) Merging two decks of cards require the prior sequencing of both decks.

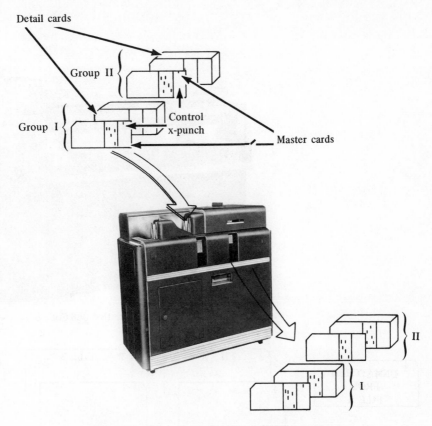

FIGURE A.7. Interspersed master card gangpunching.

3. *Matching* is an operation that compares two decks of cards. Matched cards remain separated, but unmatched cards are removed from whichever deck in which they are found (see Fig. A.9).
4. Cards containing a special punch may be *"selected-out"* of a file. The first or last card may be selected-out, as may cards containing a zero-balance in some predesignated field.

The Accounting Machine

The *accounting machine* (also referred to as the *tabulator*—see Fig. A.10) produces reports from the data found in punched cards. This machine can also add, subtract, and recognize negative numbers, and may be linked by a cable to the reproducer to create summary punched cards.

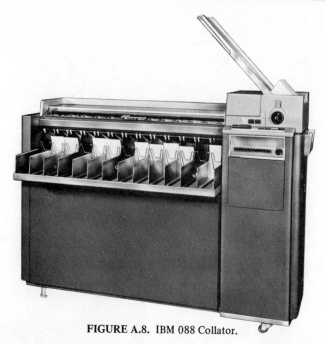

FIGURE A.8. IBM 088 Collator.

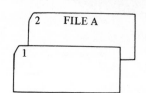
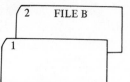

FIGURE A.9.

FIGURE A.10. IBM 407 Accounting Machine.

A.2

Computer Systems

Console Typewriter

The *console typewriter* (Fig. A.11) serves as an input/output unit, and has a keyboard that can access storage in the central processing unit or records on tape or disk files.

FIGURE A.11. IBM 1052 Printer-Keyboard.

The Central Processing Unit (CPU)

The *central processing unit* (Fig. A.12) contains main storage, arithmetic, logic units, and the control unit which verifies the accuracy of the instructions in a computer program and controls the sequence of operations performed by the computer system.

Card Read/Punch

Card readers (Fig. A.13) provide the input of punched cards for many computer systems. Card readers operate by the motion of the punched card under a read station containing a series of brushes or photoelectric cells. Data is transferred from the reading station to internal storage. Input speeds are up to 2000 cards per minute.

Card punches (Fig. A.13) are output devices for cards punched by the computer system. Output speeds are up to 300 cards per minute.

FIGURE A.12. IBM System/370 Model 145 Central Processing Unit and Console Typewriter.

The Printer

The *printer* (Fig. A.14) prints out information prepared by the central processing unit. These print-outs may include checks, forecasts, reports, listings, or even DUMPS, which are character representations of the contents of the computer's internal storage. Printer speeds are up to 1,300 lines per minute.

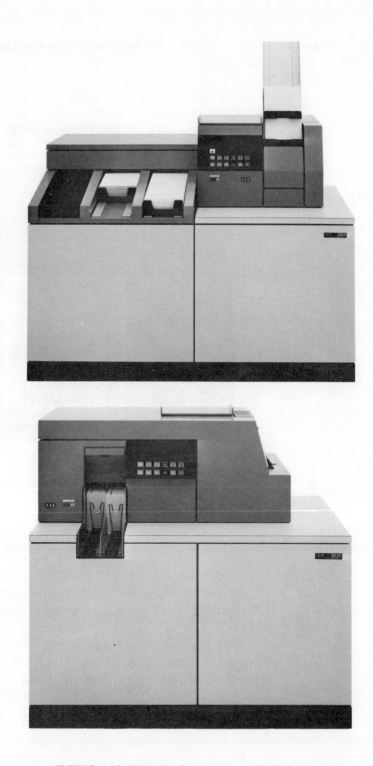

FIGURE A.13. IBM 3505 Card Reader and 3525 Card Punch.

FIGURE A.14. IBM 1403 Printer.

Tape Units

Magnetic tape is made of plastic material coated on one side with metallic oxide for the purposes of recording magnetized bits of data.

For the purpose of processing, reels of magnetic tape are mounted on *tape drives*. (Fig. A.17) During reading or writing of magnetic-tape records, the tape is moved across a *read/write head* as shown in Figs. A.15 and A.16. The motion of the tape is from the file reel to the machine reel. Speeds are up to 112.5 inches per second.

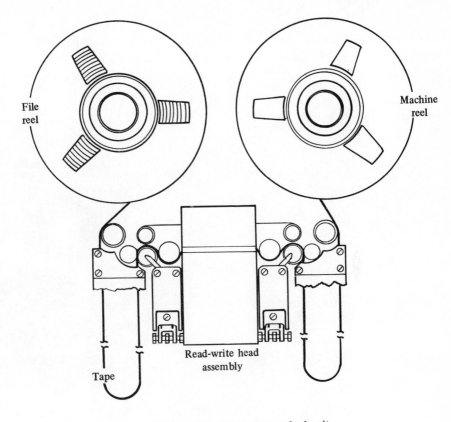

FIGURE A.15. Magnetic tape feed unit.

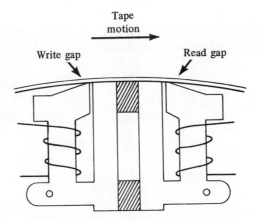

FIGURE A.16. Two-gap read-write head.

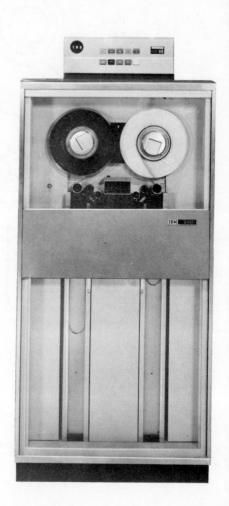

FIGURE A.17. IBM 2401 Tape Drive
                  (Magnetic Tape Unit).

FIGURE A.18. IBM 2311 Disk Storage Drive.

Magnetic Disk

A *magnetic disk* (Fig. A.18) is a thin metal disk, much like a phonograph record, but containing concentric rather than spiral tracks and mounted on a disk storage drive (see Fig. A.20). The recording surface of the disk is covered with ferrous oxide for the purpose of recording data in the form of magnetic spots.

Information may be read or written on the tracks by means of *access arms*.

Data-transfer rates are up to 156,000 characters per second.

297

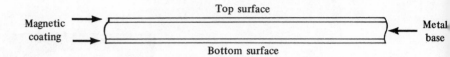

FIGURE A.19. Magnetic disk.

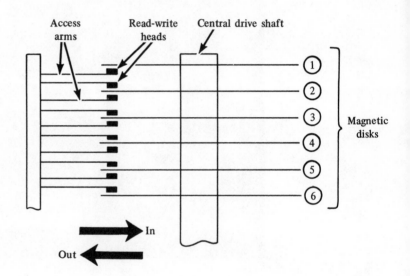

FIGURE A.20. Magnetic disk storage.

COMPUTER PROGRAM
DOCUMENTATION

Documentation for each program should contain:

1. Name of the program, the programmer's name, and the date the program became part of the program library
2. The function of the program or a concise statement of the problem to be solved
3. A description of the programmer's approach to the solution, including:
   (a) How he used the registers
   (b) Table references (tax tables, actuary tables, etc.)
4. Flowcharts of the logic used to solve the problem
5. Decision tables if required
6. A run log containing a record of serious "bugs" encountered and how they were eliminated
7. Computer operator procedures, which should indicate:
   (a) Special forms for the printer
   (b) Special punched cards
   (c) Disk packs or tape reels to be used and the disk or tape drives they are to be mounted on

(d) Carriage control tapes required

(e) A notation on the duration of the run

8. Computer-printed text of the program with comments

9. Samples of input and output

10. Storage maps or DUMPS if required

11. Memos pertinent to the program

The following is a program to provide a listing of Account Receivable. Overdue accounts are indicated by an asterisk. Note that the memo initiating this program came from the programmer's superior and is used as the problem statement.

February 10, 197

M E M O

TO: T. Watson

FROM: J. Oravec Sr. Programmer/Analyst

RE: Accounts Receivable

Provide me with a list of accounts receivable indicating by an asterisk a overdue accounts.

The print-out must include only the account number, balance due, dat of last payment, and the asterisk if required.

For example:

Acct. No.	Balance Due	Date of last Payment
123456	2000.00	12/15/69 *
694301	450.00	1/26/70

Input cards are from the card file ACCOUNTS RECEIV ABLE. The card format is shown in Fig. B.1.

Input cards will be punched from the Accounts Receivabl Report. An 11-punch in card column 72 (the units position of th Balance Due field) will appear only if a payment is overdue. (Th 11-punch can be regarded as a negative sign for overdue accounts.

After testing, send your output to the Billing Department.

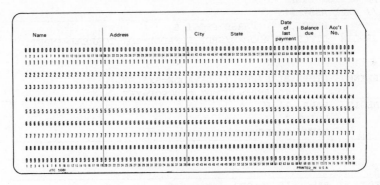

FIGURE B.1.

Approach to the Solution

Use of Registers:

Base register	register 11
Subroutine linkage	register 10

Tests:

Test sign of Balance Due field to determine the overdue accounts. If negative, continue sequentially in the program inserting an *, otherwise branch around the step inserting the *, and assemble the print line.

After the last card has been read and processed, print out an explanation for the use of the *.

PROGRAM–A LISTING OF ACCOUNTS RECEIVABLE

COMPLETION DATE–2/17/70

RUN LOG

DATE OF TEST	ERRORS	CORRECTION
2/13/70	Data exception	Packed balance due field
2/16/70	None	None

FIGURE B.2.

```
// JOB ACREC
// OPTION LINK
// EXEC ASSEMBLY
        PUNCH    '   PHASE PROG1,S  '
CARDIN  DTFCD DEVADOR=SYSRDR,EDFADDR=EDJ,IOAREA1=INPUT,                    C
              BLKSIZE=80,TYPEFLE=INPUT
*
ALINE   DTFPR BLKSIZE=132,DEVADDR=SYSLST,                                  C
              IOAREA1=OUTPUT,CONTROL=YES
BEGIN   BALR  11,0
        USING *,11
        OPEN  CARDIN,ALINE
        CNTRL ALINE,SK,1
        BC    15,START
*
EDJ     BAL   10,SPACE2
        MVC   OUTPUT+8(L'HDR4),HDR4
        BAL   10,WRITE
        CLOSE CARDIN,ALINE
        EDJ
*
*  1/10 MACROS
*
READ    GET   CARDIN
        BCR   15.10
*
WRITE   PUT   ALINE
        XC    OUTPUT,OUTPUT
        BCR   15.10
*
SPACE1  CNTRL ALINE,SP,1
        BCR   15.10
*
SPACE2  CNTRL ALINE,SP,2
        BCR   15.10
*
START   XC    OUTPUT,OUTPUT
        MVC   OUTPUT+27(L'HDR1),HDR1
        BAL   10,WRITE
        MVC   OUTPUT+23(L'HDR2),HDR2
        BAL   10,WRITE
        BAL   10,SPACE2
*
        MVC   HEADER,HDR3
        BAL   10,WRITE
*
        BAL   10,SPACE1
NEXT    BAL   10,READ               READ A CARD
*
        PACK  PAYDAY,PAYDAY
        PACK  BALANCE.BALANCE
*
        ZAP   BALANCE,BALANCE       ZAP FIELD TO SELF
```

FIGURE B.3.

```
            BC      2,GO                    TEST FOR POSITIVE
            BC      8,GO                    TEST FOR ZERO
*
            MVC     ASTER,=C'*'             SPECIAL ATTENTION REQUIRED
*
GO          MVC     ACCTNO,PATTRN1
            PACK    ACCT,ACCT
            ED      ACCTNO,ACCT+2           ASSEMBLE
            MVC     DATE,PATTRN2
            ED      DATE,PAYDAY+2           A
            MVC     BALDUE,PATTRN3
            ED      BALDUE,BALANCE+2        LINE
*
            MVC     BALDUE+1(1),=C'$'       INSERT DOLLAR SIGN
*
            BAL     10,WRITE                PRINT A LINE
*
            BAL     10,SPACE1               SINGLE SPACE
*
*
            BC      15,NEXT                 GO READ NEXT CARD
*
INPUT       DS      OCL80
            DS      CL60
PAYDAY      DS      CL6
BALANCE     DS      CL6
ACCT        DS      CL6
            DS      CL2
*
OUTPUT      DS      OCL132
            DS      CL4
HEADER      DS      OCL59
            DS      CL1
ACCTNO      DS      CL8
            DS      CL11
BALDUE      DS      CL10
            DS      CL12
DATE        DS      CL10
            DS      CL4
ASTER       DS      CL1
            DS      CL71
*
HDR1        DC      C'A LISTING OF'
HDR2        DC      C'ACCOUNTS RECEIVABLE'
HDR3        DC      C'ACCOUNT NUMBER      BALANCE DUE          DATE OF LAST PAC
                    YMENT'
HDR4        DC      C'* OVERDUE ACCOUNTS'
PATTRN1     DC      X'4020202020202020'
PATTRN2     DC      X'40202120612020612020'
PATTRN3     DC      X'40202068202021482020'
            END     BEGIN
/*
// EXEC LNKEDT
```

FIGURE B.3. (Continued)

303

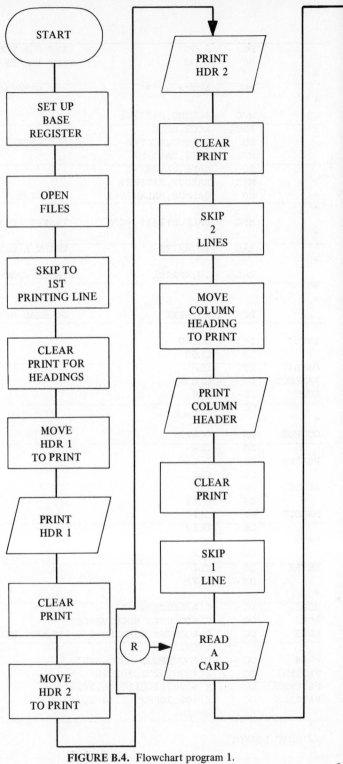

FIGURE B.4. Flowchart program 1.

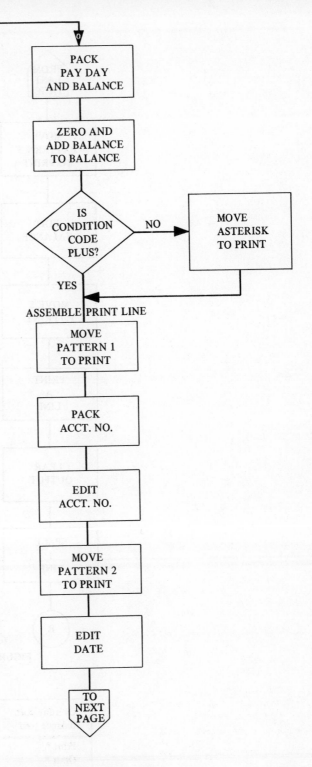

FIGURE B.4. (Continued)

305

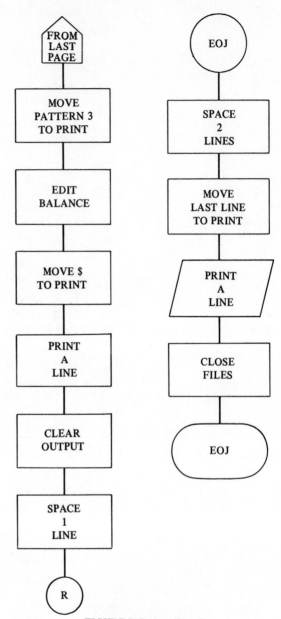

FIGURE B.4. (continued)

DECISION TABLE

Overdue acct.	Y	N
Balance paid	N	Y
Print *	X	
Omit *		X

FIGURE B.5.

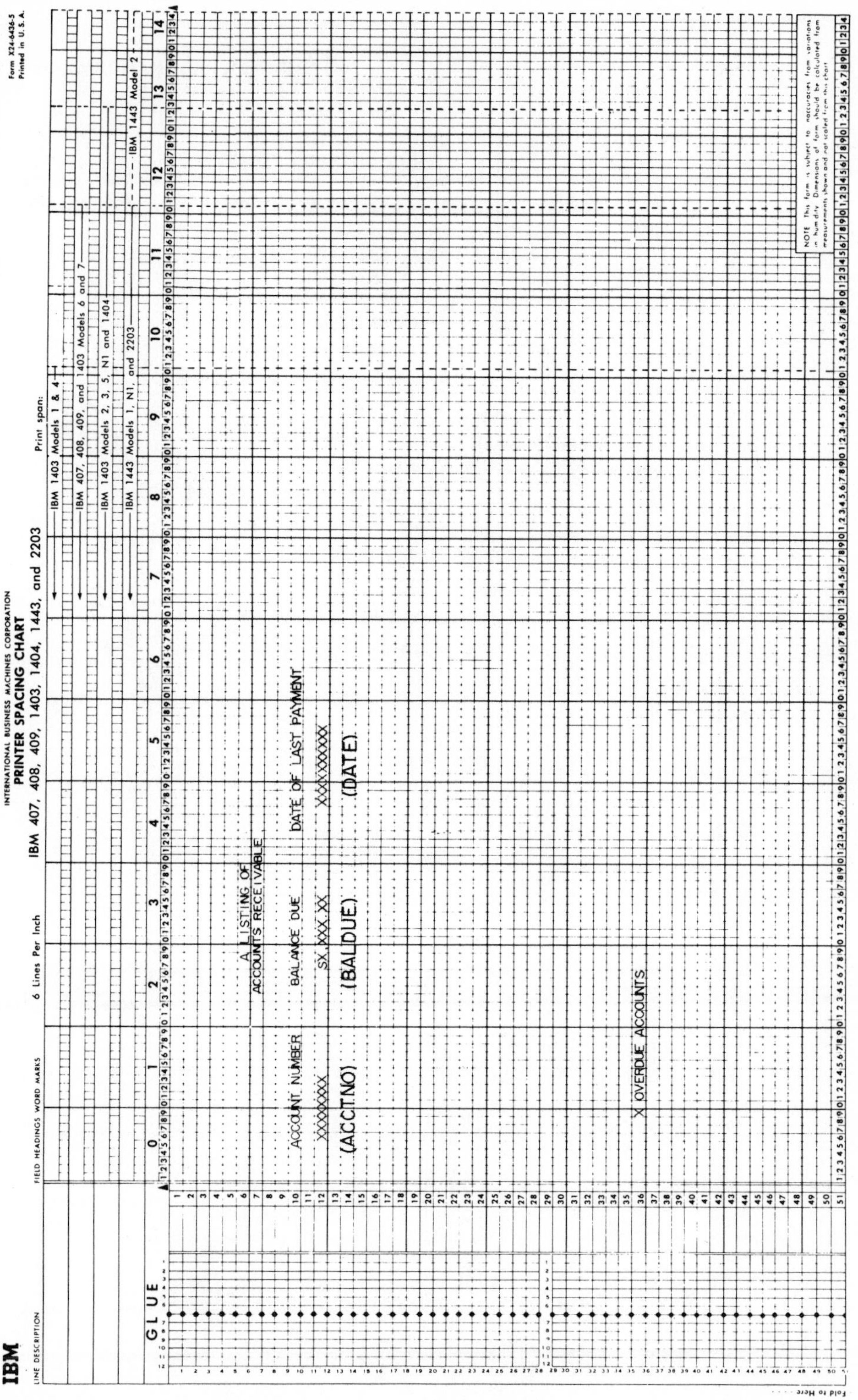
INTERNATIONAL BUSINESS MACHINES CORPORATION
PRINTER SPACING CHART
IBM 407, 408, 409, 1403, 1404, 1443, and 2203
6 Lines Per Inch
Print span:
Form X24-6436-5
Printed in U.S.A.
A LISTING OF
ACCOUNTS RECEIVABLE
ACCOUNT NUMBER
BALANCE DUE
DATE OF LAST PAYMENT
(ACCTNO)
(BALDUE)
(DATE)
X OVERDUE ACCOUNTS

FIGURE B.6.

A LISTING OF
ACCOUNTS RECEIVABLE

ACCOUNT NUMBER	BALANCE DUE	DATE OF LAST PAYMENT	
519243	$8,000.00	1/26/70	
312914	$8,000.00	1/26/70	
678112	$7,710.00	12/12/69	*
771285	$5,500.00	1/26/70	*
333948	$4,540.00	1/26/70	
561275	$6,300.00	1/26/70	
532911	$ .00		

*Overdue accounts

FIGURE B.7.   SAMPLE OUTPUT

Operator Instructions:

Use: card file A/R
standard forms on printer

PROPOSAL FOR A
COMPUTER SYSTEM

PREPARED FOR NORTH COUNTY COMMUNITY COLLEGE
BY D. ROBERTS, DIRECTOR OF DATA PROCESSING.

[In this case the proposal was prepared by one individual for an oral presentation. The text is to be narrated and the exhibits are to be prepared on flipcharts.

The questionnaire is to be handed out at the end of the presentation.]

CONTENTS

Introduction
Proposal
Broad Objectives
Specific Objectives
Immediate Objectives
Organization
Narrative

Introduction
In response to the President's request, I have prepared a bi study of data processing in an educational institution. This proj began as a proposal with costs. However, the President's memo October 10, 1968, re: an Ad Hoc Committee on Future Directi of Data Processing at North County Community College, rai questions vital to curriculum and objectives. In providing President with costs of various proposed pieces of hardware a their configurations, I have also tried to respond to his questi of October 10th.

Materials supporting this report are:

Computers In Higher Education, Report of the Presider Science Advisory Committee

Electronic Data Processing in Engineering, Science c Business, U.S. Department of Health, Education and Welf

The Proposal describes the computer system and outlines hardware and costs. The software capabilities include COBO PL/1, FORTRAN,* RPG, and BAL, which may be used to ti our students in the data processing curriculum.

The Proposal
Because of the growth predictions concerning North Cou Community College, a two-phase proposal for equipment suggested. Furthermore in a rapidly changing technology, and view of maintenance costs, computers should be leased, purchased, and commitments to any system should be flexi allowing the data processing curriculum and its accompany hardware and software to be modified in accordance with forward edge of the art.

A disk system will:

1. prepare students for random access processing, a key conc in today's data processing techniques;
2. provide a more economical system for administrative appl tions; and
3. offer greater computer language capability.

*Supplied by a private software company.

PHASE I–September, 1971

       System 360 Model 20–deliver 12-15 months

  8K Card System

	Monthly Rental
2020 Central Processing Unit	$ 599.00
2203 Printer	400.00
2560 Multi-Function Card Reader	460.00
	$1459.00/mo.
less 10% Educational Allowance	145.90
	$1313.10/mo.
Present 1130 disk system cost	1408.10
Net decrease for Card System	$ 95.00/mo.

ALTERNATIVE I

  12K One disk system

2020 Central Processing Unit	$ 976.00	
2203 Printer	400.00	
2560 Multi-Function Card Reader	460.00	
	$1836.00	
less 10% E.A.	183.60	
		$1652.40
2311 Disk Storage–1	$ 360.00	
(2.7 million char.)		
less 20% E.A.	72.00	
(1316 diskpacks required at $13.00/mo. ea.)		288.00
		$1940.40

EXHIBIT A.

A two-disk system will provide us with 14.5 million characters of disk storage suitable for student programs and administration records, with sufficient capacity to create a permanent data base on our student and faculty lasting beyond 1974.

The data base should consist of a student file, faculty file, administrator file, and staff file.

The student file can be used to generate:

311

ALTERNATIVE 2

12K Two Disk System

2020 Central Processing Unit	$ 976.00	
2203 Printer	400.00	
2560 Multi-function Card Reader	460.00	
	$1836.00	
less 10% E.A.	183.60	
		$1652.40
2311 Disk Storage—2 @ $360. ea.	$ 720.00	
(5.4 million char.)		
less 20% E.A.	144.00	
(1316 disk packs required at		576.00
$13.00/mo. ea.)		$2228.40
less 1130 cost		1408.10
Net Increase in Rental		$ 820.30/mo.

EXHIBIT B.

Grade reports

Grade summary

Class rosters

Transcripts

Dean's list

Course and grade audits for graduates

Mailing lists

The faculty, administration, and staff files can be used t
generate:

Payroll checks and supporting reports (i.e., 941a, W-2
year-to-date balances)

Employee promotion record

College Accounting programs

31

```
PHASE II–September, 1972
        System 360 Model 25 24K

        2025 Central Processing Unit        $2685.00
        1403 Printer (600 lpm)                650.00
        2540 Card Reader                      680.00
                                            $4015.00
less 10% E.A.                                 401.50
                                                        $3613.50
        2–2311 Disk Drives ($590 ea.)       $1180.00
               (14.5 million char.)
less 20% E.A.                                 236.00
                                                          944.00
        TOTAL                                           $4557.50/mo.
```

EXHIBIT C.

Broad Objectives Broad objectives are:

1. to provide a campus utility that will serve the data processing curriculum, administrative programs, the library, faculty research, the college business office, and the community; and
2. to insure that students "be employable and immediately productive in one of several entry jobs" (OE-800030, U.S. Dept. of Health, Education and Welfare).

To efficiently use any two-year college computer center, the computer *software* should provide languages that students can use in entry occupations in data processing.

Hardware in a two-year college system must be capable of producing business-like output—i.e., student programs of an accounting nature, as well as grade reports, mailing lists, class lists, advisor's lists, etc. Furthermore, data processing students should have "hands-on" experience with hardware typical in community business installations.

313

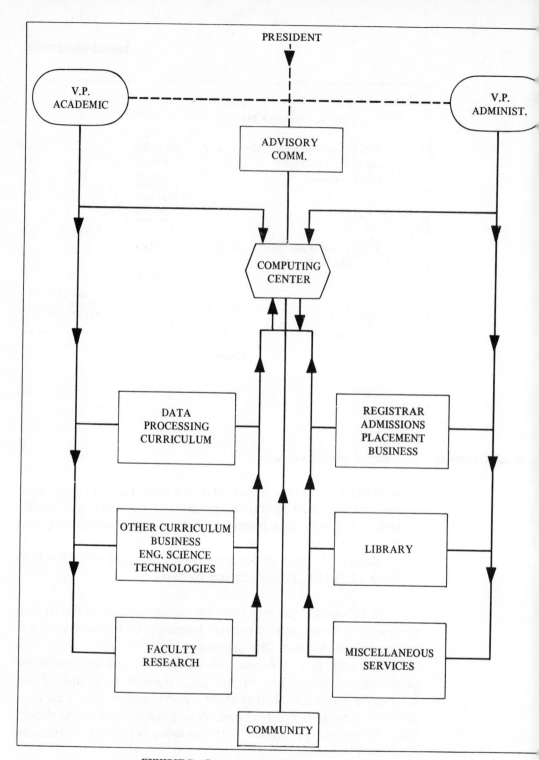

EXHIBIT D. Computer service area.

Specific Objectives

Specific objectives are:

1. to establish a *Master Plan* to consider all areas of information and communication touching upon the mission of the campus (this Master Plan should develop a cohesive and orderly approach to implement the necessary computer systems, keeping pace, if feasible, with the forward edge of this technology);
2. to determine the needs of all persons who will use or benefit from the computer system, gathering data on these needs through a questionnaire and interviews;
3. to establish communication with the State Office for Computer Education and to keep abreast of any trends in the State University system toward the centralization of data banks at the University Centers and any possible satellite status for the two-year schools;
4. to select and/or train personnel to meet the needs of administrative and instructional programs; and
5. to provide a data base for all students at North County from freshmen to alumni—such a data base would provide information on academic achievement and success in employment after graduation.

Immediate Objectives

Immediate objectives are:

1. to set priorities for use of present as well as future EDP systems (i.e., instruction, administration, library, research, community);
2. to obtain maximum benefits from this costly utility for data processing students, administration, faculty, library, and community; and
3. to put applications on existing equipment and future equipment—using the parallel approach rather than the "all-at-once" method. In the parallel method, new applications on the computer are verified against the same segment of the old system until the automated application has "proven out."

315

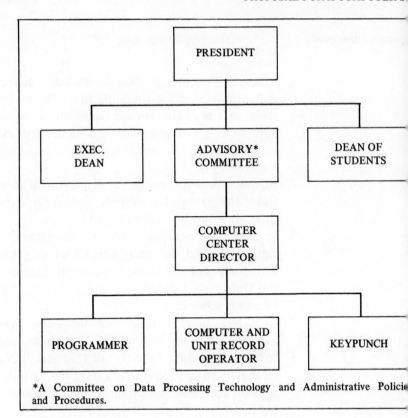

*A Committee on Data Processing Technology and Administrative Policie and Procedures.

EXHIBIT E. Suggested organization of the computer center staff (based on organizational structure at Genesee Community College).

Organization

"Computers find a widespread use in education only when well-facilities are easily available to all students and faculty members, w rapid service for all users."

—from *Computers in Higher Education,* Report of the Presiden Science Advisory Committee.

Narrative

Equipment

The equipment necessary to support a curriculum and particular objectives is subject to wide variability. It is desirable have systems with disk drives capable of accepting FORTRA

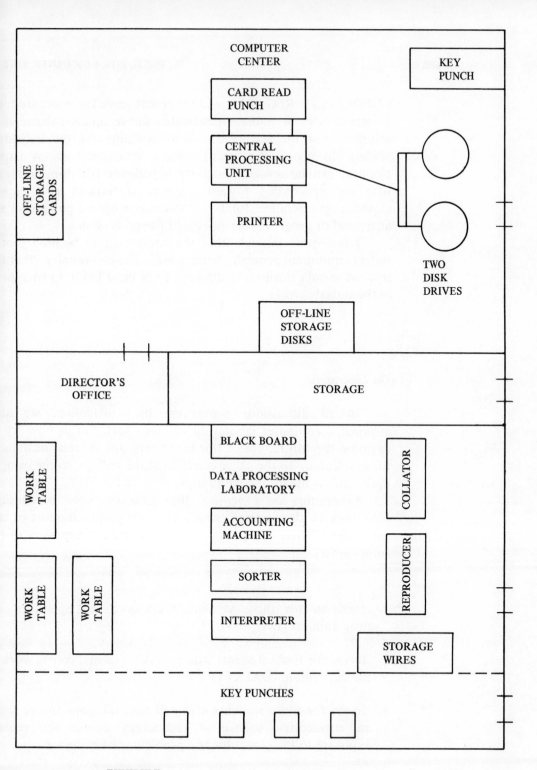

EXHIBIT F.

317

COBOL, PL/1, RPG, BAL, and other software. The more studen
in attendance, the more sophisticated the equipment that can
afforded—but the less time will be available for the individu
student to access the machine on a hands-on basis. A hap
medium can be struck: hands-on experience for those studen
who are proceeding toward machine operations as a caree
closed-shop operation for those students who are going into t
analytical or programming aspects of the profession.

I feel quite strongly that the equipment to be used shou
reflect equipment generally being used in the community—that t
student should learn on equipment he is most likely to encount
in the outside world.

The Laboratory

In all discussions concerning the curriculum, we ha
assumed a computer laboratory of some sort. Let us now try
examine the full nature of this laboratory and its relationships
the curriculum, to the other curricula at the college, to the cam
itself, and to the local community.

Computers are *expensive*; thus it makes sense to consid
their uses in all facets of campus life, not just in support of o
curriculum. There are several degrees of student exposure to t
equipment:

1. *Hands-on* for those students training to be operators a
   programmers (DAP 104)

2. *Access* for those students who are taking formal course work
   the curriculum (DAP 201)

3. *Access* for those students who will take (at some future tim
   an engineering science or technology course and requ
   exposure to the computer as a problem-solving device

4. Students in any curriculum who wish to should receive an overview or exposure course in computers (DAP 101).

Should we consider using the computer laboratory for other than course work—for example, for administrative functions of the college? It is economically and professionally indefensible to reserve the computer laboratory completely for instructional use in support of the curriculum. How better can we in the curriculum practice what we preach than by demonstrating the multi-faceted applications of the computer on the home campus? This will necessitate, of course, the presence of sufficient capability to service all the required needs, both curricula and noncurricula.

More and more we are coming to regard the actual hardware set-up as a facility for serving all the needs of a given campus—research (academic and student), instructional, administrative, library, medical, and even community. If one applies this rationale to a two-year college with a data processing curriculum, then we may safely predict that a computer laboratory will be established and that its very nature will be defined by the entire needs of that college.

The manager of this laboratory should be an administrative officer of the campus responsible for coordinating requests for service, thus insuring that all segments of the campus community are adequately supported. He should assist the instructional staff in the laboratory portions of the curriculum; help supply the problem-solving capabilities for non-data-processing courses; maintain a staff to design, program, and process the college administrative applications; and assume responsibility for long-range planning and for equipment evaluation necessary to keep his laboratory current and with *sufficient capacity* to satisfy the campus's needs.

A computer center is a total campus facility and its utilization should be for maximum benefit of the entire campus. As far as access to equipment and priorities is concerned, there is no reason why adequate access to the machine cannot be afforded all interests. If we run a computing center or laboratory in an efficient manner, we can set a good example for our students whom we are trying to train for jobs in the profession.

QUESTIONNAIRE

Check one: ☐ Faculty   ☐ Administrator   ☐ Secretaria

☐ Other _____
          Specify

1. List any computer applications that you think can support your area
   responsibility.

   Here

   Here   Your area of responsibility   Information
                                                            Flow
   Here

2. What reports generated by your office are repetitious and suitable
   machine application?

3. Are some decisions made by you repetitious and suitable for mach
   application?

4. Forms—such as student transcripts—can be filled out by machine. Can y
   list forms filled out by you that could be completed by the computer?

5. What computer hardware have you operated in the normal course of y
   activities—for example, 2260 terminal, keypunch, 1050 typewriter?

6. What applications can you audit during their first machine runs?

7. What type of statistical information does your office require?

8. Will you provide work measurement standards to a computer center?

INDEX